RESILIENCE AND TRIUMPH

A FEMINIST HISTORY SOCIETY BOOK

Resilience and Triumph

IMMIGRANT WOMEN TELL THEIR STORIES

Edited and compiled by the Book Project Collective:
RASHMI LUTHER, VANAJA DHRUVARAJAN,
IKRAM AHMED JAMA, YUMI KOTANI, MONIA MAZIGH,
PERUVEMBA S. JAYA, AND LUCYA SPENCER

Second Story Press

Library and Archives Canada Cataloguing in Publication

Resilience and triumph : immigrant women tell their stories /
edited and compiled by the Book Project Collective, Rashmi Luther,
Vanaja Dhruvarajan, Ikram Ahmed Jama, Yumi Kotani, Monia Mazigh,
Peruvemba S. Jaya, and Lucya Spencer.

Issued in print and electronic formats.
ISBN 978-1-927583-85-2 (paperback).–ISBN 978-1-77260-007-0 (bound).–
ISBN 978-1-927583-86-9 (epub)

1. Women immigrants–Canada–Anecdotes. 2. Women immigrants–
Canada–Social conditions–Anecdotes. 3. Women immigrants–Canada–
Biography. I. Luther, Rashmi, editor II. Feminist History Society, issuing
body III. Book Project Collective, editor

JV7284.R47 2015   305.48'4120971   C2015-905846-5

C2015-905847-3

Edited by Kathryn White, Carolyn Jackson
Copyedited by Shari Rutherford
Design by Melissa Kaita
Original series design by Zab Design and Typography Inc.
Cover art by Samia Ben Salah and courtesy of Immigrant Women Services Ottawa
Other art courtesy of Immigrant Women Services Ottawa
Photographs courtesy of the authors

Every effort has been made to secure permission and provide appropriate credit
for photographic material. The publisher deeply regrets any omission and pledges
to correct errors called to its attention in subsequent editions.

Printed and bound in Canada

*Second Story Press gratefully acknowledges the support of the
Ontario Arts Council and the Canada Council for the Arts for our
publishing program. We acknowledge the financial support of the
Government of Canada through the Canada Book Fund.*

Published by
Second Story Press
20 Maud Street, Suite 401
Toronto, ON M5V 2M5
www.secondstorypress.ca

*This book is dedicated to the memory of Roxana Ng.
She was an anti-racist feminist and a passionate advocate
for racialized immigrant women. She was a truth-teller
whose life, work, and spirit will inspire generations to come.*

CONTENTS

SECTION IV | EXPLORING FEMINISMS

SECTION V | ACTIVISM: SHAPING OUR WORLD

PREFACE

Yasmin Jiwani

Stories must have a home in a community of listeners for whom the story makes a claim that will be remembered.
—PARIN DOSSA (*Politics and Poetics of Migration*, 2004, p. 22)

When I was asked to write this preface, I was both thrilled and honoured. Thrilled because I had never read such an extensive collection of immigrant women's stories – stories that traversed different time periods, stories that encompassed such a diversity of styles, formats, and narratives. The honour comes from being able to comment on this brilliant collection representing women who have forged the path, clearing the way for me and others like me, and who have, in their writings, stories, and voices, mentored me in so many different ways. From them, I draw the courage to go on, to persist and like flowing water, erode the barriers of patriarchy, white dominance, and exclusion. From them, I draw the strength to continue in what sometimes seems like an endless struggle.

Resilience and Triumph: Immigrant Women Tell Their Stories, comes from a home, to use Parin Dossa's words, and is told to listeners in the wider context of a national home so as to claim space as a legitimate and valued repository of knowledge. The narratives that it recounts are of strength and resilience in the face of adversities; persistence in the face of exclusion; rejuvenation in the face of isolation; and above all, hope against all hope. It is a collection that immediately brings to mind Antonio Gramsci's powerful call for "pessimism of the intellect, optimism of the will," highlighting the myriad injustices that immigrant women have faced and their theorizing and political mobilization in countering these, but also, the fortitude of their perseverance against the odds.

This work is truly inspiring on a number of levels. On the one hand, it documents a buried history – the history of the women who have immigrated to Canada and made their second and sometimes third homes here. This strategic move effectively dislodges the normative and dominant national story – in which women who are identified as racialized minorities are often erased and their contributions minimized. The erasure and/or minimization of herstory has occupied feminist historians for several decades, and their efforts at uncovering the submerged narratives of women's lives in the making of the nation is revealing, as is evident in the series in which this present collection is featured. That herstory speaks to the hidden, yet core grounding of the nation, which women's lives represent. It is this feminist spirit that animates the stories that are compiled in this anthology.

Tactically, this collection offers enormous insight into the range of ways in which immigrant, racialized women have survived and thrived. Drawing, in many cases, from the inspiration they received from their mothers and grandmothers, their narratives gesture to the importance of cultural/familial continuity – emphasizing the role of women as reproducers of culture and nation. But more than that, this collection breathes life into the role of the mother, not simply as a reproducer, but as a strong, resilient force of power whose material and spiritual embrace one simply cannot forget, nor survive without. The mother then comes to represent all that is life-giving and affirming and where she is corporeally absent, her properties resonate with a faith community, cultural lore memory.

What is all the more remarkable is the lived history embedded in, and embroidering, the stories that are captured in *Resilience and Triumph*. Here, one gets an acute sense of not only the struggles and the achievements, but also of the broader context in which these women lived and continue to live. Their stories speak to the everyday – the lived realities at the ground level – and though short, they testify to the force of individual actions in gathering momentum for social change. The everyday organizing, similar to the organizing that went into making this collection possible, reflects the power of tactics in altering a course of history, in making institutions accountable, and in fomenting social change. Those tactics range from the very act of asserting oneself, taking voice and speaking truth to power, to collective mobilization through a multitude of forms, whether it is in the practice of everyday life or through performance in poetry, literary, or artistic productions.

The sheer diversity of this collection of narratives is enough to dismantle the discourse on homogeneity that characterizes stereotypical views of immigrant women, of racialized communities, and processes of 'fitting in.' We are made aware of what we are attempting to 'fit' into and the ingenuity with which we do this. As the stories reveal, not all of us have suffered the same hurdles, nor have all of us succumbed to traditional patriarchal impulses within our communities. Instead, many of us have chosen to walk our own paths, creating a hybrid existence that borrows from numerous sources to refashion lives worthy of living and lives worthy of remembrance.

As a woman who comes from a similar racialized immigrant background, this work makes me acutely aware that we *have* made a contribution to this country, its institutions, its practices of governance, and its evolving culture, no matter where we hailed from and no matter where we end up. That's the inspirational message I draw from the voices in this collection. These voices make me realize, more profoundly, that although the racism and sexism we face is daunting and at times paralyzing, if not deleterious to our very existence, collectively we can and do make a difference in agitating for a more just and equitable society. *Resilience and Triumph* is telling Canada that we exist, and that though the current political tide of neoliberalism seeks to eradicate our footprints, dismantling our organizations and subjecting us to all forms of exclusion, it cannot annihilate our symbolic and cultural memory of who we are and the kinds of contributions we have and continue to make to the nation. *Resilience and Triumph* is history in the making.

Yasmin Jiwani is a full Professor in the Department of Communication Studies at Concordia University. Prior to her move to Montreal, she was the Principal Researcher and Executive Coordinator of the FREDA Centre for Research on Violence Against Women and Children, a joint initiative of Simon Fraser University and the University of British Columbia. Dr. Jiwani has published widely and is the author of Discourses of Denial: Mediations of Race, Gender and Violence (2006), *and co-editor of* Girlhood, Redefining the Limits (2006), *and* Faces of Violence in the Lives of Girls (2014). *Her work has focused on media representations of race and gender in the context of systemic and intimate violence.*

INTRODUCTION:
CELEBRATING LIMINAL SPACES
Rashmi Luther

WHY A BOOK FOCUSED ON RACIALIZED IMMIGRANT AND
REFUGEE WOMEN? WHAT ARE THE CONNECTIONS TO
FEMINIST HISTORY?

The inspiration for this book comes from *Feminist Journeys*, the first book in a series being published by the Feminist History Society to document and preserve women's stories and activist history in the time frame of the second-wave feminist movement in Canada (1960s to the present). We believe this book contributes to this important initiative by sharing life stories of this period written by women who are differentiated as the "Other" based on their colour or 'dress'. Historically, they/we have been variously classified by official government policy or common perception as "immigrant," "newcomer," "visible minority," or "woman of colour." While considered "visible," their/our presence and voice have often been muted in mainstream feminist writing, despite well-intentioned attempts to the contrary. This collection, which focuses on writings by first-, second-, and third-generation racialized immigrant and refugee women, is our contribution to filling this concerning gap.

While not sufficiently recognized, racialized immigrant and refugee women have been a vital part of the history of second-wave feminism in Canada. Often feeling excluded or marginalized by mainstream feminists and feminism, they have raised important challenges to Eurocentric assumptions and dangerous generalizations embedded in Western feminism's understanding of women's experiences, issues, and proposed solutions. In many ways, these challenges have been beneficial to mainstream feminism in enabling the development of a more complex and nuanced understanding of patriarchy and gender inequities based on the intersecting and interlocking nature of gender, race, language, religion, class, and colonization. While some racialized women have raised these critical challenges as participants within mainstream women's movements, others have done so by forming parallel movements and organizations, particularly during the 1980s. Unfortunately, funding cuts beginning in the 1990s have considerably reduced their numbers and advocacy capacities.

Based on the technique of storytelling in the form of first-person narratives, this book serves as a valuable resource to supplement and enhance our collective understanding and analysis of these women's experiences from the 1960s to the present. The snapshots of women's lives, captured in specific historical moments and contexts, reveal some striking similarities and differences in women's experiences, ones influenced by factors such as when and why they came to Canada and where they settled, whether they were born here, how they negotiated their identity, changing immigration patterns, and changing political, economic, and social conditions. The rich narratives also provide new opportunities and insights for theorizations about racialized women's lives – their strength and resilience, the opportunities they have found or made, the challenges they have encountered and creatively addressed, the hopes and dreams that have inspired them, the passions and sheer determination that ground them, and the invaluable contributions they make to where they live, work, and engage as activists. Along the way, the stories present a contextually situated multidirectional mirror – reflecting how the women see themselves; how they are seen by the mainstream; and how they view mainstream individuals and systems. In many respects, this book highlights lives lived in liminal spaces, the spaces in-between – spaces of discovery, strength, resistance, and transformation, spaces in which to be and to belong.

HOW DID WE GO ABOUT MAKING IT HAPPEN?
Following encouraging meetings with members of the Feminist History Society in fall 2011, a small group of us came together to

begin discussions about this book. We wanted to focus on racialized immigrant and refugee women's lived experiences in Canada during second-wave feminism, including their engagement with women's issues and groups, as well as their understanding of tensions with feminism(s). We recognize that Aboriginal/indigenous women have also experienced racialization in their encounters with colonial powers, and we hope they will compile a similar book with respect to their experiences and activism during this period.

Through previous community organizing experiences, especially with immigrant and "visible minority" women, some of us recognized the challenges associated with outreach to diverse women's communities, especially on a national scale. We also understood that to be successful, we first had to have some personal connections and networks with different women's communities across the country. Not surprisingly, this required that we look inward at our own makeup, and to the best of our ability be reflective of the different communities we wanted to reach. With all these complicating factors, a larger collective was formed a few months later to better reflect diverse cultural, racial, linguistic (including French), and religious backgrounds, as well as ages and professional locations. Some of us were academics, others were from professional or community-based agencies or organizations, and still others were students or newly retired.

Developing our "call out," was more difficult than originally imagined. We were aware that many immigrant, refugee, and racialized women were uncomfortable with the term *feminism* and would hesitate to see themselves as "feminists." Within our collective, this evoked some stimulating discussions about how to frame our call for entries so that women would be excited to contribute their stories, including those about their active engagement with women's issues and organizations, while also respecting those who may not embrace the language of feminism. In the end, a decision was made to affirm both the plurality of women and their experiences and perspectives on feminism by pluralizing the term to *feminisms*. We also encouraged women to write about their own struggles with feminism and feminist terminologies if they so desired.

With respect to preferred forms of expression, we welcomed submissions in the form of essays, letters, poetry, drama, or artwork.

Linguistic diversity was also respected, and women were encouraged to write in either English or French. For those whose preferred language was other than these "official" ones, we agreed that we would have their submissions translated in order to provide a further incentive for women to write their stories. Recognizing that for some women an element of personal or professional risk might make them reluctant to share their stories, we later revised our call out, offering women the possibility of writing under a pseudonym. Some women very much appreciated this option, though most chose to write under their own names. Those who preferred anonymity have been identified with an asterisk (*) after their pseudonym.

Five months after our initial discussions, our call out was disseminated electronically, in both English and French, with an initial deadline of July 15, 2012. We circulated it to a carefully developed list of recipients to ensure that our outreach efforts extended to women from different provinces; different cultural, religious, linguistic, and racial backgrounds; a broad spectrum of professional and community-based locations; and a range of age groups. The deadline came and went with only a handful of submissions received. We then revised the call out and extended the deadline several times, finally establishing a firm submission date of December 31, 2013.

We had not fully appreciated the reality of women's busy lives when juggling the demands of family, work, school, and community involvement. Also, as we were writing our own stories for the collection, we were learning firsthand about the difficulty of the task we were asking others to take on. While the stories were to be brief, one major hurdle was to actually make time to reflect, focus, and write. We discovered that for many women, the autobiographical aspect required a fine balancing act between navigating the potential personal and political risks, including possible backlash, with feelings of excitement and liberation at the opportunity to share their life stories, including experiences, perceptions, and insights they had gained. Despite our numerous attempts to contact women on the identified list of potential contributors we had developed initially, our personal connections and direct relationships with women were the most fruitful in eliciting contributions. In acknowledging the value of personal networks in the development of this book, we recognize that this is also a limitation in that there are many voices, experiences, and perspectives still missing. While we thank and celebrate all the women who have so graciously and courageously shared their journeys with us, we remain hopeful that their stories will inspire others to release their inner muse at some point in the future.

HOW DID WE ORGANIZE THE BOOK?

This collection contains submissions from 47 racialized immigrant and refugee women – an eclectic mix of first, second, and third generations – ranging in age from their twenties to their seventies, of different national, cultural, and linguistic origins, socioeconomic backgrounds, and religions/faiths/spiritualities. We made a conscious decision to include all contributions, particularly in the e-book format, as long as they fit within the parameters and timeframes we had identified in our outreach efforts and editing process. We asked for clarifications and elaborations to strengthen the submissions. As there was only one French contribution that met our parameters, we decided, with the woman's consent, to have it translated into English.

All submissions were read by all members of the collective. We began to notice that there were some strong thematic patterns emerging in the stories being told. Some women highlighted their experiences as new arrivals, commenting on how they navigated different cultural norms and expectations while rebuilding home and community. Others focused on their integration experiences, especially how they manoeuvred their lives as students or professionals when confronted by the double whammy of lack of Canadian qualifications and experience. Many centred their stories on questions of identity and belonging, as well as the complexity entailed in negotiating how others see them and how they see themselves. A large number articulated their perception of tensions with feminisms, including their rich engagement with women's issues. These women clearly did not view feminism as either rigid or fixed. On the contrary, it was nuanced and varied, finding expression in women's lives in multiple ways, including by linking gender and faith. Another substantial group wrote about dealing with their engagement and activism, especially with systems of injustice that accentuate inequities and impinge on their and other racialized women's lives in Canada. Interestingly, many of the themes we noted correspond with the settlement and adaptation phases experienced by many immigrant groups, irrespective of their time of arrival.

We decided to use these thematic patterns to organize the stories: Arrival: Losses and Gains; Integration or Assimilation? A Process of Negotiation and Settlement; Identity: Women's Journeys to Becoming and Belonging; Exploring Feminisms; and Activism: Shaping Our World. Once we had established these thematic groupings, they were divided among the members of the book collective, based on their expressed interest. With this division, individual members of the collective took responsibility for maintaining ongoing communications with their respective group of women, as well as for writing an introduction to their thematic area.

While we grouped the women's stories according to these themes, we were acutely aware that many overlapping threads were woven into the stories. The pieces are richly textured, reflecting the complex nuances and flows of lives lived in the pursuit of love, hopes, and dreams of a better future for themselves and their loved ones in Canada, and back home.

With respect to the editing process, members of the book collective first reviewed the stories within their thematic areas. Two members then undertook more careful editing and fine-tuning of the entire manuscript for cohesion, clarity, and strength. In doing this, we were highly conscious of the need to honour the cadence, rhythms, and lilts of the women's voices – our goal was to promote clarity with respect to their ideas, without diluting the unique character of their voices.

WHAT DO THE STORIES TELL US?

In many respects, this collection helps renew and amplify earlier critiques of mainstream feminists for their reluctance to recognize the complexities of gender-based inequities. Through storytelling, it invites readers to experience and explore how gender intersects in complex, multiple, and nuanced ways when race, culture, class, religion, nationality, colonization, and historical context are added to the mix. In this way, we are reminded that feminism is not singular, either as an ideology or a movement. Indeed, it is complex, multifaceted, and multidimensional, as well as multiply lived and enacted. Instructively, this collection also reveals that misconceptions, stereotypes, and erroneous assumptions about each other are present among mainstream white feminists as well as racialized immigrant and refugee women. Whereas the former can hold stereotypes about the latter as being subservient, docile, and controlled by their patriarchal cultures, the latter can stereotype the former as being predominantly white, shaving their legs, and wearing high heels.

In reading the stories, we are acutely aware that each is unique. However, we are also struck by how many recurring and cross-cutting themes and patterns are present when the stories are read as a collection. While we invite readers to undertake their own analyses to better understand and address the presence of recurring patterns, we would like to highlight a few overarching ones at this point.

To begin, we must emphasize that the patterns provide us insights not only into the women's experiences but also into Canada, Canadians, and mainstream Western feminism. In many respects, the stories present us with a window to see how changes to Canada's political, economic, social, and cultural landscapes evoke corresponding changes to government policies, programs, and public attitudes toward racialized immigrants and refugees – particularly women.

These changes are most evident when comparing life stories situated in the 1960s and 1970s with those situated in the 1980s and beyond. It appears that fewer restrictions and bureaucratic red tape were encountered by those who entered Canada between the 1960s and mid-1980s, irrespective of whether they came on their own as university students and workers, or as spouses. They also found it easier to change their status from within Canada – from international student to permanent resident. This is significant because it reflects changes that were being introduced to immigration policies which, prior to the introduction of the "point system" in 1967, had actively discouraged immigrants from Asia, Africa, and Central and South America. The easing of these restrictions was based on a shift in Canada's nation-building needs reflected in an emphasis on education, skills, and linguistic abilities. With this change, doors previously closed to racialized "undesirables" were slowly being opened over the 1960s and 1970s.

It is noteworthy that during this period, when it was easier to enter and remain in Canada, the intent of most of the women who either came with male partners or followed them shortly after was not to stay but to go back after completing their studies or briefly working in Canada. After the mid-1980s, the primary purpose of such immigrants from the outset was to seek entry or refuge as permanent residents. The political and economic context of this shift is important for us to understand, for it is positioned in a period of escalating worldwide crises, driven by factors such as war, famine, natural disasters, and global restructuring under neoliberal economics. One inevitable consequence of these ongoing humanitarian crises has been large-scale displacements of people, primarily from the global South, who are forced to seek safety, security, and economic well-being elsewhere – as refugees. With more racialized individuals knocking on Canada's door as would-be immigrants or refugees, both entry into Canada and changing immigrant status from within has become more restrictive, especially since 9/11.

Another factor was the relatively more open and receptive climate of the 1960s and 1970s, which was less judgmental about "difference," especially when juxtaposed with the more hardened and increasingly less tolerant climate that has emerged since then. This is apparent when women write about experiencing a smoother integration into Canadian society during the 1960s and 1970s, of being welcomed with warmth and consideration by colleagues, managers, professors, fellow students, neighbours, and businesses. Unfortunately, beginning in the 1980s, there was a return to more restrictive immigration policies and less welcoming public attitudes, particularly toward those who look and sound different, and especially toward those who choose to wear the hijab. These later immigrants are more forthright in naming the negative impacts of racialization and discrimination.

It is striking that those writing about their arrival in Canada during the earlier decades, despite their initial intent to return to their home countries, are quite overt in stating that their desire was to integrate, to become immersed into Canadian life – to become Canadian. Some made a conscious decision to shed their cultural norms and traditions, including dress and gender-related expectations, which they saw as a liberating decision that enabled new beginnings. For others, their decision to do so was a survival mechanism, so as to not suffer the consequences of being too "visible." In contrast, those writing about experiences from the 1980s to the present, as well as some second- and third-generation women, viewed this somewhat differently: integration into Canadian society is also desired, but not at the expense of losing identification with their cultural traditions and beliefs, including their faith and how they dress. As the stories reveal, many actively sought others of their own cultural or religious communities for comfort, laughter, and belonging, as well as for collaboration in projects and activities. In many respects, it is clear that irrespective of whether or how they "chose" to integrate, what they all wanted was to belong, to be recognized and treated as Canadian. Some are also quite vocal in expressing that their colour or religious expression should not be used as a criterion to judge their "Canadianness."

Some women write about difficulties encountered in finding work commensurate with their qualifications and experiences, or about their frustrations in gaining adequate recognition for their work. Again, women highlighting experiences in the 1960s and 1970s seem to have found work with greater ease, especially compared with those writing of post-1980s experiences. In the earlier decades some women were able to find work after only a few weeks, at times even within their own professions. Such positive experiences seem much rarer in later decades.

Based on the experiences recounted, it would appear that racism toward new racialized immigrants was less overt in the 1960s and 1970s – likely because the number of racialized immigrants was smaller, enabling them to be viewed as exotic curiosities rather than as a significant threat to the white majority. However, racism was present in those earlier years in institutional systems such as hiring practices and their unequal recognition of credentials and qualifications acquired abroad. Since the 1980s, as racialized communities increased their presence numerically, concerns about discrimination, inclusion, and racialization are cited more regularly in the stories. The contributors also raise questions about the ability of policies that purport to be colour blind, such as multiculturalism, equity, and inclusion, to adequately address systemic problems of white privilege – problems that result in experiences of alienation, isolation, and devaluation of cultural/religious identity. It is interesting that for some who write about the 1960s and 1970s, racism is mentioned but gender discrimination is cited as being more problematic in that period. This suggests that, over time, racialized intersections with gender have surfaced with a greater intensity, and awareness about the presence of racism has grown correspondingly, particularly by those who feel its harmful sting most acutely.

Culture, language, ethnicity, and religion/faith are other important cross-cutting threads that are central to many of the women's identities, particularly for those of the Islamic faith. Often these traditions and values have been shaped by strong women figures who served as their mentors, guides, and teachers. For some, these were their mothers, grandmothers, and aunts. For others, these were found in ethnic organizations and through collective work on women's issues. Several women write about being inspired and guided by their feminist fathers or brothers. What was important was the experience of being valued, respected, and treated as equal to men, including ensuring that they had access to education. Another important teaching pertains to maintaining self-respect and dignity in order to resist and overcome multiple challenges and hardships. Indeed, in many respects, these teachings are vital in forming, shaping, and enacting how racialized immigrant and refugee women understand and live their feminism.

Learning about and having access to a positive sense of one's culture, traditions, and religion/faith also seem to be valued not only by first-generation immigrant and refugee women, but also by second- and third-generation Canadian-born racialized women, especially in terms of their identity development.

However, relationships with culture and religion are not uniformly positive among all the writers. Indeed, some are forthright in challenging their rigid patriarchal components and interpretations, both historically and more recently. These patriarchal (mis)interpretations are critiqued for diminishing the value of women and restricting their opportunities, and also for misrepresenting cultures and religions. In these ways, the women's stories reflect their unique journeys of self-discovery, of becoming and being, of finding ways to straddle and live in contradictory worlds – liminal spaces, where they can reclaim or challenge their cultural/religious identities while simultaneously emphasizing their Canadianness.

Finally, the women write about rejecting an imposed identity, including stereotyped assumptions, and affirming one of their own choosing. This reclamation of identity involves valuing oneself and the community of women, but also actively engaging in political and social projects and activities that support women and build communities. Struggles against racist attitudes and practices, including within mainstream feminism, are a central component of this activism. In this way, on a daily basis, the authors are articulating and living their feminisms. They do this by linking the personal (who they are) with the political (challenging social beliefs and systems).

While these stories indicate that we still have a long way to go before achieving respect, recognition, and equity as racialized immigrant and refugee women, they are replete with examples of progress that has been made, often in response to growing activism. Though still a numeric minority, more racialized women continue to make inroads into the academy as students, professors, and researchers. Their presence and activism have resulted in some curricular changes to programs and have forced an examination of existing practices with respect to faculty hiring, student admissions, community engagement, and research support, among other things. Similar challenges and developments have also taken place in other areas including journalism, education, social services, police services, nursing, social policy, community services, and so on. In addition to making inroads into established professions and mainstream organizations, racialized immigrant and refugee women have been instrumental in establishing vibrant women-centred and culturally appropriate programs and services, as well as advocacy bodies, in response to growing needs and existing gaps.

HOW DOES THE BOOK CONTRIBUTE TO FEMINISM AND FEMINIST HISTORY?

This book unveils a rich tapestry that displays the complex and nuanced nature of racialized women's lives in Canada during the period of second-wave feminism. As such, it offers us glimpses into their lived experiences, including their hopes and dreams, struggles and achievements. It also offers us different lenses, sometimes uncomfortable ones, from which to view ourselves and our society – a society that, contrary to popular belief, has become more racialized over time. More importantly, the stories present us with an opportunity to enhance our understanding of feminism, recognizing that it is not a single movement, but plural and varied, informed and shaped by a mixture of gender, culture, religion/faith, and historical context. In many respects, feminisms are shaped and expressed by being grounded in and challenging the ideas, beliefs, and values of the culture from which they originate, as well as by exposure to other societies and belief systems. We are hopeful that the experiences and insights shared by women in this collection will challenge and encourage us all to reframe our feminist lenses, inspiring the emergence of a more inclusive and vibrant movement – a new wave – one that is responsive to and embracing of multiple expressions of feminism.

We are extremely excited by this collection. We see this as an unfinished project, because there are so many more stories to be told, so many more voices to be heard. We encourage others to write, to find their inner muse, so that we can continue to enhance and deepen knowledge, challenge assumptions, build cohesive movements, celebrate successes, and strengthen support for our collective struggles.

RESILIENCE AND TRIUMPH

ARRIVAL: LOSSES AND GAINS

INTRODUCTION
Monia Mazigh

Once again she would arrive at a foreign place. Once again be the newcomer, an outsider, the one who did not belong. She knew from experience that she would quickly have to ingratiate herself with her new masters to avoid being rejected or, in more dire cases, punished. Then there would be the phase where she would have to sharpen her senses in order to see and hear as acutely as possible so that she could assimilate quickly all the new customs and the words most frequently used by the group she was to become a part of – so that finally, she would be judged on her own merits.
—LAURA ESQUIVEL, *Malinche* (p. 18)

Uprooting one's home and way of life to start anew in a foreign land, whether as an immigrant or a refugee, is a daunting experience, filled with mixed emotions of hope and excitement as well as sadness and loss. On the one hand there is hope for safety and acceptance, economic security, new adventures, new opportunities, fulfillment of dreams, and the creation of brighter futures. On the other, there is a sense of anxiety at leaving loved ones and lives that are familiar and venturing into the unknown and the uncertain to begin anew. These emotions and experiences, related to arrivals and adjustments, are explored by the contributors grouped in this section.

Nostalgia is a recurring theme across the stories: women speak fondly of their villages, their cities, their parents, and families. However different, each woman describes the same process:

< Samia Ben Salah
Awakening
2014

- the pain of leaving home
- the first excitement of the new place
- reality hits
- the slow and hard adjustment

The decision to leave home for whatever reason is accompanied by pain, tears, and intense emotions – a woman leaves her country of birth, her family and friends, and her memories, to travel a long distance and live among strangers in another country. But along with the pain, there is excitement in discovering the new place. Then disenchantment slowly crawls in; feelings of loss and awkwardness reappear. Nostalgia throws the women into a sort of a cognitive dissonance. Yes, they decided to come to Canada, to follow their dreams or their loves, but they did not necessarily want to lose their cultural habits and traditions of dressing, eating, or even their mother tongue.

These authors, referred to as "brown women," "South Asian women," and more recently "racialized women," live in an ongoing dilemma as their strong attachment to their roots confronts their discovery and burgeoning love for their new adopted country, Canada. This dilemma haunts them. It follows them daily at work, when talking to new friends, and at university when they start studying. Everywhere they go, they are faced with inner conflict and sometimes guilt: Will they forget their home country? Will they really forget who they are? Can they forge a new identity that melds their home and Canadian cultures?

At the same time, these women have positive stories to tell us about Canada – the snow, the weather, or the kindness of a neighbour, a fellow student, or a coworker. These uplifting moments seem to have a soothing effect on the wounds the women carry in their hearts. But the effect is only temporary.

In the language of "experts," this complex process of adjustment is called acculturation. Much of the scholarly literature depicts acculturation as "a one-way process": the immigrant acquires new culture and loses her native culture (Berry, et al, 2006). However some authors (such as Birman, 1998) suggest that there exists a bi-dimensional aspect to the acculturation process whereby the immigrant retains her ethnic identity while acquiring a new cultural identity. This is the experience of our contributors. They struggled to find a place of belonging.

Immigrant stories of arrivals and adjustments include the full range of experiences. In addition to happy moments of learning and connection, there are stories of painful memories, of longing for home and the familiar, of feeling guilty, and, perhaps, of experiencing recurring bouts of depression. And then, amidst this sadness, there is a twinkling light, a sense of hope and optimism – through fulfilling work, a new child, a new beginning, or fond reflections of lives well lived in their new home.

WALKING A TIGHTROPE IN ILL-FITTING SHOES
Pramila Aggarwal

I arrived at 6:30 p.m. on September 5, 1981, at Pearson International Airport, Toronto, Canada. After a brief interview at the immigration counter, I was given permission to enter Canada as a visa student. I proceeded to the baggage claim area. I scooped up my suitcases as they tumbled off the chute. I piled the two suitcases, one piece of hand luggage, one small knapsack, and a shoulder bag onto a trolley. I took a deep breath and started toward the customs clearance area. I repeated to myself what my much-travelled friend Renu had instructed me to do when dealing with immigration and customs officials. "Be calm, be composed. Don't look down but don't look too confident either. Be somewhere in between; pleasant, confident, and secure" – all the things I was not feeling. To my great surprise and relief, I was waved on.

It was nearing dusk when I came out into the arrival area of the airport. I ducked my head outdoors to measure the temperature, found it comfortable, and let my navy blue gloves remain in my hand luggage. They had been knitted with love by Mrs. Sethi, a colleague with whom I had taught in a public high school for gifted children in Delhi. I had been told to be prepared for cold. Though not quite cold, a chill of loneliness sent a shiver through me.

My next step was to decide whether to pay for a taxi or sacrifice convenience and take a bus downtown. This was the start of watching every penny I spent – not that I had ever been careless with money. I decided to take the airport bus to the Royal York Hotel and from there a cab to the International Student Centre on the University of Toronto campus. This saved me $20.

At the centre, I sat on the hard bench, jet lagged, my senses numb and my brain in overdrive. The person at the reception desk informed me that my application for the graduate residence had not been received due to a mail strike. Unless I had friends with whom I could stay, my only option was to pay $40 a night at the YMCA.

• • • • • • • • •

Only twenty-four hours earlier, in the wee hours of the morning at my parents' home, hours before taking the flight to Toronto via London, I brushed my teeth at the sink, tears flowing down my cheeks into the drain. I could hear my mother crying in the other room. My father had ordered a taxi to take us to the airport. I was having a hard time composing myself. I wished I were not going anywhere. "I am twenty-nine years old. I have two master's degrees. I have a job I like, and friends I love. Do I really want to go so far away, a place of no return, for a PhD?" I knew that graduate school was just a ruse, a good cover story for leaving Delhi so that I did not have to face publicly my marriage breakup. And so I was leaving my home and my family. At the airport, the flight was announced, and I boarded the plane just as the sun was rising behind me. I flew alone on a one-way ticket, on a continuous passage from India to Toronto.

I had no friends or relatives in Toronto. Luckily, before I left Delhi, Vinod, a family friend, gave me contact information for two people who were friends of friends of his. They asked me to come over to their apartment. There I went, lugging my heavy hand bag-gage and a heavier heart. In the subway, I stood the entire way from St. George to Jane for fear of missing the station. By this time it was getting quite dark. From the Jane station, I boarded bus #35. I had to peer hard to discern the street numbers from the moving bus. Street numbers, I learned, were odd on one side and even on the other.

It was a relief to finally step into an Indian apartment. They made room for me where their two children slept. My first night in Toronto, I lay awake to the gentle breathing of two little girls and wondered what was going to become of me. I did not know that this was the start of many months of sleepless nights.

The second person I met was a local, a white Canadian graduate student, Pat. She drove me around in her secondhand, metallic blue sports car and treated me to lunch that consisted of a dainty salad in a deli in Yorkville. It struck me as odd to see tall white women with shaved legs in high heels, going about their business very purposefully. I had expected to see women's liberation in the street. I wondered aloud, "What happened to the women's movement that they are still subjecting themselves to these ridiculous shoes and shaving their legs? Aren't these women feminists?" It did not take me long to learn a thing or two about the Canadian women's movement and its struggles on issues such as abortion, pay equity, and violence against women. I learned that women may have more personal freedom in Canada but here, too, capitalism colludes with patriarchy to keep women in their place.

Later the same evening, Pat brought me to a party where I was the only brown person. Everyone was friendly and curious, and I reciprocated in kind. I was introduced to eating boiled, buttered corn on the cob and drinking beer straight out of bottles that were half the size of beer bottles in India.

My first year in, I got a good dose of "white magic." It had started with millions of lights shining on the drive from the airport to the Student Centre. The bus had moved smoothly, and cars, all big and new, glided by silently. The university library was stocked full of journals and magazines and books, all current. The dispensing machines magically turned money into chocolate bars, bags of potato chips, and cans of pop. I could have my fill of unobstructed views of flowers in planters and of tidy front lawns of houses in the Annex. The wide sidewalks made it really pleasurable to walk, and to cross the street, all I had to do was stick my hand out and cars would come to a halt. My ears experienced great relief at no longer having to cope with the excessive honking on roads in Delhi.

"Dear Amma," I wrote. "It is so clean here. They even wash the streets. There are no power outages either. All the buildings have lights on all day and night, and windows do not open. People use a lot of very good quality white paper, and wash their driveways. You would really like the trees. They are huge: maples and oaks and birch trees which have white trunks. Newspapers are at least double the size of what we have. I made friends with a Greek student. She lives with her family, quite far away. She and her husband are both students. Do you know there is a girl from Guyana who so much looks like me. Her last name is Rambachan. Where did she get that, do you think? Living in residence, I share a room with a student from Thailand. Can you believe that she is here without her two-year-old daughter? Sometimes I see her cry, being so far away and all. Ma, there are no showers in the residence, just baths. So I bought a small bucket to bathe.

"Amma, when I first arrived and went looking for a place to

stay, it took all day to find a place which I could afford; a lawyer couple had advertised for a student to stay in their basement for $40 a week and occasional babysitting of their two young children. You know, I have never taken care of babies. And these little girls are rude. I could not figure out how to close the sofa bed so I just left it open as a bed. I did not like any of the food, so I just ate bread with butter, and sometimes jam. I was there for barely a week and was finding everything to be just too much: the dark room, the dingy shower in stark contrast to the spacious quarters of the landlord." I decided not to send this letter.

"My Amma, I met a couple from Bihar. Vibha and Parmeshwar Mishra are both graduate students too. They rescued me from my misery by offering me the couch in their living room. Vinod is here in Toronto for some work, and I wish I could just fly back home with him. The other day, some friends of the Mishras were visiting, and they are leaving for India shortly. I was so upset. I should be the one who should board that plane! I find myself unable to control my sense of ownership and proprietorship over India. How absurd is that? The Mishras have two boys and only two rooms. I sleep on a little couch in the living room. No problem. Vibha and I cook together in the evening. I feel so grateful but also feel so burdened by that gratitude.

"I feel like an outsider. My entire life savings I brought with me are running out despite my thriftiness. Most of it went to pay the tuition fee. You know, thousands of rupees come to nothing in dollars. I am experiencing a situation for which I was neither prepared, nor know how to overcome – being a very poor student. I feel lost, anxious, unhappy, and homesick."

I decided it was better not to send the above letter as well. I thought it was better to write to my mother about my observations of life in Toronto than tell her about my feelings, and thus save her from worrying about me.

So I told her about how I loved the anonymity and the athletic facilities of the university. I was really taken by the ease women of all shapes and sizes had with their bodies. They would walk around naked in the change room, shave their legs in the shower in full view, quite unconscious of their nudity. A few hours a week all my worries would disappear as I moved to the music of Tina Turner in aerobics class. I described how all signs of people are erased to keep the city clinically clean and that an army of cleaners and cleaning equipment followed all the events which drew crowds: be it an International Women's Day march, Labour Day parade, Santa Claus parade, or Caribana. Anyone walking even an hour later would find no sign of any activity – celebration or protest alike. And I told her how I feasted on the fall colours, even as a knot began to form in my stomach. I knew that when the lush green leaves changed into red, yellow, brown, and orange, and then fell, they would remain fallen. The days would become shorter and for a long time all would be bare and desolate.

"Amma dearest, I, the invincible, my father's jewel, am yearning for the sound of your glass bangles as you roll chapattis; I miss hanging out with our friends and aunts and the water-laden breeze from the east, and the fragrance of the first monsoon showers on parched earth. I miss sitting out on our front lawn savouring the sun and eating roasted peanuts in winter and listening to All India Radio. I miss listening to fellow travellers in buses and trains engaged in animated conversations and vendors calling out their wares on streets, in buses, and on railway platforms, all in Hindi. Here, I have no one I can speak to in Hindi. Also, I hate having to wear shoes all the time. It is almost never warm enough to wear *chappals*."

My mother had taught me that the winds from the east brought rains, and the winds from the west dried up the rain, and the wind from the north brought the cold air from the Himalayas. In Toronto, I could not predict if it was going to be cold or warm or rainy by smelling the air. Canadian intonation was another challenge as sentences would just peter out, leaving me grasping for the punchline. I could not interpret, decode, or even understand certain verbal and non-verbal expressions. Having to speak in English all the time and punctuating every interaction with "please" and "thank you" was getting on my nerves. Addressing professors by their first name was another thing I could not get used to. I had a hard time pretending not to stare at people in elevators or in public transport.

· · · · · · · · ·

In less than a year I had been transformed from a regular woman to a Third World immigrant, a visible minority woman, a Paki, South Asian, a woman of colour, and more recently into a racialized woman. These descriptors, together and separately, signified how the "real Canadians" saw me. I was not only the "different Other" but somehow inferior as a result of being different. "You don't look like an Indian; how come you speak such good English?" they would exclaim in disbelief. I could never be sure whether to take offence or accept it as a compliment. I had a choice of being a West Indian, an East Indian, or a Native Indian but none of the Indians enjoyed much status in Toronto anyway! So it didn't really matter.

In 1982 I decided to run for office in the Students' Association and organize against differential tuition fees for foreign students. I also worked outside the university as an occasional interpreter for trade unions. That work took me to factories with no windows, where a hundred workers shared one toilet, and where the only telephone did not work. There was no pretence of equality or democracy in that environment. This was the other Toronto, where my fellow Indians toiled, day after day. The women were my age but looked ten years older due to stress, hard labour, and lack of sunlight.

They were fighting for equality and their right to be paid the same wages as those who worked on the day shift. After eight months of organizing, the workers lost the union drive by a mere two votes. Subsequently, most of the organizers lost their jobs due to their union activism. This experience took away any vestiges of the "white magic of democracy" I still clung to. It was all a sleight of hand – a case of democracy limited.

My ability to speak Hindi and Punjabi resulted in a part-time job. I got hired by a union to teach English to Punjabi-speaking sewing machine operators in a garment factory. Most of the machine operators were Indian and Italian immigrant women. Once a week, the teacher for the Italian women gave me a ride to the factory.

The plant manager had picked one of the corners of a very shabby cafeteria for the English classes. It was bare except for a few run-down metal chairs and tables, a phone, and a vending machine that was mostly out of order. Every week, I would set up a flip chart and wait for the women's shift to be over. We sat around a table and shared jokes about their bosses, their concerns and confusion about their children's schools, and their complaints about their husbands and mothers-in-law. They expressed interest in having some control over their earnings, so we went to open accounts in a bank close to the factory. "Now, we have our own accounts so we can deposit at least the overtime cheque in it and our husbands need not know." Once, I was teaching about prefixes and titles such as Mr., Mrs., and Ms. They were really intrigued and asked, "Can any woman put Ms. before her name?" When I answered in the affirmative, one of them mischievously observed, "Wait till I tell my husband that I am not Mrs. You." Everyone had a good laugh. While they loved their work, they also hoped and wished for better working conditions. So we talked about their collective agreement. They wanted to know about getting involved in the union. A good opportunity presented itself. An election for the president of the union and other executive positions was in the works. Hitherto, the president's position had not been contested. For thirty-five years, the president had been acclaimed.

As the election drew nearer, the women in the class wanted to talk to their coworkers about getting involved so they decided to meet in the Sikh temple on a Sunday morning. They compiled a "shopping list" of their demands. They found an ingenious method to circulate the shopping list around to their coworkers under the very noses of management. When questioned by their line supervisor about what that piece of paper was, they said it was a recipe they were sharing with the other women. They identified women who would speak to the demands in the forthcoming general membership meeting. Their most pressing concern was the possibility of losing their wage rate and being paid at a piece rate.

At the union meeting, to the surprise of the union officials, women from the English class stood up and expressed their concerns and handed the shopping list to the chair of the bargaining committee. The union officials had not expected these women to participate so actively in the union. Some of the surprise was due to the fact that in Canada there are a lot of stereotypes about Indian women – that Indian women are shy, subservient, docile, traditional, and controlled by their men.

· · · · · · · · ·

For the last twenty years I have been a full-time professor at a community college. At my college, quite frequently, students and colleagues ask with honest curiosity, "How did you get this job?" I want to retort, "What do you really want to know?" but I keep my annoyance to myself. Not only am I a very visible minority at work, I have the same experience in community meetings and social functions. I am called upon to explain everything from bindi, henna, sari, salwar kameez, and Hindu and Muslim fundamentalism, to the Indo-Pakistan dispute about Kashmir. I could be flattered that I am deemed an expert in all things cultural and political, but I am not. It is part of a larger picture of ongoing discrimination. The frequent discriminatory treatment I receive from service providers – be they government officials or shopkeepers – in my white middle-class neighbourhood is a constant irritation and a persistent reminder of my colour and gender.

In Toronto, a lot has changed in the last three decades. Indian culture has become more popular, what with all the Indian restaurants, Bollywood movies, cultural festivals, and a whole month dedicated to South Asian-ness, including readings by Indian authors. However, I am tired of monitoring my everyday conduct because I represent and am expected to stand in for all South Asians. I have to put up with Canadian confusion about Hindu and Hindi. I still cannot discern the difference in the sounds of "w" and "v."

The last five years have been particularly challenging as I have lost my only sibling, my older sister. She had watched over our parents for all the years I have been away. In her absence, I am trying to care for them by visiting twice a year and by arranging a care team. I fear that when my parents are no more, I will lose my home and country. I have seen it happen to my immigrant friends. It is a terrible loss to have to prepare for. I feel in perpetual transit. I draw some comfort that there are only twenty hours between here and there. But it is a constant process of being unsettled, settled, and unsettled again. Thirty years later, I am still walking, flinching, and faltering in ill-fitting migrant shoes.

Postscript: Since writing this piece, both of my parents have passed away and thus I begin a new phase of my life without the anchor of their love and guidance. As a result, I will not have pressing reasons to travel back to India as frequently. It is hard to tell at this point how this will affect my relationship to my home and country.

Pramila Aggarwal, PhD (candidate) was born and educated in Delhi, India. She is a professor in the Community Worker Program at George Brown College, Toronto. For more than thirty years, Pramila has worked locally, nationally, and internationally for immigrant workers' rights, anti-racism, human rights, and community development. She is currently doing research on the contribution of Punjabi grandmothers to Canadian society. Pramila is a recipient of CASSA's Excellence in Equity Award for economic justice, the City of Toronto's William P. Hubbard Award for Race Relations, the Board of Governors' Award of George Brown College for Excellence in Service to the Community, and the NRI Welfare Society of India's 2014 Mahatma Gandhi Pravasi Samman award. She has several publications to her credit.

MEMORIES

Vijay Agnew

This excerpt about India, Indian diasporas, and cross-cultural rela-tionships is from a book of creative fiction that I am currently writing, tentatively entitled Love and All That. *It was presented as a paper at the International Council for Canadian Studies conference in Ottawa, May 22, 2012.*

The loss of home makes people sad and nostalgic. Memories haunt them as they go about making new homes in countries and cultures, distant and different, from where they were born. Others chafe against the restrictions of home and long to disentangle themselves and discover new ways of being and becoming that will redefine them.

The book begins with an advertisement by Rahul, a widowed

physician living in Canada, for a companion from India. Lila answers it. Rahul, after a lifetime of being away from India, is nostalgic about "home," but the India that exists in his imagination is very different from the one that Lila experiences day-to-day. The letters that they exchange juxtapose two contradictory sentiments: a desire to return home against a wish to leave home.

Rahul falls in love with Lila through the letters but she begins to doubt her decision to leave India and home. Rahul asks his friend, Ayesha, to write to Lila and try to convince her to come and live in Toronto.

· · · · · · · · · ·

To: Lila Gulati
From: Ayesha Ali

Dear Lila,
I am a friend of Rahul's and am writing to you at his request. Iqbal, my husband, and Rahul are colleagues at the hospital and we have known each other for several years now.

Let me begin by saying that I was astounded when Rahul revealed how you had both met. I was outraged that he had done something so morally questionable and in such poor taste. Men who advertise for companions and housekeepers do so, most commonly, to exploit them. Rahul does not fit that stereotype. He has been lonely since his wife died a few years ago and has been feeling nostalgic about India. Still I do not condone what he did. If you are looking for a character reference I am happy to give Rahul one without any reservations. He is a decent man, a man of honour and integrity. You are lucky to find yourself such a nice man.

Rahul wants me to reassure you about coming to live in Toronto. Images of glamour and affluence of the West abound in media and social interactions at home. I will not speak about that. Instead I will tell you a little bit about my own experiences.

Coming to live in Toronto was a marvellous adventure for me. Like you, Lila, I grew up in Delhi and went to university there. I still think of Delhi as my home although I have a home and a family here in Toronto. Rahul and Iqbal are forever talking about "back home," quite oblivious to how it has changed since they left. They often respond to situations by comparing how they would be assessed "back home" versus how they are thought of here in Toronto. They are nostalgic about their youth and as they go on (and dare I say become middle-aged) their memories have taken on an increasingly romantic hue. Conveniently they have edited out all the dull and difficult moments. Reminiscing about the past makes them happy, so why should I be a curmudgeon and insist on a reality check?

I had an arranged marriage with Iqbal. He had come to Delhi to find a bride and he chose me. After a quick though grand wedding and a three-day honeymoon I followed him, after a few weeks, to Toronto. Lila, I am confessing this to you. Usually I do not reveal the arranged part of my marriage to friends here at the university. It is not that I am ashamed of it, rather I wish to avoid the shock and expressions of dismay that such a confession usually evokes. I am immediately transformed in their eyes into a victim, for they jump to the conclusion that I was coerced into the marriage. It is far from the truth. I could have said no but why would I?

I expected to have an arranged marriage and had been anxiously waiting for *Abba* (father) to find a prince for me to marry. A handsome physician chooses me and offers to take me with him to a world full of glamour and romance (not to mention it being the Mecca of shopping) – why would I say no? Other girls, prettier than me, were clamouring to be the chosen ones and were envious of my good fortune. I was thrilled to be chosen as a wife. It would be hard, however, to convince my friends here at the university about it. Your situation fits another stereotype and many will be ready to "rescue" you if things go awry. Perhaps you can derive some comfort from this fact. However, I am convinced that there will be no such need with Rahul.

When I first came to Toronto I was very young and had never travelled outside of India. Not even very much within India. The sights and sounds of the city enthralled me; imagine a road with no crowds, no pedestrians, and no vendors. It was all so neat and clean; not a speck of garbage could be seen anywhere. I cannot truthfully say I loved it, although I should have. I missed the chaos and confusion of the narrow streets of Old Delhi where I grew up. I missed the vendors and the beggars. I even missed the touts, those aggressive street vendors and taxi/rickshaw drivers and their harassment. I felt alone and isolated. When I walked along the road I could think, without being interrupted or disturbed by others, of whatever pleased my fancy. Mostly though I thought of Iqbal, so enthralled was I in my newfound love for him and enmeshed in exploring and discovering each other and Toronto.

One day, while we were in a restaurant and being served by a white Canadian waiter I happened to remark that he had an accent. Iqbal laughed his head off and said, "Ayesha, it is you who is having the accent."

Dumbfounded, I answered, "How you are saying that, Iqbal? I am speaking just like other people who are going to an English-speaking convent school."

"Yes, you are speaking just like your friends. People here are not talking like that."

"You are saying I am having an accent?"

"Yes. You are mispronouncing vowels, mixing up the *v*'s and the *w*'s. You are talking in a sing-song voice and not crisply like a Canadian. They are thinking you are not knowing how to speak good English."

That silenced me for a bit. In Delhi I had been a super confident young woman, propelled by the privileges bestowed on me by my parents. It was a shock to realize that in Toronto, I did not quite meet the standard of approval or acceptance by others. It was a humbling realization but perhaps, in retrospect, a well-deserved one. I had been quite a pampered brat when I lived in Delhi and, at the time, was an arrogant young woman.

Iqbal had a few friends like Rahul but I knew no one here. Surprisingly I found it not intimidating but very liberating. I could do what I liked! My Delhi family was overprotective and I had felt constrained by their expectations. I was hesitant and insecure and afraid to disappoint my parents by stepping away from tradition. My little niche in Delhi had been populated with girls just like me. We spent our time dreaming of the handsome princes who would soon come galloping in and rescue us from stodgy old parents. In Toronto there was just Iqbal and me! I revelled in the freedom. I could do my own thing and be the person I dreamed of becoming. It was heaven!

My experience of the first snowfall was very exciting. I had only seen snow in movies. I remember standing at the window, watching the branches that had earlier looked dull and forlorn be transformed into a thing of beauty by the gently falling snowdrops. I waited impatiently for Iqbal to get home so I could go outside and feel the snow. He helped bundle me up in a heavy scarf and hat. Together hand-in-hand, we went out. As soon as we stepped outside the front door I slipped but I did not fall. Iqbal had been holding on tightly to my arm. Hesitantly I bent down to feel the snow while Iqbal made a snowball and playfully threw it at me. We got into a snow fight! Laughing and giggling we fell into each other's arms and kissed amorously.

Imagine that, Lila! Kissing and hugging when the desire moved you rather than worrying about propriety. Iqbal and I cared not a whit who saw us or didn't. At home I was always so concerned with what other people would say and think about me. In Toronto, why care? I knew nobody. Besides, we were just two more anonymous immigrants in the city. We could do just as we pleased. Glorious, glorious freedom to be just me!

I arrived in Toronto with suitcases full of beautiful saris and *salwar kameez* that had formed part of my dowry. What was I thinking? Did I imagine that I would be caught in a swirl of parties, banquets, galas, and weddings every night of the week? I certainly had enough clothes for that kind of lifestyle. In Toronto, we knew no one; who then was going to send us these invitations? In the excitement of getting married and leaving home for the glamorous West I had not taken time to think. Neither had Ammi (mother) and Abba for that matter. They sent me off to Toronto just as they would have to my marital home in Delhi, expecting me to engage in the lunch and dinner rituals of the rich and leisurely women of their set. The clothes that I brought with me were far from appropriate for a woman who sat alone in her apartment dreaming of love and romance. There was no one with whom I could share my happiness. There was no Ammi and Abba; there were no friends. (Lila you must remember this was in the days before the Internet and Skype.)

When I wore a sari with thick clunky boots my legs felt cold and uncomfortable. I missed not having Abba's driver to take me where I wanted to go. Instead, I had to drag myself around in a sari on snow-covered sidewalks and in subways and buses. It did not feel glamorous at all. Rather, it was all a bit of a trial. Lila, try to avoid that mistake. Leave behind all your fancy clothes and buy yourself something useful and practical. Most important, however, leave behind your *memsahib* sensibilities for you will have to do all your own chores – even clean your own toilet!

In the summer I bought my first miniskirt. Imagine that! Perhaps if I had gone shopping on my own I might not have been so adventurous, but Iqbal was with me and anxious that I adopt the local fashion scene. He encouraged me to buy the miniskirt, along with shorts and jeans, hoping that they would blend me in with the others on the street. When I modelled them for Iqbal at home he whistled. I felt embarrassed for the miniskirt exposed most of my legs and it felt as if I was walking around naked. Iqbal said that I looked leggy and sexy and had to wear it on the weekend when we went out together.

All week I wore the miniskirt at home trying to get used to the feel of bare legs. I imagined the horror of my Ammi and Abba if they ever saw me wear one. My Ammi would, even in the privacy of our house, refuse to look at me. I could imagine her bewailing that I had brought shame not only to Abba and her but to all our ancestors. I had besmirched their honour for generations to come. Such thoughts brought to mind all my youthful rebellions. At home, in Delhi, Ammi and I had argued endlessly about modesty and decorum and Abba tried valiantly to broker a compromise between the two of us. Despite his efforts it had always ended up with either Ammi or me in tears. In Toronto, I could wear what I liked, yet I missed the battle of words. Without Ammi to fight and win against, it was just not as exciting to wear the miniskirt.

I felt self-conscious when I wore the miniskirt on the street, but nobody seemed to notice or care. What was I expecting, anyhow? It is not the culture here to whistle or to pass rude remarks. People are, of course, free to stare and they often convey their approval or lack of it by how they look at you. Besides, the miniskirt drew far fewer curious stares than the sari.

Lila, what I am trying to say in this letter is that much depends on your attitude. You can make yourself miserable thinking of all the familiar sights and sounds, friends and relatives that you will have left behind (and I did plenty of that as well in the first years that I spent in Toronto). Perhaps you are familiar with the writings of v.s. Naipaul who I like to claim as an Indian despite his Trinidadian roots and British residence and citizenship. Naipaul captured his departure from Trinidad in this memorable sentence: "I left them all and walked briskly towards the aeroplane, not looking back, looking only at the shadow before me, a dancing dwarf on the tarmac."

In Toronto it was easy enough for Iqbal and me to move into a brick-and-mortar home, but finding an emotional anchor and becoming "at home" was a much more complex task. It took many years. Salman Rushdie (2002, 336), another expatriate writer, describes what happens to people like you and me when we leave home:

> The migrant, severed from his roots, often transplanted into a new language, always obliged to learn the ways of a new community, is forced to confront the great questions of change and adaptation; but many migrants, faced with the sheer existential difficulty of making such changes, and also, often, with the sheer alienness and defensive hostility of the peoples among whom they find themselves, retreat from such questions behind the walls of the old culture they have both brought along and left behind.

Lila, I do not know enough of the circumstances that led you to answer Rahul's advertisement. Regardless, I imagine you to be having a dream for yourself and are now wondering if it can be realized at all. Coming to Toronto to live with Rahul will undoubtedly be a challenge. At the same time it will be an opportunity to make a new life, reinvent yourself in ways that suit your fancy, and for you to be your own person.

Is happiness assured in this new adventure that you are contemplating? I cannot answer that for you. The question, as I see it, is a simple and a difficult one – does Lila want to submit to fate or does she want to take the future in hand and make her own fate?

Lila, I am cognizant that as a live-in (and I assume financially compensated) companion to Rahul you will be crossing the boundary of what, in India, we think of as respectable. You will undoubtedly encounter dilemmas that are physical and metaphorical, known and unknown, visible and invisible. Crossing boundaries requires courage, I grant you that. But why be afraid?

The allure and the excitement of becoming part of a new society and fashioning a new life lies in the dream and in the quest to follow that dream. The quest might illuminate desires, longings, and strengths that, at the moment, are hidden even from you. Who is to know what you might become in the future? It is the quest, the journey, that is consequential and not our success or lack thereof in it. It is the journey that shapes and moulds us to become the person that we are today. The Grail is a chimera. The quest for the Grail is the Grail. The point of the Odyssey is the Odyssey.

Lila, I am looking forward to getting to know you. Please feel free to write to me if you have any questions or need to address some doubts. I promise to be as honest and as supportive as I know how.

Sincerely,
Ayesha Ali

· · · · · · · · ·

To: Ayesha Ali
From: Lila Gulati

Dear Ayesha,
Thank you so much for writing to me. I was a little embarrassed that someone other than Rahul and I knows how we met. What must you think of me? I am a morally upright woman, even if I say so myself, who has fallen on hard times. Since you are originally from India you must have come across many poignant and heartbreaking stories. I do not want to add to that treasure trove. Besides, we all struggle with our own particular demons, thus not much is to be gained by competing to determine whose pain is more onerous or requires greater courage to bear. I do what I can.

I found your letter to be very encouraging. I am a staid forty-year-old woman and cannot imagine myself in a miniskirt. Perhaps they are no more in vogue. When Western customers come to the boutique where I work, they invariably have very nice things to say about the elegance of a well-draped sari. They are probably not visualizing a sari-clad woman having a snowball-throwing match with a loved one. Does it make a quaint sight or a hopelessly tantalizing one?

I have never consciously thought of a sari in one way or another for it is simply what I wear most days. I can visualize myself in jeans and a shirt (preferably in a bright red, blue, or green colour with an Indian motif). I do not fancy wearing black and brown but perhaps might change my mind if I come to live in Toronto. Who is to know?

Since I work in a boutique where many Western tourists shop, I have developed some understanding of what they encounter in India and how they usually react. However, it is hard for me to imagine the reverse – how does it feel to be an Indian in Toronto? When you wear jeans and a miniskirt do you blend in with the local people? Are you indistinguishable from them? Do you feel self-conscious of who you are? Do you have, what a customer described to me, the equivalent of white-skin privilege by being brown-skinned? Does it get you extra dispensation in things you do outside the home?

You have lived in Toronto for many years and undoubtedly have many friends; does it, however, feel like home? I am wondering if, despite the passage of years, you miss Delhi and your friends here.

Ayesha, you have perceptively identified my dilemma. Fate has dealt me a heavy hand and I am torn between accepting it as my karma or striking out and making a new niche for myself. I have responsibilities that I am loath to shirk yet I cannot stop myself from dreaming of a better, happier tomorrow.

It would be a pleasure for me to meet you in person and perhaps we may do so in Toronto. In the meantime, however, if you come to Delhi I hope you will take the time to meet with me.

Thank you once again for writing to me.

Sincerely,
Lila Gulati

• • • • • • • •

From: Ayesha Ali
To: Lila Gulati

Dear Lila,

Writing to you made me reminisce about the past. Memories of the young woman that I once was play in my mind. I find myself reflecting on things that, without knowing or wanting to, I have, over the years, come to accept as normal and routine. Your query about whether I felt at home in Toronto has compelled me to reflect on being a brown-skinned Muslim woman in Toronto. When I first came in the 1980s there were far fewer immigrants from our part of the world than at the present time. The horrific event of 9/11 has changed life and heightened sensitivities but I will save that sad and painful story for another day.

A few years after I had been living in Toronto, I enrolled for a PhD in political science from Smith University, here in the city. Although I had two infant sons, Rahim and Salim, my parents had sent a trusted maid to help take care of them. My Ammi and Abba were distressed that I was alone in a foreign country and burdened with tasks that, in their home, are taken care of by servants and *ayahs*. They found Farida and made all the arrangements for her to come and live with us in Toronto. At the time I did not know enough about Toronto or about mothers like myself to appreciate the privilege. (Now that I am part of the university I know that the word privilege is a loaded term and evokes all kinds of confessions and distressful acknowledgment of guilt in right-minded people.)

Farida pretty much took over all the housework and childcare and so I had plenty of spare time. Iqbal wanted me to continue with my education rather than waste time shopping, watching television, and complaining about how much I missed home. Enrolling for a graduate degree was a bit of a switch. When I attended the university in Delhi, I was a dilettante, not a serious student at all. I had spent all my time gossiping, smoking cigarettes clandestinely, going to the movies instead of classes, and hanging out with friends in the cafeteria. Why not, I would say, you are only young once! Live and let live was my motto though, I must add, not of Ammi and Abba. My flightiness was a trial to them.

A few days prior to the start of classes at Smith University there was a departmental meeting for incoming graduate students. This was to be followed up by a wine and cheese party to allow professors and students to get to know each other informally. I thought that I would attend the meeting but skip the party. Although I was curious to meet the other students, I felt shy and insecure about being in an environment that was totally unfamiliar to me. Besides, I had no way of knowing what to expect. Would anyone be interested in speaking with me, a married woman with children? What would I say to the other students? Talking about the weather ("It's so cold!") is not exactly scintillating conversation. How many times would I have to answer the polite query, "Where do you come from?"

I have had experience with this question among my neighbours. They are friendly and want to welcome me but the conversation usually goes like this:

"Where are you from?"

"India."

"Not from Pakistan; I thought Ayesha was a Muslim name. It tells you how much I know."

"No, no, no. You are right I am a Muslim but from India."

"Oh."

Lila, I have found it is not of much use to give people a quick history lesson so I usually let the remark slide. Besides, my neighbours are only trying to be gracious and welcoming so why should I harangue them?

Iqbal would not hear of my missing the party and insisted that I stay for it and get to know the other students. Iqbal is a very friendly man who converses easily with different kinds of people. It is not the same for me. Can you imagine me, a well-brought up Muslim woman from Old Delhi, going up to a strange man and introducing myself? Was I socialized to act, in what my Ammi would call, such a brazen manner? Was I to disgrace my parents and heritage all in one go! My entreaties to skip the party fell on the very deaf ears of Iqbal. I do not like to disappoint Iqbal and thus mostly agree to whatsoever he wants me to do. (Is that not what a good Muslim wife does? Or even a Hindu one? I have, over the years, unlearned some of that good behaviour much to Iqbal's chagrin. At such moments he regrets encouraging me to attend university).

On the day of the meeting I dressed carefully. By this time I knew enough not to attract attention by wearing a silk sari or a salwar kameez. Instead I dressed in jeans and a sweater. I added a few gold bangles and some jingly earrings. (Lila, I have found that you can never completely leave the past behind.) When I looked in the mirror I did not see a "Muslim" or an "Indian," just the regular old me (though a rather pretty one, I must add). At the entrance of the room, where the meeting was to be held, there was a table with rows of neatly placed nametags. A middle-aged woman was sitting there and smiled broadly as she handed me a nametag. She said, "Ah, there you go, Ayesha." After a few seconds she added, "If you need anything just let me know. Don't be afraid to ask for help." I was amazed that she knew my name; how was that possible? I had no clue as to who she might be. Feeling confused and jittery, I put the nametag in my purse instead of sticking it on my sweater. If I could have, I would have stuffed my face into the purse as well.

I made my way to one corner of the room hoping to sit there inconspicuously.

A man in a rumpled tweed jacket, baggy pants, and with a full head of salt and pepper hair stopped to speak with me and said, "Hello Ayesha. I am Andrew Whittaker, the graduate program director."

Hastily I got up from my chair and said, "Hullo, Professor Whittaker."

"Don't be so formal. Call me Andy like everyone else."

"Okay," I mumbled.

Andy went on: "I am delighted that you are taking my course on Third World politics. It will be good to have you in the class and get a different perspective." He looked around at the room that was by now nearly full of white-skinned people and said, "We'll speak later during the wine and cheese." Having said that, he ambled along followed by my nervous eyes.

How was it possible that Andy and others knew my name? What was I missing? I could hardly distinguish one person from the next. They were all white and looked the same. (Not factually true – they had different coloured hair and eyes, but in my stressed-out condition I missed all that. Now after all these years I can hardly believe that of myself.) There was no one there who looked like me and with whom I could relate, however tangentially. I felt alone in this sea of white faces. I needed a raft but there were none that I could identify. I wondered if aspiring for a PhD was a good idea after all. My little boys would certainly love to have me play and laugh with them at home. Instead I was sitting alone, with an aching knot in my stomach, feeling like a stranger in a strange land.

I was on tenterhooks throughout the meeting though nothing much was expected of me other than to sit quietly and listen to others. My anxiety was so intense that I could hardly make sense of the conversation. It sounded like gobbledygook to me. I kept wiping sweaty hands on my jeans. Frustrated with myself. I vowed not to be guided by Iqbal in the future. Did he know what it feels like to be alone among strangers? What was he thinking, advising and encouraging me to attend university? Silly man! Henceforth, I would follow my instincts and stand up for myself. Hai Allah! Why have you brought me here?

Once the meeting was over, the wine was passed around and the room came alive with people milling about greeting friends and associates. Everyone seemed to know one another; there was an aura of camaraderie among them. I stood in one corner – a wallflower – afraid to speak with anyone. Instead of undergoing the ordeal of this party I could be at home listening to the plaintive melodies of *ghazals* and dreaming. In my mind's eye, I was back in Delhi, dressed up in a fancy sari with loads of jewellery and flitting about like a butterfly at a social event. Why had courage (and words) suddenly forsaken me? Why was I quivering and feeling insecure and uncertain? Where were Ammi and Abba when I needed them? Where was Iqbal? Safe at home entertaining himself! Foolish man.

I was sorely tempted to slip out of the reception but Andy expected to speak with me and that posed a dilemma. Besides, I wanted Iqbal to think well of me. I was not a coward, not really. It is just that being alone among so many strangers had completely flummoxed me. I teared up. But I was determined not to cry. If anyone saw me with tears, how in the name of Allah would I explain them?

I must have looked a bit scared or perhaps just out of place. A female professor, Joanne, strolled up to me and introduced herself. She was dressed in comfortable-looking clothing and that should have put me at ease; however, my heart continued to pound and my face felt hot and flushed. Longingly I looked at the door wanting to escape from the room. Instead I remained rooted in front of Joanne, wishing desperately for the party to be over.

Helpfully, Joanne offered information about the campus and herself. Shyly I informed her that I had enrolled in the Women and Politics course that she was teaching that year. She responded with a laugh in her voice, "I remember seeing your name on the class list." Not only that, she seemed to have read my application file and for some unknowable reason, remembered its details. Joanne continued by saying, "It's great to have you with us, Ayesha. We need more women like you to continue with their education. I am looking forward to having some lively discussions with you in the class." I was totally dumbfounded and could only respond with an unintelligible mumble.

Lila, I was anticipating sitting quietly in a corner taking in the information that would be presented in class. I had nothing to share. I was not knowledgeable and learned as I imagined everyone else in the room to be. Now I felt sorry that I had wasted my undergraduate years being irresponsible. If I had been a better student I would not have felt so scared of embarrassing myself and all Muslims (in the bargain) with my lack of knowledge. How would I camouflage my ignorance in a small classroom? What was I going to do?

Seeing me quiet, Joanne went on to say, "I noticed from your file that you have children; do you plan on enrolling them in the campus daycare?"

"Oh, no," said I, taken aback once again. "I have a maid who takes care of them."

"Oh," she responded. She seemed to be curiously disappointed by my reply. It made me feel even more confused and anxious, for it was clear from her face that I had said something wrong. I had no idea what it might be.

Only months later I learned that it is not quite the done thing in academic circles to confess to having paid help. It is considered be morally reprehensible and exploitative of other women, particularly if they come from a poor country. How was I to know that, Lila? In Delhi we have maids, servants, drivers, and all that. No one is ashamed of employing them. Rather, for a family like mine, it would have been shameful not to have them. Our community would condemn us as miserly and miserable human beings if we did not have servants. So, you get an idea, Lila, how values change when you leave the comfort of home. Everything is questionable and negotiable. You have to decide for yourself what you believe rather than blindly act on received wisdom. The old signposts from home become redundant though they continue to nestle in our hearts. All decisions, trivial and not so trivial, become difficult, complex, and perplexing. Sometimes, I am left feeling like a traitor.

Andy now came and joined us. He said, "Ayesha, there is also coffee and soft drinks; can I get you something?"

"Thank you, Sir. I am fine."

"Sure you don't want some coffee?" he enquired again.

"I'm fine," I replied, feeling awkward and tongue-tied.

Joanne continued to twirl her wineglass as she looked on watchfully at me. Why? What was she expecting?

After a few minutes of chitchat Andy said, "I was born in Britain but when I was two years old I went to live in Darjeeling with my parents. They were missionaries there."

"Oh!"

"Yes, I know it must be a surprise for you to hear that. I lived in Darjeeling till I was twelve and attended school there. I have some very pleasant memories of Darjeeling. Have you ever been there?"

"No."

Lila, if up to that time I was feeling conflicted and out of my depth, now I truly panicked. Andy was expecting to make conversation on my turf – India – but I knew little, if anything, about Darjeeling. I had lived in Delhi and had until then few occasions to visit other parts of India. All I knew about Darjeeling was that it was in the mountains and had many foreign-owned tea plantations. Lila, I don't mind revealing my ignorance to you. At the time I knew nothing about tribal people who live in Darjeeling or about the exploitative wages earned by women who pick tea leaves. Can you blame me for being nervous and feeling ignorant?

Joanne came to my rescue and talked a bit more about Andy. She said, "Andy was educated in Britain and came to Canada after he obtained his PhD. He still has a British accent, can't you tell?"

"No," I replied, feeling increasingly more stupid and dumb.

Should I have known? Lila, I don't want you to think poorly of me. Like you, I, too, can tell the difference between a Bengali and a Punjabi accent, and between a convent-educated and non-convent-educated person. But how was I to distinguish between a British and a Canadian accent? How many Britishers had I met, anyhow, to know the difference? I had no clue, or more accurately was truly clueless. Silently, I wondered if enrolling for a PhD was a good idea after all.

Joanne added, "Andy is an immigrant just like you."

I said nothing, just looked politely at them.

(In my mind, however, I said, "Really! You could have fooled me! In what way is this confident, well-educated white man just like me?")

Andy went on to say, "Lila, I have a picture of my mother wearing a sari. It was taken while we lived in India. It's in my office, I'd like to show it to you."

"Okay," I mumbled. The best I could do at that moment was to agree to whatever was being proposed. All possibility of making an independent judgment had long since fled my mind.

Turning to Joanne, Andy said, "Do you mind if I take Ayesha to my office for a few minutes?"

Joanne looked enquiringly at me and asked, "Would you like me to come along as well? I can if you so want."

"Oh no, please don't trouble yourself. I am fine."

Andy led the way out of the lounge. My heart was palpitating. I would have to make conversation with Andy, one-to-one. What could I talk to him about? How could I make myself sound interesting? To my great relief, as we walked along the corridor to his office, Andy gave me a conducted tour of the premises. Thankfully I could get along by muttering polite responses. In a few minutes we were at Andy's large office, with its wide windows and shelves stacked with books. Some shelves were neatly arranged while others had books piled up every which way.

The picture of his mother was proudly displayed on one of the bookcases. It showed a white woman clad in a simple cotton sari with her hair pulled back sternly. Her demeanour exuded a gentle kindness. It was a quaint photograph. Despite the sari she looked different from anyone that was known or familiar to me. The portrait surprised me in another way as well. If I were to display a picture of my Ammi it would show her wearing a fine silk sari and looking regal. It would do me proud. Though the picture perplexed me, I was able to make timid but admiring comments.

I then turned my attention to the books lined up alongside it. Noticing this, Andy said, "I'll let you browse for a few minutes while I go and check my mail. I'll be back in no time." He half closed the door behind him.

Sighing with relief at this brief respite from attention I looked around curiously. You will not believe this Lila, but one wall of his office displayed tribal costumes and elaborate brocade jackets like those that used to be worn by the Maharajas in bygone days. Andy had simply spread them out and stapled (or nailed) them on to the wall. A kirpan with a filigreed case had been given pride of place. I was bemused by the decor. It did, however, put me at ease. Andy obviously had good memories of India and Indians. He would not judge me harshly and might be sympathetic. I was sure that I would make many mistakes as I went about my studies; perhaps Andy might help and guide me. The room endeared Andy to me, yet it did not dissipate my self-consciousness or insecurity about saying and doing the right thing. My conundrum was that I had no idea what the "right" thing might be.

As my eye travelled around Andy's office I saw a poster that was half-obscured with a coat hanging over it. I thought it might be a scene of India and thus moved the coat aside to have a look. The poster had the image of a bare-chested man, wearing low-slung jean shorts, long dreadlocks brought together in a ponytail, and strumming on a guitar. Lila, we see enough bedraggled men with few clothes in Delhi so the nakedness by itself was not a shock. Rather it was the raw pride with which the man was displaying his body that caught my attention.

"Hai Allah!" said I, hand held over mouth. I must have stood still for a few minutes for Andy found me there when he came in. He seemed a bit dismayed at first but recovered and smiled sheepishly at me. He said, "Oh, I forgot all about that poster. I am very sorry, Ayesha. Please forgive me. Usually I never shut the door when students come to my office, so no one other than me sees the poster. I'm sorry if it has upset you."

"It's alright," I mumbled. Embarrassed, I kept my eyes glued to the ground and refused to look at him.

"You have nothing to fear from me Ayesha. As you can probably tell I am a gay man."

"What!" I said as my eyebrows shot up.

He laughed freely for several seconds. Eventually I joined him in the laughter. That broke the ice and I felt more at ease than anytime earlier that evening. We now conversed more easily about books that he thought might interest me. Very kindly he lent them and then guided us back to the party. He left me in the company of Joanne and a group of other students.

I slipped out of the party soon thereafter. Iqbal, as he had promised, was waiting for me in the car, outside the building. Hastily I got in, rested my stiff and aching back against the car seat and exhaled a huge sigh of relief. Iqbal laughed and said, "You are looking flushed and excited; what happened?"

"Iqbal you are never believing what all is happening to me."

Out came the story of Andy.

Iqbal was not perturbed, instead he said, "I am wanting you to have new experiences and meet different people. That is why I am encouraging you to do a PhD."

"Iqbal, I am dropping out. I am not knowing much about anything. Why I am going through all this stress and anxiety? I am not thinking of taking up a job, so why I am bothering?"

"Ayesha, why to give up so easily...you think I am not feeling uncomfortable when I am first coming here? You are getting over it."

"Iqbal, I am not wanting to go through with this. I am happy at home."

"Ayesha, you are getting used to it, I promise. Years from now you are looking back and laughing at yourself."

I did not drop out of the program and am now a professor. Andy helped me over the years and our common interest in India brought us together. Even after all these years he comes with his partner to visit Iqbal and me. He loves Farida's cooking and always teases that I have made a career for myself by leaning very heavily on another woman. That is undoubtedly true, but Farida and I are both happy. So there!

How are your plans coming along, Lila? If I can be of any help
let me know.

Sincerely,
Ayesha Ali

*Vijay Agnew is a professor of social science at York University. She
has written extensively on immigrant women in Canada, race and
racism, and the South Asian diaspora. Some of her publications are:*
Racialized Migrant Women in Canada, *edited (University of Toronto
Press, 2009);* Interrogating Race and Racism, *edited (University of
Toronto Press, 2007);* Diaspora, Memory and Identity: A Search
for Home, *edited (University of Toronto Press, 2005);* Where I
Come From *(Wilfred Laurier University Press, 2003);* In Search
of a Safe Place *(University of Toronto Press, 1998); and* Resisting
Discrimination *(University of Toronto Press, 1996).*

OVERCOMING HARDSHIP

Hanako Honda*

I was born in a small town in Kagawa prefecture in Japan. I grew
up in that same town and lived there for twenty-two years with
my family. All my schooling was in Kagawa. Naturally, I lived in
my parents' house. Generally in Japan, people try to have some
independence by choosing a university outside of their hometown.
However, I wanted to stay in my hometown because my parents
had always told me that life with one's family together was the best
idea. I thought that my future would involve living in the same area,
close to my family. This perception completely changed when, in
the middle of my university life, I met a Canadian man at my private
English-language school.

My decision to attend a private English-language school was
inspired by my best friend, who had decided to study abroad in

Australia. This had started me thinking about going to a foreign country to bring excitement and adventure into my life. After my friend left for Australia, I made the decision to attend the private English school while I attended university. This meant working hard in a part-time job between university classes in order to pay the expensive tuition for the private English school. I was also trying to save for a ticket to go abroad. Even though it was a very busy period, I was very excited about the thought of new adventures in my near future.

My English teacher was from Canada. When he left our school, he extended a friendly invitation to every student to visit him whenever they wanted. I immediately decided to visit him as my first trip. It made me feel safer knowing that there would be someone I could ask for help if needed. It was also easier to convince my parents to let me go to a foreign country all by myself, knowing that I would be safe with someone they knew.

During the two weeks of staying with my teacher and his family in Ottawa, all the things that I saw, felt, and experienced gave me a different outlook on life. Before the trip I had only one option for my life – living in my hometown with my family with a nine-to-five job. The trip gave me a lot of new possibilities: working in a different country, going to get a master's degree in English, travelling around the world, and so on. The turning point in my life was when I started to date my former teacher while I was visiting in Ottawa. We continued to date when he moved back to Japan to take up another job.

After two years of dating, we married. In the last year of my university program, we talked about where was the best place for both of us to live after my graduation. I remembered the great experience I had during my previous trip to Canada. Immigrating to Canada sounded like an adventure. The idea of both of us living in his country was both very natural and exciting. This was the biggest decision of my life. However, at the time, I was too immature to understand how hard it would be to live an independent life outside my home country, without my family and friends. I thought that I was going to have the same feelings I had experienced on my vacation to Canada.

In November 2008, my husband and I landed in Ottawa. I

had already completed the process of applying for my permanent residency as an immigrant; therefore, I was eager to start looking for a job, or going to school if I wanted. Nothing seemed difficult. Nothing was difficult. I believed, at least in the first month or so, that everything about my life in Canada was going to be perfect.

However, it did not take a long time before I began to be frustrated by living in Canada. At the beginning, my English skills were not strong enough even for daily interactions. Moreover, I had no idea where to go for fun or how to help myself without asking for my husband's aid. It felt like nothing was under my control. The days were just passing by and I was not doing anything special. "What am I doing here?" I thought. I was not a student anymore and I did not yet have a job. I felt useless and helpless, a nuisance to my husband. I started to lose my confidence and began to feel that immigrant people were in a weak position without the skill of English.

My first winter in Ottawa came with a lot of snow. In my hometown in southern Japan it was very rare to have snow. I experienced Canadian snow as if it was my first time. I could not really enjoy the first snow or winter but, at that time, did not know why. Now I know that I was feeling lost and experiencing loss living as an immigrant. I remember that I tried really hard to show my enjoyment to my husband and his family even though, in the bottom of my heart, I was not really feeling it. I did not want to disappoint them, so I acted happy and had a fake smile all the time. Little by little, I started to feel more and more tired. Nobody noticed that I was getting depressed.

I needed something, anything, to make me enjoy life and help fight the depression. I started to think about what could make me comfortable in Canada. The answer was easy – make some connections with Japanese people. I decided to work for a Japanese restaurant in downtown Ottawa. That way I could also get the work experience I needed.

The smell of Japanese food, speaking Japanese, and feeling Japanese culture made me so comfortable. I could actually communicate with people as I had hoped, and gradually, that gave me back my confidence. Another positive was that I started to practice English to communicate with the customers.

After a few months of working at the restaurant, I found out about my first pregnancy. I had to quit my job because it was not really safe for a pregnant woman. The restaurant had a kitchen and an eating area on a different floor, and the stairs were always wet. I felt it was very dangerous. I would have liked to work as long as possible, but I could not ask the owner for a different position, one that was safer for me. I was afraid of making a bad impression, especially with Japanese people. Also, I did not want to bother them. So I was stuck at home doing nothing again. This second depression was the biggest thing in my life. I hid that depression in exactly the same way as the first, by pretending that I was not depressed.

Unfortunately, at that time, I completely believed that only something related to being Japanese would make me feel better. I became addicted to Japanese television and watched all day long. I did not want to do anything else. I just cooked dinner for my husband. I rarely cleaned or went out for shopping. Now I think that I could not have done anything else because of the terrible depression I was feeling. Watching Japanese television was a way to keep busy and avoid being depressed and stressed. However, my husband started to show his disappointment in me. He saw me as a lazy housewife, day in and day out. He started to tell me how energetic and active I used to be in Japan. But I did not want to hear about that. My husband and I argued a lot. I do not know how many times I felt that I wanted to go back to Japan. I cried through many nights. I was very frustrated that our relationship was getting worse and worse. It was one year later that I was finally able to show my honest feelings to my husband. We started to talk seriously about my problems every night and tried to find what I needed to have a better life in Ottawa.

When my first child was born, my mother travelled from Japan to help me out. She stayed with us for one month. That one month passed so fast. On the last day at the airport, when I was seeing her off with my son, I had an epiphany. I do not know how I can say this but the feeling at the airport made me feel strong. I realized that my family's lives are in Japan, but I don't live there anymore. This was my own choice. In that moment at the airport, I finally realized what it means to live in a foreign country without family and friends. For me it means that I have to be tough and ready to face any difficulty, and that I have to be tougher than ever for my son.

It has been almost four years since I first landed in Ottawa. Now I am pregnant with my third child. My first son is three years old and goes to a preschool in Ottawa. In the meantime, my English skills have gotten much better. I no longer have daily problems when going to see a doctor, communicating with my son's teacher, and so on. I no longer feel that I am weak or stupid because of mistakes I make with English. I've made more and more Japanese friends by joining the playgroup organized by the Ottawa Japanese Cultural Centre with my second son and am enjoying being in the Japanese community.

I am also enjoying my life in Ottawa more and more. There are a lot of reasons for this. Now I know what is fun for myself, what is comfortable, and what can help me to feel better. I have been asking myself what I want or what I should want for myself. I am studying to write the TOEFL (Test of English as a Foreign Language) as a first step to going on for my master's degree, and to open up more job possibilities. Even though I am busy with my two boys and housework, I am eager to find the time for my career, including studying English, researching universities, and working on this writing project as volunteer work. Now I do not have even a minute to be depressed or complain about my situation. I am satisfied with my fulfilling life.

No matter where you live, the bottom line is to keep asking yourself, what do you want to do to make your life better? The answer will be always different, because it depends on what problem you are facing at that moment. You cannot just be depressed. If you keep asking what you want to better your life, you will find something better.

I understand my long depression was necessary to get this strong positive mind. No experience is wasted, even if the depression was actually very tough. At the same time I really appreciate my husband's support and patience. Moreover he always trusts me and gives me the right advice. Our unshakable trust in each other was actually the biggest help for our better relationship and for fixing my depression. Be yourself. This phrase is for all the people who are reading my life story right now. No matter where you live, the bottom line is to keep asking to yourself, what do you want to better your life?

Hanako Honda is a pseudonym I have chosen for myself. I am twenty-eight years old, and five years ago I immigrated to Ottawa from Japan. Once in Canada we decided to start a family and I have been at home raising my three wonderful kids, ages five, three, and one. I also have a degree in international relations from a university in Japan, and I have been studying to become an early childhood educator in my free time. I hope to begin working when my youngest starts to attend school.

GOING BEYOND EXPECTATIONS

Usha G. Rao

I came to Saskatoon, Saskatchewan, in March 1965 to join my husband, Gururaja, who was a PhD student in mechanical engineering. A few weeks after my arrival, I started working in the computer area on the University of Saskatchewan (U of S) campus.

I had some prior experience, having worked for a year in a computer department in Bangalore, India. My bachelor's degree in physics, chemistry, and mathematics from the University of Mysore, India, was also helpful in getting into this area.

At that time, U of S had the earliest generation of IBM computers, magnetic tape drives, and punch card machines. Working there, I was happy to learn whatever I could about programming in order to improve my skills and learn how to operate new computing technologies that were being acquired. This continued until early 1969 when my husband completed his thesis.

After completing his doctorate, my husband applied for jobs in companies in Canada and the United States. Even though he was overqualified for many jobs, he was not successful in his applications. We were packed to leave Saskatoon. As a last effort, we were planning to stop in Toronto to apply for jobs before returning to Bangalore, India. To our surprise, he was called for an interview from Saskatchewan Power Corporation (SPC). Just one day before we were to leave Saskatoon, he received a job offer from SPC to work in their Saskatoon office. At that time, Srikantha, our eldest son, who was born in July 1964, was five years old and living with my parents in Bangalore. His brother, Vasudeva, born in Saskatoon in May 1966, was three years old.

We had left Srikantha in Bangalore because we had always intended to go back to India. As soon as my husband joined SPC, we made arrangements for our son to join us. After all the formalities were completed in India for his travel, my parents sent him to Saskatoon, alone, under the care of the airlines. He successfully made his maiden trip across the continents at the young age of five years old. Finally the time had come for all of us to be together as a family.

Srikantha was scheduled to arrive on January 7, 1970, late at night, on a cold winter day. The plane arrived on time and my heart pumped faster with impatience to see him. All the passengers arrived and there was no sign of him. Then we saw him on the top of the stairs with a stewardess. He started to walk down the stairs slowly. My tears came down with so much joy. He knew that we were his parents and his brother was there too. We drove to our apartment. We fed him and tucked him in to have a good night's sleep. He and his brother slept in bunk beds.

Srikantha knew everything about us. Our families in Bangalore had constantly told him about his younger brother and us. We had always looked forward to our parents' frequent letters. They provided the details of his growing up and sometimes included photos. We missed seeing his first few years, and he missed being with us too. It was very expensive to bring him and our financial resources were barely enough to survive. Many families in our situation had to be away from their children in those times.

The suffering of not being with our first son was the hardest part of my life, even though he had been well looked after by my parents and my seven siblings with lots of love and affection. My mother told me that they wanted to keep him safe and in good health, to return him to us at any time. They worried any time he got sick and were relieved when we received him safe and sound. He was looked after like a precious jewel.

Even now, whenever I hear about children left behind by

parents due to circumstances beyond their control, my stomach starts to churn and my heart feels the pain. This will never leave me as long as I live. At present, the communication options that one has at their fingertips, to see and talk to their children virtually, is a great advantage to parents. The sixties, when we were dealing with this, was a very difficult period for communication. The only tool we had was to go through the telephone exchange in Montreal and book the call through to Bangalore and wait and wait. Only a high-ranking official or business in the neighbourhood had a phone in India. Every household had to go to these places to make or receive a phone call, with prior arrangement. The fastest means of overseas communication was through telegrams, which were delivered by the mailman.

I had a new experience when we had our second son, Vasudeva. I had to go back to work and we did not know what to do. Having a babysitter was unheard of for us. At that time, the concept of babysitters did not exist in India. We grew up in large joint families and there were always some members of the family staying home. Luckily we found good babysitters to look after him until he was eighteen months and then we put him up in the daycare on the U of S campus.

Being a vegetarian in the sixties and seventies created challenges. The grocery items we were accustomed to using in Bangalore, such as spices and lentils, were not available in Saskatoon. Through our friends' network, we found out that they were available in Vancouver and Toronto. So, together with our vegetarian friends, we would send a big list of grocery items to the stores for mail order delivery to us in Saskatoon. Eventually, one or two Indian grocery stores opened in our own cities.

In January 1972, we moved from Saskatoon to Regina as my husband started working in the head office of SPC. Our third son, Krishna, was born in August 1972 in Regina, and we became Canadian citizens in 1973.

I rejoined the workforce with Saskatchewan's provincial government in May 1976. By this time, computer technology had advanced significantly. First I worked as a secretary with duties to look after some computer-related work. I was given training for three months in computer programming. After this, I was given a position as a programmer analyst. That was the turning point in starting my career in Information Technology (IT), which ended in August 2000 when I retired. I was very proud to be part of that era when I saw the start of many things and was able to work with the programming languages and databases in the "leading edge" IBM mainframe IT environment.

In order to succeed in my career, I had to overcome many of my shortcomings. First of all, I am basically a shy person. I had fear of expressing myself in meetings and presenting my ideas. I always thought that my English was not good. The "not good enough feeling" I had when I compared myself to others who were such good communicators was hurting me.

To overcome this fear, I joined a Dale Carnegie course to improve my speaking skills. This was a great help to me. Also, I needed some accounting skills to undertake some computer projects. I started taking business administration courses in Regina and got my certificate in Business Administration from the University of Regina in May 1984. My husband encouraged me to become a Certified Management Accountant (CMA). Even though I do not hold a CMA designation, I completed all the required courses, which were very helpful to me in my work. During those working days, my managers and coworkers were very supportive. I considered myself lucky to be in that environment.

We are very proud of our three children and their achievements. We had always encouraged our children to participate in local community and neighbourhood activities including hockey, cubs, and the Boy Scouts. During their high school years, they all joined the Royal Canadian Air Cadet program and attained their private pilot licences and prestigious scholarships. They continue to be immersed in the Canadian way of life and culture.

After retirement, we moved from Regina to Ottawa in 2002 to have the pleasure of being with our eldest son and his family. We have enjoyed seeing our grandchildren grow up and have participated in their school and other activities. Being close to our family has made our retirement days more pleasurable. Our son and daughter-in-law have given us so much of love and care (and still do) that we do not feel out of place in the new surroundings.

I have learned to see only the good things in others, to think positively, and to accept failures as stepping-stones for success. I am grateful for all of the opportunities and experiences that I have gained in life and in the nearly fifty years that I have lived in Canada. I am, without question, very proud to be a Canadian.

Acknowledgement:
I would like to thank Nandini, my daughter-in-law in Ottawa, my three children, and my husband, who helped me to bring this article to this final stage. I remain grateful to them, my two grandchildren, and other family members for their support and love.

Usha G. Rao came to Saskatoon, Saskatchewan, from Bangalore, India, in March 1965 to join her husband, who had begun his PhD studies in the Faculty of Mechanical Engineering. She started her career in the information technology field at University of Saskatchewan Computer Centre, Saskatoon, in 1965. In 1973 both she and her husband became Canadian citizens. Usha retired from Information Systems Management Corporation, Regina, Saskatchewan, in September 2000.

MIGRATIONS

Amarinder Kaur*

As the youngest child and the only daughter of my parents, I was very special to them. I could do no wrong. Even though we had little wealth, I had all the love in the world while growing up in a beautiful hilly village in northern India. Since there was no television at home, for entertainment we told stories, sang folk songs, read books, sat around a fireplace, and occasionally went to an old, smelly theatre to watch a three-hour movie that we critiqued and discussed until there was not much left to talk about. We had a few friends, and did not feel the need for more. We were well occupied in just being together. I had learned well, both from my parents and at school. I had a master's degree and a prestigious job in the only undergraduate program for women in a nearby town.

I was twenty-three when I met Surinder. He confused my heart and overwhelmed my thought processes. I spent my time thinking of him, or silently wondering if he might be thinking of me. He had lived alone ever since his parents and siblings had moved to Canada. He was planning to move there as well, after he had finished his bachelor's degree in science. As a result of my attraction to him, I absorbed myself completely into understanding Canada: its geography and its system of education. I dreamed of being admitted to a Canadian university.

At that time, there were no visa requirements for citizens from Commonwealth countries, so all I would need was a passport. I forgot, of course, that there was the question of funds for my air passage, and details such as what it would cost me to live over there. To my young mind, these barriers could be crossed when they came around. It was decided that Surinder would go there first and speak to his parents, and I would apply as a student. Once there, marriage would follow as the obvious next step.

Two anxious years passed, during which I submitted several applications to Canadian universities. One of them offered me admission and a small scholarship with a waiver of tuition fees. My friend lent me the money to pay for a one-way ticket from Delhi to Montreal, the city where Surinder and his parents lived. Things seemed to be moving along well, very much as I had planned them. I was, of course, devastated at having to leave my beautiful village and my loving family, especially my parents. However, my mind was no longer in India; it was flying over what I had imagined to be the streets of Montreal.

My flight from Delhi to Montreal was an eventful one, especially as I had never been on a plane. I had left with only a few dollars in my purse, and I experienced unfortunate delays while in transit. However, it all seemed worthwhile when I arrived in Montreal and found it even more awe-inspiring than I had imagined. The city was huge in comparison to my small village. It had an underground train right in the middle of town. It had shopping centres with endless rows of massive stores. One could buy many different kinds of bread, much more delicious than the thinly sliced Wonder bread brought every other day to our home by the "bread man" we had known for years. I could not stop admiring all that Montreal had to offer: the amusement park, the palladium, the waterfront, the people, the languages, the churches, and the mountains that were so much smaller than the ones I had grown up with.

I loved Montreal. I found shared accommodation with another university student. Everything seemed fine, except that Surinder had not yet introduced me to his family. I thought we had been clear that he would speak about our relationship to his parents. I had assumed they would be delighted, and that we would soon have a short and simple marriage ceremony. What seemed clear to me, however, was not that clear to him. He told me that there had never been a "love" marriage in his family, and that he did not know how to approach it. I was frustrated by this barrier and offered to approach his parents myself, a rather unusual task for a prospective bride. He agreed.

One day, armed with the confidence of a twenty-five-year-old, I arranged to meet his father and explained to him that Surinder and I had been dating for more than two years. I told him that I had left my job in India to come as a student to Montreal so that we could be together before getting married. Surinder's father did not say much to me. I thought at the time that he was perhaps shy, and therefore did not know how to respond appropriately to his future daughter-in-law's unusual proposal. Unfortunately, I had no choice but to broach the difficult topic since Surinder did not feel he could address it, and I had no one from my family to raise it. I guess it was a mistake since it created the very incorrect impression that I was "chasing" after their "naive" son, and "pushing" him into a relationship. It did not matter that Surinder was unemployed at the time, or that I still had a permanent job back in India. It was difficult for his parents to accept the joint decision made by the two of us without any parental consultation. It was an insult that could not be forgotten.

I was at an age when one conveniently chooses to ignore barriers. Surinder's hesitation and reluctance to approach his parents and their concerns just did not seem to matter before our ultimate dream of being together. These hurdles crossed, we were married. However, Surinder came through without tarnishing his image as a "dutiful son." I was the one who had seemingly led him astray. After marriage, I took on my responsibilities with renewed energy. I was fortunate to find a reasonably good job.

Soon, however, I began to feel that there was something missing in the skyline of the great city of Montreal. I was, of course, missing my parents and family. I felt lonesome just thinking of what I had left behind on the cone-covered slopes of my village. But it was not just that. There was a missing sense of language, and the experience of hearing it spoken by everyone around me; of breaking into song without feeling uncomfortable among people I knew would understand. I missed the music, especially the sound of drums echoing around dusk, calling people from one village to another in unison, as one great system of communication and connectedness across the mountains.

I found some of what I was missing by engaging with a community of women with similar experiences. People here called this the "South Asian" community. Many of these women wanted to express their feelings and share their stories, very much like I did. One of the most critical challenges we faced was control. Most of our lives had been controlled by others or by external factors, and we had accepted that as part of the deal of being a woman. It seemed that education and fluency in English or French enabled us to take greater control over our lives, and economic stability through steady employment made it easier for us to make some decisions. However, even when we had all the means and resources to control our lives, we found it difficult to confront the men in our lives. It was difficult for us to answer the apparently simple question "What is it that you would like to do?" We could not find a response since we had never felt the need to ask that question of ourselves.

I came to love my community of friends and increasingly sought collective strength from them. I began to lead two lives – one at home with Surinder and his family and the other with the South Asian women's community where I began to spend a lot of time as a volunteer. There was silent acquiescence from my in-laws. We did not speak about it, nor did I expect anyone to understand. It was work that generated no income, and which was, for the most part, ridiculed or disliked by the more "well-adjusted" men and women within mainstream circles of South Asian families. It was generally felt that South Asian women's groups dealt with controversial topics that only increased divorce statistics among the community; supported abortion under the label of what was called "pro-choice;" promoted gay and lesbian rights in the community; and failed to generate interest in traditional cultural values. Such activities made most people uncomfortable. They saw these activities as creating problems where there were none, and resulting in unnecessary controversy within the community.

Years passed by, and Canada grew into another home. I went back to my village every other year and found that it was no longer the same. Urban development had crept in, and the once pristine slopes were now covered with plastic bags and "lost" garbage. Gradually, I stopped going to my village since it only made me feel sad and helpless. Surinder and I stayed together and built a fairly stable home for our children. I felt we had made some gains in the community. There was greater acceptance of diversity, and although the country was still not willing to legally accept that women have control over their lives through a pro-choice approach, it was prepared to not obstruct access to medical services for pro-choice decisions. Even today, we are not prepared to confront the issue of abortion and unwanted pregnancies on a national or provincial basis. We choose, instead, to not address it. Perhaps this is our "Canadian" response to a topic that has the potential to tear a country apart.

Our children have now grown into adults, and there are far more second-generation men and women of South Asian descent in this country. Many of them now have spouses from diverse backgrounds. Hopefully, this generation of Canadians will better understand, and be more sensitive to, the needs of women from minority communities. However, our efforts to gain control over our lives still remain tentative at best. Addressing this through South Asian community centres or counselling services does not seem to have worked. We need, instead, to find more encompassing ways to look at this and other such issues. For example, do we still identify ourselves as South Asian women, or have we now created a new culture or shared legacy from South Asia, Canada, and North America? We need to examine our new identity that makes us as distant, if not more, from our countries of origin as from what we have come to know as "mainstream" Canadian culture. Ours is a world community formed of those who have left behind countries and cultures to adopt new ones. This community is no longer set apart from the "mainstream" Canadian community. It is strong, resilient, and well able to succeed, not only in North America, but in other lands as well. We need to acknowledge this strength, and to use it to overcome barriers with the confidence and attitude of a twenty-five-year-old enthusiastic woman, ready to take on the world.

This author has chosen to write under a pseudonym because in writing this piece, she is also writing about those who are still very much a part of her life. She believes that by revealing her identity, she might seriously offend those who are still close to her and jeopardize her relationships with them. However, although names have been replaced, the facts and feelings expressed are very real. The author currently volunteers as an editor, writer, and activist in adult literacy. She is also dedicated to supporting the rights of indigenous populations and marginalized communities.

INTEGRATION OR ASSIMILATION?
A PROCESS OF NEGOTIATION
AND SETTLEMENT

INTRODUCTION
Peruvemba S. Jaya

In an effort to integrate feminist and anti-racist perspectives, we suggest there is value in seeing integration as a process of acquiring "racialized and gender parity." Such a yardstick helps us assess the integration process of the women in our study…a methodologically individualist approach which focuses on individual immigrant women's experiences, because it is on that level that we can gain an understanding of the concrete processes and barriers to integration as they are identified by the individual immigrant women, as well as their resistances or strategies in overcoming them, both as individuals and in groups. (Miedema and Tastsoglou, 84:2000)

One of the main challenges that immigrant and racialized women face is integration, whether it be economic, cultural, or social. Many studies have examined the Canadian immigration journey as experienced by women immigrants, while the impact of Canadian policy and practice on immigrant women has also been studied.

A feminist and equity perspective has been adopted by some scholars while discussing economic integration. The key findings are that education does not always increase immigrant women's labour force participation – immigrant women are more likely to be unemployed than immigrant men. Occupational patterns show segmentation in the occupations of Canadian-born women and immigrant women, with immigrant women being employed more in manual occupations and earning less than their Canadian-born counterparts. Barriers to integration faced by immigrant women include systemic obstacles such as racism, sexism, language, and accent.

The social factor is another important aspect of integration. Having social networks and support systems provides social capital for immigrants and refugees. The many formal and informal social and familial networks that refugee women have provide them with a sense of active agency in their own settlement and resettlement process (Lamba and Krahn, 2003). Da (2008) reported that Chinese immigrant women found social support through religious participation. This activity provided both emotional comfort and psychological support to deal with the many challenges faced in the process of immigration and settlement.

Interesting and overlapping themes emerge from the stories and contributions of the authors in this section. There are experiences of friendships formed and integration processes that are joyful and positive. There are challenges in gaining economic integration, finding employment, and the unsettled feelings evoked when foreign credentials are not recognized.

Themes of shifting and conflicting identities, of being caught between two different worlds, highlight the difficulties of cultural adjustment. The theme of family is one that runs through almost all of the stories.

The exclusionary practices of racialization processes that require women to make choices about their identities, cultural traditions, and so on in order to achieve a degree of acceptance and belonging cause some women to opt for assimilation as a way of coping and fitting in.

Gender and racial discrimination, as experienced in Canada in the 1960s and again in the 1980s, provide a longitudinal perspective that examines the challenges of racialized immigrant women through different decades of the twentieth century as they navigate the different barriers faced in achieving, social, cultural, and economic integration.

The experiences of settlement and integration, including the range of barriers and challenges that are encountered, as well as the opportunities and benefits that are present, are varied and complex. While each experience is unique, the commonalities highlight the power of broader political and economic contexts to shape relations between racialized immigrant women and Canadian society. Most importantly, this group of stories reveals that, despite the varied experiences of those who immigrated earlier and those who came more recently to Canada, racialized immigrant women are succeeding. When knocked down, they pick themselves up and become stronger in the process.

FINDING GROUND BENEATH THE SNOW

Zebunnisha Valiani

Today is the first of May 2012, International Workers' Day. I recently retired from the workforce, making room for younger people. I am sitting at my kitchen table with my laptop, looking outside, enjoying a morning coffee as the sun shines on the May Day tree, which has more flowers than leaves, swaying back and forth. This is a tree I did not plant; it grew itself. The apple tree is in full bloom with pink flowers. All the snow has gone. I am admiring all this and thinking how to start my story.

I am writing about my arrival in Canada way back in the winter of 1967, when I landed in Toronto with my husband, Aziz Valiani. Aziz had a passion for travelling. We met in London, England, through his sister, who was my friend. Aziz was teaching in London, and I was attending a commercial training college in Maidenhead, Berkshire. He travelled all over Europe and then decided that he wanted to go to North America. One day he saw an advertisement in the *Times Educational Supplement* for a teaching position in Saskatchewan. He submitted an application. There were about 4,000 applications and only 400 were selected. He was one of them! He left England on August 31, 1966.

We had been friends for two and a half years. We had thought of getting married, but it was not financially viable. By November 1966, I was planning to return to Kampala, Uganda, to work and look after my mom. I received a telephone call at work from Aziz telling me that he was coming back to London. He added that he liked the little town where he was teaching, that he found people very friendly, and that the salary was much better than in London. He also said our married life would be better than in England.

So the plan to go back to Uganda changed, and I had a month to prepare for the wedding.

I telephoned my father in Kampala to get his blessing. He was not pleased with the idea that we were getting married in such a short time. According to custom, the wedding should take place at the home of the bride's parents. He urged me to travel to Kampala for the wedding so that the whole family could take part. I was the first girl in the family to get married. I told him that Aziz had only a two-week break from school, and it would be difficult to manage it all, in addition to travelling.

Then I had to look for fabric for my wedding dress. Luckily, Aziz's mother was a seamstress, so we went to D.H. Evans on Oxford Street in London. We looked at many pieces of fabric and chose white Chantilly lace from France. She took my measurements and started working on the dress immediately. Meanwhile I was taking care of catering, accommodation, the marriage license, and invitation cards. In about ten days my dress was ready.

I thought I had taken care of everything but, when Aziz came back to London on December 15, he said he wanted me to wear a sari, not a dress. There was hardly any time left to look for a new sari and blouse so I resorted to the sari I had worn when I arrived in London from Kampala in 1964.

We had a civil marriage on December 19 and an Ismaili wedding and cultural ceremonies on December 24. As soon as we got the marriage certificate, we went to Canada House in Trafalgar Square and started our immigration process. All my medical and security checks were done within a week and I was ready to come to Canada.

Aziz and I arrived in Toronto on January 2, 1967. We now had freedom to plan our lives – a new experience for both of us. We stayed with friends for a few days. They took us around Toronto and to Niagara Falls, which was an exciting experience for us. We went skating, organized dinner parties, and sat for hours and hours discussing various world and personal issues.

We arrived in Saskatoon on Ukrainian Christmas. The entire town was bright and beautiful with lights and snow, and I was with someone I loved. We stayed overnight to wait for our ride to Naicam, Saskatchewan, where Aziz was now living. I was standing in the window of the hotel lobby looking outside. There was so much snow on the ground that I thought, "Is there ground under all that snow?" I did not wait to do my own research. I turned to Aziz with my question. From then on, this became an inside joke between us.

When Aziz's teacher friend arrived we drove a couple of hours to the little village of Naicam. I saw a few houses on either side of the street, far away from each other, and bare trees shivering in the cold wind, wanting to be covered. The population was 700. I became number 701.

Aziz had told me that we would have to stay with his landlady as there was no flat for us to rent in Naicam. When we arrived, Aziz's friend David McRoberts drove us to the home of the assistant principal of the school. Here we were told that the Melfort School Board had prepared a flat for us. It was a very pleasant surprise.

The next day, the principal and his wife, Stella, came to welcome us. Eventually, Stella and I became friends. We met for coffee and if she was preparing some interesting dishes from Ukraine, she would call me because I had told her that I liked to cook. Another neighbour, Karen, was also very friendly. In those early days there was something in the making although I did not know it. Every time I told Stella I was going shopping because I needed some things, she would ask what, and then say, "Don't buy that, I will give you one. I have extra." I didn't mind, but I wondered, "Why won't she let me go shopping?"

In mid-January, we received an invitation for dinner from the Browns (Mr. Brown was a school board trustee). I was asked to wear my wedding sari. I was surprised at the request, but I love my saris and I said to myself, "Why not?" I was newly married and loved dressing up (even now, I like dressing up in my saris). The Browns came to pick us up and took us to the Naicam High School Auditorium. It was completely dark as we entered. Suddenly the auditorium light came on and the whole community was there. Even though it was *-20° and blowing snow*, it didn't stop the community from attending the event.

Usually, a shower is given to the bride-to-be before the wedding, but this was a unique shower for both bride and groom. There were a few presentations and then came the music. One of the teachers had composed some lyrics to the melodies of "My Bonnie Lies over the Ocean" and some other popular songs. As the band played, our new friends sang:

MEN
My sweetheart was over the ocean
My sweetheart was over the sea.

But I went to England at Christmas
And brought her to Naicam with me.

CHORUS – ALL
Aziz, Zebun, A couple so lovely to see, to see.
Aziz, Zebun, We think you're as nice as can be.

MEN
Now I'll get some good old home-cooking,
And someone to fuss over me,
And I'll get my clothes washed and ironed
All these things I'll now get for free.

LADIES
Yes, I was far over the ocean,
Yes, I was far over the sea,
But Aziz came over to England
and that ended "FREEDOM" for me.

After all this came a huge surprise – boxes full of gifts. They
were the household items that I had mentioned to Stella and Karen.
I was so touched, I was speechless. Thank goodness for Aziz, who
made a speech on our behalf.

During my six-month stay in Naicam, we were invited by parents for dinners. Some were well-to-do farmers and some not so
well-to-do. We were taken skating and curling and invited to farms,
picnics, and other events. There were many celebrations because
1967 was Canada's centennial year. The village organized a parade,
and I was invited to be on one of the community floats.

One thing I learned is that one cannot do any wrong or anything out of the ordinary in a village because all eyes and ears will
see and hear of it. Here is a little story: On Valentine's Day, Aziz left
me a card before going to school. I did not wake up to have a cup of
tea with him as usual, as I had the flu. When I woke up and saw the
card, I thought I would go to the store and get a card too. As I was
walking, I slipped a few times. My so-called English winter boots
had no grip but that's all I had. I got the card and when Aziz came
for lunch I gave it to him. At 3:30 p.m., when he came home, he

was laughing and asked me: Did you go out? How many times did you fall? I asked him how he knew and he replied that his students told him I had fallen five times. I did not keep count, but apparently others did!

After a few months, I got tired of being at home with nothing much to do. I decided I wanted to go out and work. I tried to look for a job. In the village there was a bank, a Co-op grocery and department store, a cinema, a one-man operated railway station, a small auto dealer, a store specializing in farm equipment, and a few family-owned businesses. One day I saw an ad in the Naicam paper for a bank clerk, so I applied. I saw the bank manager, and as he was showing me around a telephone call came for him. Before taking the call he told me to stay away from money and papers. I was surprised but did not say anything to him. I came home and told Aziz about the incident. He was shocked.

Later that day, Karen invited me for coffee. As I opened the door, a delicious aroma greeted me. With coffee, Karen served me freshly baked sticky buns. I asked her for the recipe and she said it was very difficult to make these buns. I went home, my curiosity killing me, and leafed through the recipe book that was one of the shower gifts. I made a list of ingredients for Sticky Buns and went shopping at the Co-op. After a couple of days, there was nothing to do so I opened up the recipe book, took out the ingredients, and followed the recipe precisely. I invited Karen and Stella for coffee, and I served them samosas and sticky buns. Karen asked Stella if she had made the buns. Stella said, "No, Zebun made them." Then Karen asked, "Did you help her?" Stella replied, "No. Zebun is a very good cook. She grew up in a big family where lots of cooking took place."

So the clerk job was kept from me, but not the road to sticky buns! Still, I needed something more interesting and challenging to do. I hungered to be more productive again.

In the meantime Aziz was considering going to university to top up his teacher-training diploma with a degree in education. To do this, he would have to travel to Saskatoon after school, which would have taken almost two hours several times a week. This would have been difficult in the winter, so I suggested we move to a city where he could attend university and I would have more opportunity to find a job. There was one issue about moving away – a condition in his contract that he had to stay in Naicam for two years, as the school board had paid his moving expenses and airfare. We decided he should talk to Mr. Brown. When Aziz explained the situation, Mr. Brown was very supportive and said he would try his best to help us. A few days later, we were given the green light, but he had to pay back half of his airfare. I was very happy and we started sending out his résumé. He received job offers from Winnipeg, Vancouver, Edmonton, and Calgary.

Now we had to select which one to accept. Winnipeg was out because it was too cold. Having grown up in a British colony, Aziz was against anything to do with the British, so Vancouver was out too. Edmonton was too cold, so we chose Calgary. Our landlord advised that Calgary was a nice little city. Pointing out it is not too far from the famous Rocky Mountains and gets winter-shortening Chinook winds, he emphasized, "And you will be closer to us."

At the end of June 1967, we packed all our belongings in preparation for the move to Calgary and left them in the landlord's basement. We found an apartment near Aziz's new school and with good access to public transport for me to get around. I also got my first job, with Canada Post, sorting Christmas mail. There I met many university students working during Christmas break. While working at the post office, I received a phone call from a hospital for an interview which led to a job. I worked there for four months and quit. I found another job with a company operated by a daughter and father but there was not enough work for all of us so I was laid off. But through all of this, I did get so-called Canadian experience.

In September 1968 I got a job with Montreal Trust. While working there I found out that I was pregnant with our first child. When I let my supervisor and coworkers know, they were very happy for me and eager to help in any way possible. They would not let me carry anything heavy and made sure I was all right.

We started looking for a two-bedroom apartment and noticed that the increased rent would be just a few dollars less than that required to buy our own house. So we looked into purchasing a home. The existing houses were a little bit over our budget and did not have all of the facilities I was looking for. Finally the realtor got a bit facetious and said, "Mrs. Valiani, you don't seem to like the old houses very much. Why don't you consider building your own house?"

This gave us the idea to look at houses under construction. We managed to find a style in an area we liked. We made a few changes and made an offer. The offer was accepted and construction began. When the mortgage documents arrived, upon perusing them I noticed that our mortgage's amortization was for forty years instead of twenty-five. I telephoned our agent and voiced my concern. He replied, "Mrs. Valiani, first of all, most people here don't stay in the same house for longer than three years. Regarding your mortgage, your total household income was not high enough for you to qualify for a twenty-five year mortgage." This, of course, was back in 1969, and most people went out of their way to help us. As an aside, our agent was correct; after two and a half years, we moved into another house.

I went back to work when my daughter Salimah was only three months old. I arranged for childcare with my neighbour, who was home with her own child. When I got back to work I found out that my assistant had gone to my manager and said, "Zebun will not be able to do this work with the baby and will be tired." She had all sorts of reasons, but my manager told her, "Zebun was hired for this position and it's hers at the moment. I will decide after I see how it is going." The whole office was happy to see me back and Salimah became the baby of the department.

After fifteen months I resigned from the position because I received news that my mom was very sick and would not live long. I took off to Kampala where I stayed for four months. When I returned to Calgary I got pregnant, and my son, Arafaat, was born in August 1972.

After various jobs, I landed a secretary position in the purchasing department of a major Canadian engineering company active in the first round of Alberta's oil sands development. While working there, I realized I liked the work and was able to execute the buyer's duties quite easily. I spoke to one of my bosses and expressed my desire to become a buyer. He fully supported me, giving me information on some courses I should take.

After a while, an opening came up for a secretary position for the head of one of the company's engineering projects. I was given this position. I gained a lot of invaluable hands-on experience. My boss was very helpful if I had questions related to the work or my courses. Later, when I finally received my certificate, I showed it to him. He was impressed and laughingly said, "I knew you were up to something."

I formally assumed the responsibilities of a buyer and was assigned to projects. Then came the recession of 1982. We were badly affected and lay-offs started taking place. In nine months I was laid off.

Following a year of unemployment I restarted my career, this time in the federal public service's, National Defence Department. After I had worked for fourteen years, holding positions in various departments of the Canadian Armed Forces base in Calgary, the federal government decided to close the base and move all its operations to Edmonton.

Once again, I went through a lay-off. But this time, protected by a union, I and others like me were offered an excellent early retirement package with good benefits, which I accepted at age fifty-five. I stayed home for a while but one day met an old boss while shopping. He asked me what I was doing, and I replied nothing much. He said, "Come work for us, we need you." The federal government was rehiring public servants because their labour was still needed, but this time I was hired through an employment agency, ostensibly to avoid "double-dipping." As an agency-worker I certainly did not have the benefits that I did as a unionized public servant.

During the G8 Summit Canada hosted in Calgary in 2002, I was still employed as a contract federal public servant and was responsible for arranging the back-up office operations. Meanwhile, my daughter was on "the other side," protesting the "anti-people" development plan for Africa that the Canadian government and G8 were proposing. A relative in Toronto saw her in protests on television.

One day, shortly after the G8, having managed to keep my job despite my daughter's political activity, a requisition crossed my desk for a contractor to take on operations of a previously publicly operated cafeteria in a federal scientific research institute. From a contract public servant, I now became a sub-contractor after winning the bid.

In the cafeteria, I did not only serve sandwiches, soup, and other continental entrées. I offered a forty-item menu of international cuisine that changed every week. I hosted celebrations for a range of ethnic events including Id, Nawruz, Chinese New Year, Diwali, Christmas, and Carnival. Workers at the institute proposed events to me, I worked with them to create a menu, and the director would do research around the event and make a presentation prior to the highlight – eating the food. The cafeteria became a cultural meeting place where colleagues of the institute came to know each other in a way Canadians rarely seem to – despite living side-by-side. After almost ten years of running the cafeteria, I decided to retire once and for all at age seventy.

Reflecting on my very full history of work and contributions to Canada, particularly on May Day, I feel that my story is unique and very unlike the stories of people who immigrated to Canada after me. Unlike now, when I came to Canada there was ample demand for workers and barriers seemed few to us. Ironically, today even our highly educated, Canadian-born children face far more racial discrimination than we did, and I feel the weight of my choice of having my children in Canada. Still, as the product of British colonialism in Africa, I am not sure where it might have been better to have them. But that is another story for another time....

Zebunnisha was born in a small village of Uganda named Mitaramaria, East Africa. She has lived on three continents and worked in a range of sectors including finance, engineering, and public service. She also enjoys cooking, singing, and entertaining. Her next writing project is a recipe-cum-story.

REDEFINING THE FUTURE
Aruba Mustafa

Stories by Aruba Mustafa and Preeti Nayak were submitted jointly. Preeti's story can be found in Section III. They state: "Together, our experiences reflect only a fraction of the larger issues at stake. As high school classmates, our dialogue about racialized, feminized spaces began to emerge via our search for self-understanding. Our hunger for mentorship and support has only grown with time, and we hope our reflections will serve as a reminder to all women of colour that we have gaps to fill and roles to play, for future generations of truth seekers."

After moving to Canada at the age of ten, I remember a constant desire for someone to teach me how to reconcile my conflicting worlds. All I remember is being different. Whether it was my religious beliefs or my homemade lunch, the differences were conspicuous. I grew up wanting to confide in someone, someone to help me make sense of my otherness at home and outside.

I am not quite sure when I became aware of my different ethnicity. There isn't a pivotal moment. My earliest memories of Canada are crowded by rhetoric of multiculturalism and equality, the superficiality of which was hidden behind "So, where are you really from?" or "Ha-ha, your last name sounds like Mufasa." The mostly innocent queries and initiatives of kids and adults alike are so ingrained in me that despite the passing of time, I don't expect to shed this skin of otherness.

I remember the sexual innuendos and the scandalous talks that matured my vocabulary in a matter of months. I learned what a "BJ" was, and the benefits of wearing a skirt on a date. None of this was relevant to me, and I did not want to learn it. Before I could learn what my own values were, I learned that they had to be flexible, letting the strongest cultural forces mould them into their imitation.

As a reaction, at home I was withdrawn. And at school I worked hard to appear enigmatic about my upbringing and roots, arrogant toward parents or any authority, comfortable dismissing my religion as if it was baby fat, the disappearance of which was long overdue. It was a battle between wild, uninhibited individuality, and suffocating paternalism. There was no middle ground, and there was no middle woman.

I speak as if this were in the past. We have a tendency to compartmentalize our lives into neat chronological sections, each ending with a conquering. I do it because it is easier to retroactively analyze the ways in which I have assimilated myself in order to blend in. It is much more painful to expose my current insecurities, my inability to articulate my acceptance of arranged marriages, or my ambivalence toward late-night partying. There are versions of my life edited differently to suit different readers.

As I enter graduate school and wonder what kind of a lawyer I want to be, or what kind of a woman I want to become, I have trouble finding examples. There's a residual tiredness that makes me feel much older than twenty. And no matter how much I appreciate my success, I feel the same skin of otherness. The desire to have a mentor seems juvenile, these reflections, isolating. While I haven't reconciled the conflicting identities, I have learned that I am not unique in this journey. It's not an individual issue, but a collective one. Knowing that is empowering, because it becomes more than a personal struggle; it's a cause.

Thinking of my younger, more susceptible self conjures feelings of loss, but it also creates a sense of responsibility. I think about the young girl on the bus wearing a hijab, and I imagine her spending her energy defending her decision of modesty. Or the girl smoking behind the garbage dump. I wonder how many spritzes of perfume or drops of Visine she will use to cover up the signs of being high. And I wonder how much effort the daughter I hope to have one day will spend thinking about whether to explain her differences or hide them. I wonder if she will feel different, whether she will embrace her otherness or deny it.

There must be a mother who is teaching her daughter how to be an immigrant Canadian, how to embrace her two histories and be at peace with the clashing roles we are prescribed, producing categories more accurate than "woman of colour," and creating vocabularies that empower her daughter. I want to find that mother. I want to be that mother. We all have to be that mother, that teacher.

Aruba Mustafa is a Pakistani Canadian. She recently completed her juris doctor. She loves to cook, paint, and tackle adventures like bungee jumping. Aruba is passionate about mentoring young people and staying involved in local community development initiatives.

WAITING FOR THE SUNSET

Nnene Ikejiani

The first question I am asked as an immigrant woman in Canada – more often than not – is "What brought you to Canada?" Naturally, people are curious and want to hear your story. At first I wondered why this question. After a while, the question became a constant reminder that I did not belong here – in Canada that is. At the time I was unaware that Canada was and still is being built by immigration. Certain stories were expected; I sensed the anticipation to hear something about the desperate need to flee my home country – a tale about escaping an African war, famine, or perhaps both, in search of a better life in Canada. This is why, when I answer the question, I often find their enthusiasm wavers. Somehow, in stating truth, I fail to meet their expectations and disappoint them. I can almost hear their thoughts, laced with doubt about my story. *If life was that good for her then why doesn't she go back to Nigeria?*

I am the second of seven children, five girls and two boys. My large extended family – uncles, aunts, cousins, nieces, and nephews – all lived within a twenty-five-mile radius. We could have breakfast at our parents' home and lunch and dinner at an aunt's, with no invitation or notice. We were welcome to stay the night too, as long as someone knew where we were. My mother was a strong woman, ahead of her time but still subject to it; she was married off at fourteen without the chance for education beyond primary school. By twenty-five she had borne four of her seven children, the boys being the last. She was unfairly treated by her husband and his family for years, simply because she had borne girls with no boy yet. She was practically abandoned financially and forced to raise her girls alone. But she was determined that no man would treat her daughters the same way, and wise enough to know that education for her girls was key to their freedom from oppression by any man. My mother did everything in her power to make sure her girls went to school. When her husband said he would not educate his daughters beyond primary school, she swore that would only happen over her dead body.

Despite her own negligible education, she was simultaneously a businesswoman, a farmer, and a contractor. She became a self-proclaimed feminist in our small town in the mid-sixties. This did not gain our family a good reputation, but she did not care what others thought about her. She would say to us, "Don't let anyone, man or woman, tell you that you can't be whatever you want to be because you are a woman. I will make sure each and every one of you goes to university and gets your first degree. With that, I know you can feed yourself and your children, with or without a man." Nothing made her happier than her daughters coming home with A's on their report cards. And so we all did. I went to college on a four-year federal government scholarship; my tuition, books, accommodation, and transportation allowance were paid. As a student, what else could you ask for? All you had to do was study.

I was young, beautiful, brilliant, and had dreams – lots of them. I had recently graduated from Polytechnic with a higher diploma in nutrition and dietetic studies and was excited about the stage of life about to unfold. But I had obligations to fulfill before I could pursue any of my personal dreams. The National Youth Service Corp was a federal government program designed to promote unity among Nigerian youth, and hence the nation. After graduation from university or college you were required, by law, to serve your country for one calendar year in a state outside of your home state, before you could proceed to graduate school or begin a career in your field of study. I was due to begin my service in September of 1980, but before then, I made a trip to Charleston, West Virginia, in the United States. En route, I stopped over in London to visit an uncle at Reading University where I planned to go for my master's in food chemistry. I planned to work until I could save some money to move to London or the States to further my education. I wanted to work for a food manufacturing company, like Cadbury, and ultimately build my own business in the food packaging industry.

I thought I had it all planned out, at least until one summer day in June 1979 when I met a Nigerian Canadian at Heathrow Airport. The course of the rest of my life was changed by that chance meeting and the intense family pressure to marry. These were the catalysts to my coming to Canada. I did not marry the Canadian I met at the airport. I married his brother.

I arrived in Calgary, Alberta, in the summer of 1985 with my nine-month-old. The eighteen-hour journey was tiring; my son cried clear across the Atlantic Ocean and on through to Calgary. Welcome to Canada! Life took a sharp turn. I desperately missed the few years after my youth service when I loved my job as a dietician in Enugu, where I had my own flat, shopped at the best department stores in the country, and travelled to London, Italy, and America often. I had lost all that was familiar. New country, new husband, new friends, and then there was the sun that would not set! Coming from the tropics where the sun always sets at 6:00 p.m. and almost instantly leaves the sky and roads in a thick and deep dark, the summer in Western Canada was peculiar; when time for sleep arrived the sun hung, fat, glowing, and, to me, almost defiant. What do you do when the sun refuses to set? You wait. Studying world geography did not prepare me for the sleepless nights of my first summer in Canada. I waited until the fall, when the sun finally retreated at the end of the day, and I met the cold and the winter, which came with challenges, but I slept.

I did my best to adjust to my new country and was eager to get back to work or school. But reality struck, I could not work as a dietician nor was I permitted to write the exam that would allow me to practice as a dietician in Alberta. I spent more than a year applying for countless positions in the Dietary Department at the Calgary General and Peter Lougheed Hospital in Calgary. I was willing to work as a dietary aide, porter, or supervisor – every position but the one I was trained for, had worked at, but was no longer qualified for. I did not receive a single call back.

Two years after my arrival in Calgary I became pregnant and gave birth to my daughter. Oh, how I wished I could go home – just run away with my children to the life I was used to. But that was another dream, not a possibility without a job. Attaining airfare for myself was far-fetched enough, let alone for two children! My husband could stay in Canada if he desired. My only concern was for my children. How could I work with two children and no family support? I could hear my mother's voice; "Don't let anyone tell you...." And so I persevered.

My friends told me that I could get childcare subsidy from social services. "Perfect," I thought, "I can finally get back to work." Again I started applying to the hospitals and heard nothing but silence in return. I was at the daycare dropping off the children one day when I overheard the manager say they needed to hire new staff. I asked if I could apply and was hired on the spot. I loved seeing my children while at work but I still wanted to work in a hospital and kept applying. It was the thirteenth application before I finally got an interview and was hired as a dietary aide. I found myself assembling food trays that were sent up to patients. Yes, that was what my degree got me in Canada. The initial excitement about this achievement swiftly evaporated. I attempted to walk my other chosen path and attain my master's. However the University of Alberta informed me that my degree from Nigeria was not recognized in Alberta and that I needed to take high-school-level mathematics, chemistry, physics, and biology to be admitted for a first degree in Nutrition. Reality struck again. My degree was worth absolutely nothing in Canada. I would be set back twelve years. I could see and feel the dream of a master's degree and anything beyond slipping farther and farther away. What I had was two children and a husband whose health was beginning to fail. I came to a pivotal moment in my life where I could either be selfish for once or choose to sacrifice my dreams for the most important people in my life. I chose the latter, for my young children.

It was 1993 and a cool November day in Edmonton. By this time, my marriage had dissolved, but the relationship my children had with their father was strong and full of love. They were excited for him to come and pick them up for the Remembrance Day long weekend. I had packed clothes, favourite stuffed animals, and children's books for their visit to Calgary. Their father was supposed to pick the kids up by noon. I watched the time pass – half past noon to four to seven to eight and he did not show. I had tried to call, but his line was busy all afternoon and into the evening. We never saw him or spoke with him again. My husband died of a brain aneurysm. As if I had not lost or sacrificed enough during my seven years in Canada, I was faced with another life-changing event – I was widowed at thirty-six. My son was only nine and my daughter was seven.

It was time for another tough decision. With absolutely no family support in Canada, I was under tremendous pressure to return home, especially after my mom visited us. "This is no life you are living here," she said. "Why are you suffering here alone as if you have no family? You are going to work yourself to death! All you people do here is work, eat, sleep, wake up, and repeat the cycle all over again. That's no life!" I did not want to put my children through yet another change; they would have to adjust to a new country, new school system, new friends, and going from a family of three to countless extended family members. "Mama," I said, "I will come home when they are grown."

Today those kids are grown. My daughter graduated from Carleton University with a major in psychology and a minor in English. My son is a University of Ottawa Law School graduate. I have a single regret about choosing to stay in Canada – losing my career. But that is what a mother does. It is a sacrifice! I have two amazing children that I am so proud of. Our experience in Canada strengthened us, and today we are very closely knit. As I look forward to the sunset of my life, I find myself asking, "Is it time to go home?" The more I ponder this question the more convinced I am that while Nigeria is home to me, so is Canada. My roots and the sun that I know are in two continents. I visit my mother and family every couple of years and it seems to suffice for now. But my Mama still asks, "When are you coming home?"

Nnene Ikejiani has called Edmonton, Alberta, home for the last thirty years. She is a mother of two adult children. Chigbo, her son, is a lawyer in Ottawa, and Ralueke, her daughter, is currently working with the Edmonton Public School Board. Nnene has worn many hats in her work career. In Nigeria she was a clinical dietician. In Canada, she has owned a business, worked as a banker and is now a financial security advisor. Like most immigrant women in Canada, she carved a new career for herself after having worked at numerous odd jobs. Despite the setbacks, she is grateful for the experience of life in Canada because it has made her the strong woman she is today.

CHANGES IN OPPORTUNITIES BETWEEN THE 1960S AND THE 1980S
Uma Parameswaran and Janaki Balakrishnan

This is a conversation between two women of fairly similar backgrounds who had very dissimilar experiences in Canadian society and in their workplaces. The major difference between them is that they arrived in Canada twenty years apart. Their experiences seem to show that for racialized immigrant women the Canada of the 1960s was a very different place from the Canada of the 1980s, and that the 2010s are perhaps more friendly to newcomers than the 1980s. Of course, this is only one such conversation on the subject.

UMA: Let me start with some personal background and my arrival in Canada. I am the fifth of a family of four boys and two girls. My father was a professor of physics and my mother a homemaker. Looking back, it seems to me that gender equality was practised as a matter of course in my family. My father handed over his salary to my mother on the first of every month, and she made all the decisions related to household expenditures. I assume she consulted my father on major budget decisions, but since they never owned a house or car or business, I doubt there was any occasion when she had to discuss or "get permission" as to how, when, and where the money was spent. Though we lived in a fair degree of comfort compared to most others, the family still lived frugally, from paycheque to paycheque.

Because a good education was the top priority for my parents, all of us were educated in private mission schools, all of us went to college at our parents' expense, and all of us earned our master's degree. I taught at a women's college for a couple of years, got a

Smith-Mundt Fulbright Scholarship in 1963, and left for the US. I met and married my husband in the US and, after spending a year in India, we immigrated to Winnipeg in 1966. I came as the wife of a person who already had a job offer, so we got our landed immigrant status without much delay.

I was working on my doctoral dissertation and thoroughly enjoyed the first year. We lived in a luxurious sublet furnished apartment and I was welcomed into the local badminton club. There were frequent parties within my husband's department, where there was collegiality and cordiality all round.

JANAKI: I am the fourth child, the second daughter in a family of five children. My father had lost both his parents at a very young age and was brought up by his elder sister, a divorcée with no children of her own. He was a government servant and my mother was a homemaker. Both my parents were from poor families with rich values of culture and tradition. With my aunt almost in the place of a grandmother, we grew up in Delhi, away from all the other relatives who were in South India. At home, we had to speak Tamil, eat Tamil food, and learn prayers in Sanskrit. Outside our home, we spoke Hindi and English. So, to some extent, living as a South Indian in North India was my first experience of being an outsider.

Even though I wanted to be a medical doctor, my father decided that he would not be able to afford it, and that I'd be better off being a teacher, and so I ended up training for that. I was the only one in my family who was not the top of the class, but I was also the only one who got scholarships, from grade six all the way through university. I was the only one who never needed any financial help from my parents for my studies or for my marriage.

I had an arranged marriage in 1985 to my husband, who was already a professor at the University of Manitoba. It took about a year to get my papers processed and I arrived in 1986. My daughter was born the next year, and my son three years later. I taught Sanskrit at the University of Manitoba for a year, and then settled down to the life of a housewife and a mom of two kids.

UMA: In the 1960s, one could get into academia without a PhD, and I was offered a lecturer's job at the University of Winnipeg in

1967. My salary was more than that of a male colleague who was appointed the same year to the same department because I had completed all but my dissertation. The following year, I was made assistant professor on tenure track, and in due time I earned my PhD. In short, I had a red-carpet treatment from day one. Neither my gender nor my skin colour seemed to have any negative impact on those who employed me.

JANAKI: Getting into the workforce was a long and tedious process for me. When my son started preschool, I stumbled upon the opportunity to do a post-baccalaureate certificate in education at the University of Manitoba. I was told that if I did that, I would be able to teach in Winnipeg. Seven months and $5,000 later, I waited patiently in line to graduate. Just as I was wondering why I was given a different coloured gown than my peers, I was informed that it was because I had a master's! So, they recognized my education from India! I was on top of the world. Finally, I would be able to do what I enjoyed the most: teach.

Sadly, it was not that simple. I was given the highest classification for teachers, which meant that I would have to be paid a high salary as well. My balloon of enthusiasm deflated when I heard that I had become too expensive. Determined as I was, I went to a branch of the Winnipeg Transition Centre after seeing an ad in the local newspaper. I learned how to write a résumé, how to make cold calls, and how to answer questions in an interview. I would walk into the nearby high schools with my 'résumé' and ask if I could substitute in their school. I did not have the "dress pants and shirts" recommended by the Transition Centre. At that time I generally wore salwar kameez, the northern Indian attire of long pants and shirts that were very loose fitting, or I would wear Western clothes: blue jeans and a loose t-shirt. That first year in 1995–1996, I got called to substitute only three times.

Since I wanted more opportunity to work, I went to a junior high school near my house. I was interviewed by the vice principal, as he was in charge of calling the substitutes. He repeatedly asked me one question: "Where are you from?" I tried to tell him that I am from Winnipeg/Canada/my neighbourhood, but none of these answers satisfied him. When he asked the same question for the fifth time, I asked if he wanted to know where I had obtained most of my education. He immediately sat up and said, "Yes." So, I told him that most of my education was from India and my latest degree was from the University of Manitoba. Immediately he told me that I could not sub in his school, as he had heard that teachers beat up children in India! I was furious. I informed him that whatever he had "heard" was wrong and his blanket statement was discriminatory. I complained against him, but the case was dismissed as he denied saying anything like that, and I had no witness.

Then, in January 1998, I got my first break: a term job! I was assigned a lot of different courses with no prep, but I was not going to complain. Soon after starting, the principal called me to his office. He had the female vice principal with him. He sat me down and then the vice principal informed me that I was expected to wear work clothes and what I was wearing (salwar kameez) was not appropriate. They gave me the rest of the day off to go find some "work clothes." I called my husband and he took me to Sears and asked the staff to help me find some "work clothes" as neither of us had any idea of what those were. That lady picked some clothes off shelves and we paid for them. I wore those clothes to work from that day on. All I knew was that in that same school another younger teacher would wear short shorts and a tank top with a sweater on top (that she'd take off during the class, claiming that it was very hot), and nobody said anything to her. My baggy Indian clothes were not work wear, but my young white colleague's attire was. Years later when I was telling someone this story, they told me that it was discrimination and was against human rights. My daughter would look at me and ask, "Amma, why are you wearing old people clothes? Why don't you wear clothes like my teachers?" I had no answer for her at that time. Looking back, I realize that the lady who had helped me was elderly, and she had picked the clothes that she'd wear to work!

UMA: There was no question that my generation had to suffer gender discrimination, but I can't say I suffered racial discrimination. I have friends who have told me about discrimination from employers who did not believe a woman could manage a family and a job. My whole generation of women gave rise to a lost, unborn generation, as it were, because often by the time they were settled in an academic job, their reproductive life was behind them. In practice it became a choice between career and having a family. Things have changed a lot since then, with labour unions and our new laws that ensure not only maternity but paternity leaves. In my early days in academia, there was no question of anyone getting maternity leave; even getting unpaid leave depended on the employer's attitude! Again, I was lucky to have a department head who accommodated my needs when I became pregnant and said he would arrange for someone else to take my classes during the second term. However, it so happened that my daughter decided to arrive six weeks early and was born in late November. By the time the university reopened after the Christmas break, I was ready to teach again. So I missed only three weeks of classes.

As regards dress codes, I know many offices and businesses even in my early days had a written or unwritten dress code that women wear "office attire." In my own case, when I was a graduate student at Indiana and Michigan State Universities, my saris generated nothing but friendly and sometimes pleasantly curious conversation. It never struck me that I should wear anything but my saris when I started working in Canada. I always wore my saris and the red bindi on my forehead when I went to class.

On my non-teaching days, I would sometimes wear a pantsuit. I have an anecdote from those very early days. One day, when I wore a rather elegant pantsuit, I thought a bindi looked out of place and so decided not to wear the very Indian bindi with the very Western outfit. One of my colleagues looked very concerned as he came up to greet me – "Uma, are you unwell? You don't seem yourself today." I told him I was fine, and he looked at me more closely and said I didn't look myself. I pointed out that I was not wearing a bindi! He had not noticed my pantsuit but had noticed that my face was not my usual face. That clinched the matter for me; from then on, I had no hesitation wearing my bindi with pantsuits or jeans or shorts or whatever Western outfit I chose to wear, whether for work or elsewhere.

JANAKI: Either you have been very lucky or things were different at that time. All I got during my first years in the workforce were part-time stipend jobs at the university, teaching Sanskrit and Hindi. After fourteen years of working term jobs, I got a part-time but permanent job, teaching adults at Red River College. In 1994 I was informed by the associate dean of education that I should specialize in teaching English as a second language since I had a master's in English literature, rather than trying to find a job teaching English. Even though I was told that it would not be easy to find jobs teaching English as a non-native English speaker, I took his advice. Today, I am an English as an additional language teacher! So things have changed even since I came to Canada.

UMA: Let us talk about discrimination in the workplace. I have had some battles in the workplace on issues of gender discrimination. My discipline – English literature – has a long history of using what I call slave labour – part-time positions that are poorly paid and where the class size is large, with a huge marking load, and the remuneration less than half of what those in tenure-track positions got for the same job. Because English is popular among women, many women go all the way to a PhD in the discipline. But when it came to getting hired, men always seemed to get the full-time job. Granted the 1980s were lean years for many universities, with budget restrictions that prevented new vacancies. Even so, it was obviously unfair that the few vacancies that did come up were always filled by male candidates. So one of my battles was to get more women hired full time into the department. I also introduced the first women's literature course, and a few years later introduced four more women's literature courses with the help of three part-time women colleagues. I also initiated and chaired a women-focused research group and edited a beautiful volume at the end of it, after a national conference on women-focused research.

I was active on the board of The Writers' Union of Canada and of the Canadian Ethnic Studies Association. Always aware that more recent immigrants had more negative arrival experiences than my own, in the 1980s I was active in the Immigrant Women's Association of Manitoba, and worked to expand its services with a counselling section. When the provincial government cut off all funding in 2000, I once again took an active role and as president helped get the organization on its feet again. My work within the community has been recognized at my workplace. In short, in my own life, I cannot recall being targeted on the basis of race, though perhaps I have sometimes been shortchanged because of my gender.

JANAKI: I wish I could say the same. I have volunteered extensively to work with children who have come to Canada from war-torn countries, and hosted and mentored many refugee children, but my work has seldom been recognized or rewarded by administrators. It is as though one is expected to do a lot of community volunteerism as part of one's job. I have been passed over when it comes to promotions and other development opportunities. But I persist because the work I do – helping new immigrant and underprivileged children – is its own reward.

Today I often wear my Indian clothes to work, especially when the weather gets warm. In 2007, I was working with a group of kids from grades 3 to 6. It was summertime and I was wearing my Indian clothes to work daily. One day we had cooler weather and I went to work wearing pants and a shirt. One of my students would always come to my door to say a cheerful "good morning" to me every day. That day she also poked her head in but did not say anything at all, and then left. Later that day I went to her class to work with her. I asked her why she did not greet me that morning. All this time she had not looked up at me but was only hearing my voice. She looked up and said, "Oh, Mrs. B! I did not recognize you, as you are wearing regular clothes! I was looking to see if you were in your office this morning and I did not see your special clothes." Now I do not get recognized if I wear "regular" clothes. Mrs. B has got to be seen in her "special" clothes!

UMA: Could we say, then, that Canada of the 1960s was a friendlier place for racialized immigrants than the Canada of the 1980s? And that today's Canada is better than the Canada of the 1980s?

JANAKI: From your experience and mine, perhaps that is true. No doubt, a fuller picture will emerge when sociologists and analysts draw conclusions from a wider spectrum of life stories from people like us.

Uma Parameswaran was born and educated in India. She went to the US as a Smith-Mund Fulbright student in 1963 and returned to India in 1965. She came to Winnipeg in 1966 and retired as professor of English. She has published extensively in the fields of postcolonial literatures, including Writing the Diaspora: Essays on Culture and Identity *(2007). She is a writer and author of award-winning fiction,* including A Cycle of the Moon *(2010) and* What Was Always Hers *(1999). She has been on various national boards, including The Writers' Union of Canada and Canadian Ethnic Studies Association. She lives in Winnipeg with her husband. They have a daughter and two grandchildren.*

Janaki Balakrishnan is a teacher, originally from New Delhi, India. She came to Canada in 1986 after an arranged marriage in June, 1985 to Dr. S. Balakrishnan. Initially, she spent time with her two children as her teaching credentials from India (BSc. (Hons.), MA, BEd) were not recognized in Manitoba. It took fourteen years of working in temporary part-time positions in schools, university, and college to finally land a part-time but permanent job at Red River College. Today she is a qualified special educator for children and adults with special needs, an adult educator (in the fields of sciences and mathematics), as well as a specialist in intensive literacy and numeracy for people with extensive language needs.

LEARNING THE TREES

Phedra Deonarine

My family and I moved from Gulf View, Trinidad, to Vancouver, Canada, in 2002. We are a Muslim family, which made it an odd time to emigrate. But we were moving to Canada, and the Caribbean isn't the Middle East. Canadians, at least, seemed to have a sense of geography. I was ashamed in a way to be from the Caribbean, but still pleased to clarify that "No, my family is from Trinidad, not India," because here, it seemed that India was seen as poorer even than the Caribbean, and that seemed far more shameful. I did little things like hide the fact that I didn't eat pork, but I never lied about what I was. Concealment was easier and a carryover from Trinidad. In some regards, it was easier to be a Muslim here than in Trinidad.

I don't know if I was happy in Trinidad. I left when I was eighteen, and teenagers aren't known for bubbling with joy. I grew to like the move to Canada. I wasn't fond of the tropical sun, and Vancouver was fairly comfortable. People in Vancouver seemed to favour size-zero girls, which wasn't the case in Trinidad, where thickness and shape were much admired. It was lovely to be the right size, if not the right shade. I just had to remember what my mother told me, "Walk like a strong black woman," which was odd considering that we were East Indians. Odder still considering the tense relationship between black people and East Indians in Trinidad. But my mother wasn't raised to be a racist, and I never heard the 'N-word' in my house until an East Indian girl used it at my primary school.

There were things I missed – books I'd read as a child, certain fruits that were native to Trinidad. But that was to be expected. If I ever mentioned something that I missed, my mother countered by saying, "What you want? You rather be in Trinidad with chicken costing sixty dollars a pound? You forget about that?" My mother seemed pleased with the price of food in Canada. It was much cheaper to buy meat for every meal, even beef, which was a special-occasion meat in Trinidad. She used to consider meat for every meal gluttony, but after moving she bought as much as she wanted. She did say, though, that the chickens were sweeter in Trinidad and the meat "looked different." She raised chickens as a child and was a bit concerned about the diet of the chickens in Canada, and whether or not they got to roam about.

I was supposed to miss Trinidadian food more than I actually did. I started eating food from different countries in Vancouver, options I'd never had before. I grew impatient with the constant taste of cilantro and hot pepper at home. Although my mother was always willing to make a pot of dhal or stew chicken, I was more interested in going for sushi. My mother didn't like sushi. She approved of my mixing with Asian girls because she thought that Asian girls were "very decent." So it was all right to go out with them for food because they "appreciate food and were raised in a home."

She forgave my culinary explorations faster than my sister's sudden aversion to food. My mother couldn't understand why a person would choose not to eat. Every day my mother cooked pots of food, but my sister dawdled with it and never ate. She wasn't fat, my sister, at least not by Trinidadian standards – she had "shape and size." I was "finny-bone" and harassed by strangers to "eat more" and "watch yourself in case you fly away" if it was windy. People said I wouldn't be able to have children and "What boy go want a finny-bone girl for?"

So I continued to gorge on foreign food while my sister starved herself, sleeping away hours in an unmade bed. For my mother this meant that her pots remained full. She kept going back for seconds and thirds. She didn't want to try new foods. She refused to see my sister's anorexia as a serious problem. We got calls from the school counsellor, but my mother insisted that my sister's behaviour was a choice, not a disease. "Why you behaving white like that for?" she asked. "Whoever hear of someone starving theyself? Stop playing movie star. I cook all this food. You think it fall from the sky?"

I didn't think at the time what moving would have meant for my mother. My father had to work in a different province because Vancouver had so few jobs and none that paid enough for an immigrant with a family of four children trying to rebuild a life. While he was away, my mother started going to the thrift store. She was amazed at how little it cost to decorate a house in North America. This was wonderful because our house in Trinidad had been unfinished for a long time. We lived with painted cement floors and only tiled them when we needed to sell our house to move to Vancouver.

My mother started leaving the house an hour earlier to pick us up from school, so that she could spend time in the thrift store. She made a "nest of lights" out of a second-hand basket and old Christmas lights and ornaments. Then came the little village with Christmas carollers and gingerbread houses in snowy lanes. She called it "the winter village" and her "winter-time decorations" because we couldn't celebrate Christmas. It didn't matter what she called it because it was the middle of September and nothing was season appropriate.

No one in my family commented on the Christmas wreath on the back door in August, or the Thanksgiving centrepieces year-round. She kept a tidy house, my mother. She had the carpets shampooed once a month and couldn't stand clutter. The most frightening TV show, and perhaps her favourite, was *Hoarders*. She didn't understand how people could live in such a mess and disrespect property like that. She admitted that she understood "the high people feel when they in the thrift store. You don't understand that. When you lonely and you don't have to spend too much money to make your place nice. It does be a nice rush and does give you a moment of happiness. It does be a nice, nice happiness, but it don't last. You don't know what that loneliness like."

My mother was alone, perhaps in ways I couldn't understand. Her siblings were not with her, nor her husband. I missed my friends and my boyfriend but I see now that didn't compare. The little problems I faced were tripled for her. I had trouble getting makeup due to my skin tone, little things like that. We moved from being part of a majority group to suddenly being a minority, but these things seemed like small sacrifices to be safe. Children in Trinidad were being kidnapped, and the atmosphere of the country around elections was violent. I told people in Trinidad how safe it was here, but they got defensive and said things like, "We might have high crime and thing. But them foreigners does have crazy killings. They like to collect body parts and thing. I hear they have one killer there who did feed people to pigs."

That was true, and for a second I was embarrassed. Only it *was* much safer here. You just had to know where to avoid. Here, you didn't need to plan to go out only when your male friends were going. At least here cars driven by girls weren't spotted by men on the street who would fling nails on the road to cause the tires to pop and the car to stop. It was safer to be a girl here, and like everywhere else, safety increased with how much money you had.

I still spent the majority of my weekends at my mother's house. Out of respect for my mother and fear of her finding it, I refused to go on birth control. There were certain things that you didn't discuss because it meant you were acting "big woman," and even in my twenties and in a foreign country, I didn't want the stigma I'd internalized from Trinidad's social structure. Most of my friends were immigrant girls and none of us talked about things like that with our parents. Once, at university, my friend told me that she overheard our Canadian floor-mate discussing sex with her boyfriend – with her mother. My friend wrinkled her brow and said, "I could never do that. It's so disrespectful. How come they don't understand the difference between a mother and a friend?"

I wasn't jealous of daughters with that kind of relationship. The distance in the roles was important, and didn't signify a lack of compassion. How could it, considering that my mother left her home country in midlife, left her family and the comfort of being in a land she knew? She moved to a foreign country in order to send her children to school, and to keep us safe from the crime and blatant racism of Trinidad. She had four children and one miscarriage. She almost died giving birth to my baby brother and forever lost her trust in Trinidadian doctors.

My mother's first three children were girls. She made sure that my eldest sister and I learned to drive stick-shift cars, because she saw no reason why "only boy should learn on manual." She sent all of us to school because she didn't think boys should get special privileges. There were morals to adhere to, but she gave us the tools to be independent. She didn't want us to think anyone was better than we were. She sent all of us to university. We changed in school. None of us lived at home, and all of us lived with men before marriage. I think in a number of ways, we broke her heart, but at the same time, none of us grew up racist and we all knew that you never hate a person for something they cannot change. We all owe that to her. And if it sounds too fundamental to mention, you didn't grow up in Trinidad.

I never saw the point of studying Trinidadian literature. To me, greatness didn't happen on the island. We were small, with no history and a high crime rate. Moving didn't change my lack of interest in Trinidadian authors. But later on I wanted to be a writer, and it seemed only fitting to read work from my country. How odd it was to read of places I knew and to understand the characters; odder still to see that most of the books were published in Canada, America, or the United Kingdom. I knew Trinidad though, and I knew those people the way a child does, and in some regards, this will remain so for me. But I'm not ashamed anymore. We are a small nation, but we gave the world fine writers. There aren't many women writers from the Indo-Caribbean, but gaps can be filled, even at a distance.

Sometimes my mother wonders if the move was worth it, but I think she knows it was. I am very glad we moved. I never would have wanted to be a writer if we hadn't. I came across a passage in a book by a Trinidadian writer, V.S. Naipal, who said – I'm paraphrasing – that one knows the trees of one's homeland in a complete way because one grew up with them. You can learn the birch and the oak, but you know the cocoa tree because you grew up together.

It's hard to make a new land home. You have to learn that new place in a way you didn't learn your birth country. But hard isn't impossible and everyone learns eventually what is and isn't acceptable. I haven't gone back to my home country in almost a decade and have no plans to do so. It isn't ingratitude or shame, just the way things go. People move. They grow up. These things happen. This is my home now. I will make this my home now.

Phedra Deonarine grew up in Trinidad and moved to Vancouver, BC, when she was eighteen. She completed her BA in English at the University of British Columbia. She was the Truman Capote Fellow in the Rutgers-Newark MFA in the Creative Writing Program. Her work has appeared in Indiana Review, Canada Writes, *and* Cuizine. *She is currently studying Caribbean literature at Rutgers University–New Brunswick, New Jersey.*

ADJUSTMENT AND ACCOMMODATION
Sheila Nirmala Denetto

I arrived in Canada on a wintry day in February. It was my first encounter with ice and snow and, wearing improper footwear, I slid and fell on the tarmac. Right away there was the adjustment to be made to the harsh climate. I was in a world very different from the one I grew up in. In the more than half century I have lived here, there were many, many accommodations that had to be made.

To begin with, there was the work world, and how I entered it and continued to progress in it through many years of education. Given my career choice, I was able to widen my horizons as I engaged in activities that would help my personal growth and the well-being of my family. My most profound influences came from good women friends, and often world figures and books that inspired me. From these, I gathered insights that helped me endure hardships that came my way inevitably, as this was, I understood, a life condition. The raging public discourse on women's rights and feminism from the 1960s onwards had an impact on how I conducted my public and private life. Another tier was added to my development when I joined the teachers' union and became aware of inequalities in the workplace and also the responsibility I had in the classroom to provide equal access for girls in non-traditional activities. I learned that being a visible minority citizen meant there were barriers in the workplace and in how one was perceived by the dominant culture.

My husband of three months met me at Dorval Airport in Montreal. It was February 1965. As I exited the terminal, I could see him peering at the crowds that had just emerged from the last checkpoint. I don't think he recognized me in my fur-collared coat, hat, and other winter wear. He still imagined me as he had last seen me, wearing my beautiful tropical clothing, which at the time was a sari. He chuckled at the sight of me and I, in turn, noted his attire – a heavy winter coat and an Afghan-style hat. I immediately sensed a crucial part of my identity was compromised.

The way I dressed was so much a part of my identity. Over

the next year, transforming my wardrobe was a slow and painful adjustment. I grew up in a small Christian community in India, where I remember very well the missionaries who abounded in my life. They never gave up their Western dress, not even stockings, which must have been extremely uncomfortable in the heat. These comparisons crossed my mind, and I wondered what made me change as opposed to those who clung to their traditions, good or bad, from dress to ideas to food. The difference, I realized, was that the Europeans would never go "native" – an acknowledgement of surrender to a "lesser" culture. They were at the time the colonists and, therefore, felt superior to us. Now my coming as an immigrant to Canada was de facto an acknowledgement that I was here to better my life in a promised land. Within this understanding, my own and Canadian society's, is the basis for all our interactions. It is an underdog labelling of "visible minority" that happens at every level of interaction between me and the new society in which I now live, imposing social pressure that pushed me to make the choices I did – to assimilate.

I chose to wear Western clothes when I ventured out, for practical reasons and so that I was not as visible or open to extra attention, good and bad. In the mid-sixties when there were few South Asians in Montreal, one really stood out wearing a sari. Of course it was extremely uncomfortable attire to be wearing in the dead of winter. I heard many Canadians remark on how lovely the costume was, but one also heard comments such as, "Are you warm enough?" or "Is this a cultural requirement?" In these questions were judgments about one's choices and the very real problems such a choice might create in this society. I felt the best thing to do was to wear my cherished saris at home and for special occasions. This was my first step towards "Canadianization."

There was an internal dialogue going on in my mind about how better to fit in. It seemed crucial that I do so in the workplace. I had barely landed in Canada when, ten days later, I was at work in a school. At the time there was a shortage of teachers, and my qualifications were accepted by the Montreal Catholic School Board. I had three years of post-secondary education in India, two of which were spent acquiring a teaching diploma. At the time, some English medium convents in India were providing teacher training that was valid in Commonwealth countries. It was a coveted certificate, enabling one to teach, ostensibly, in all Commonwealth countries.

My first assignment in Montreal was to teach a grade seven class. These children ranged from thirteen to fourteen years old. The students' reaction to my accent, which at the time was very British sounding, was painful. I had just administered a spelling test, and what started as snickering turned ugly as the students yelled that they didn't understand what I was saying. The principal was called in, and there was some discussion about differing accents and how students needed to tolerate such differences. It was good to have a helpful principal. I enlisted his help in other matters such as classroom management and in understanding the very different school culture that existed in the Canadian system. There was no automatic respect for the teacher as was the case in India.

It is crucial to understand this difference if one is to navigate difficult situations, and it is best to enlist the help of good mentors. Learning to recognize those who will help and guide you is a very important aspect of progressing toward healthy adjustments to a new culture. Thanks to this principal, I learned some early lessons in how to manage a tough situation. The first three months at this school were a trial by fire. However, they made a good foundation for future improvements and learning. I made a conscious choice to change my accent. It helped that I was a pretty good mimic. My next assignment was with a lovely bunch of third graders still in awe of their teachers. This second transformation helped me communicate effectively with my small students. In their forgiving hearts, any mistakes I made were easily overlooked. Very different from the cruelty of pre-teens!

Moving to Ontario was good for my husband but a disaster for me. Ontario had no teacher shortage and my qualifications were thrown out as useless, even though I had taught for the better part of five years in Montreal and my certificate stated clearly that I could teach in Commonwealth countries. Thus began my long journey into procuring my teacher's certification in Ontario. I tried to branch out into another profession but found that for all practical purposes, to continue in education was my best option. I felt adrift and insecure as I was now totally dependent on my husband for my financial well-being. This was not a comfortable position, given that my husband was spiraling down the path of alcoholism. I felt terrified for my family and, without a job, quite powerless. I think my husband did realize I needed to get back on my feet professionally; he understood it would be good for the economic well-being of our family. He, therefore, was glad to fund my education.

I had difficulties enrolling in a Canadian university. Even though I had obtained five university courses during my stay in Montreal, I was told I did not have the equivalent of an Ontario grade thirteen certificate! After a couple of years of stalling, Lakehead University enrolled me in their undergraduate degree program, even recognizing the university credits I had obtained in Montreal. It might have been low enrolment numbers that prompted this change of heart! I do not know for sure. I finally received my Canadian BA and BEd in 1976, six years after arriving in Ontario. I was able to get my first teaching job soon after I graduated. I later obtained an MEd. Over the years I studied to become a well-rounded teacher by taking courses specifically designed for teachers' professional development. I took one of my last university courses in 1996, two years before my retirement.

The opportunity to improve oneself and progress in one's career is something I treasured, and I doubt I would have been able to do this easily in India. I exited my profession having taught all grades – one to eight – and having been a curriculum consultant and a vice principal of a fair-sized school. By this time I had the qualifications and experience to apply for a principal's position. I did not pass the rigorous interview process. I had reached the visible-minority glass ceiling. I heard from a friend on the interviewing panel that one of the important and influential panel members had determined that Thunder Bay communities, where we resided at the time, were "not ready" for a person such as myself – read, "not ready" for a "visible minority" individual! All the positions I had held in my career were extremely rewarding, but the career pinnacle, the coveted role of principal, was kept from me.

All this progress in my career co-existed with the obligations and duties of raising a family. My husband's liking for alcohol turned into a full-fledged addiction. I felt myself swimming upstream trying to keep hearth and home together for the best part of forty years. Suffice it to say, having a career, though very hard in light of my domestic problems, was a godsend. I felt secure because I had a job and earned good money. I felt rewarded in the accolades I received for work well done. I must say that my decisions early on to emulate "mainstream" Canadians in accent and dress made acceptance in the workplace easier. Were there any overt attempts to require this of me? No. I had deduced this as a requirement from my interactions with Canadian society at large. I never wanted to stand out. It was just easier to assimilate! It was my comfort level that was important.

I was an accidental recruit to be an active member of the teacher's union. I believe visible minority participation was encouraged. Despite my reluctance to become politically active, I did learn about employment equity and pay equity for women through my participation in the Union. There were discussions about and activism around these issues. I realized that being a woman and a visible minority person put one at a disadvantage; my participation helped both causes.

My first enlightenment around women's issues came from reading *The Female Eunuch* and then other feminist works that enjoyed media attention in the early seventies. In the classroom I made sure girls were never assigned gender-type roles. I tried to encourage girls and boys, by example and persuasion, to question assumptions about what girls and boys could and could not do. I took seriously my mentorship in encouraging boys and, particularly, girls to shine in science and mathematics. I had a thriving science program and found every opportunity for girls, who were generally reluctant to enter and engage in competitions, to showcase their work.

I believe that dinner table discussions about gender issues formed the basis for how my own children conduct their lives today. My legacy to my children has been the model I provided both by a life lived and by guidance through discussion. They are enlightened about the issues and try to not fall into old patterns of male dominance. Their support during very trying times was invaluable.

I became a citizen of Canada in 1970, five years after my arrival. The first adjustments of dress and accent were pragmatic ones, and whatever their underlying reasons, they set a course for success in work and at home. If this is a kind of "racialization," then I was a willing participant. I obviously read the cues and codes that lay beneath the surface in Canadian society and I made the decision to change because I did not want to be any more "visible" than I already was. One's visible status does not ever go away – after all, it is based on the colour of one's skin. It does irritate, sometimes infuriate, as the status it affords you is one of a second-class citizen.

There are many examples I can provide as to why I believe this. When in a line up, if by chance one is at the counter beside a white person, the server visibly struggles with whom to serve first. I was asked by a twenty-something nurse's aide how I enjoyed living in Canada…she obviously had lived in Canada for less than half the time I had! She felt a sense of entitlement to her "Canadianness" that my colour precludes me from.

In the almost half century I have been here, I have been invited into the homes of friends from the dominant culture about a dozen times – a little more than twice a decade! I came from a society where inviting friends into our homes happens without much fuss. People drop in unannounced (at least when I lived there) and are frequently fed before they leave. I have visited India many times over the years and I see that in urban areas, where men and women have work and obligations outside the home, there are time constraints and, therefore, some limits on informal "dropping in." Over here, both my husband and I kept up our tradition of inviting friends over for social events. We were seldom asked back to the homes of these people. The only exception was when, for twenty years, we lived in a rural community outside Thunder Bay. Much to our delight, our immediate neighbours were prone to dropping in without warning. At first, I think there was a lot of curiosity about us. For whatever reasons it happened, we accepted and returned the hospitality during those years. But this experience was not duplicated in urban situations. Our Thunder Bay experience was a testament to lives lived away from the demands of urban centres.

I still hear many South Asians and immigrants from other countries say they have stopped inviting people over because they never get invited back! As a visible minority person, one does exist in a sort of parallel universe here. We end up associating with our own kind more often than not because there is a reciprocity in such friendships that is not available from those of the mainstream community. Even though I have all the legal rights of being a Canadian citizen, I feel

I am not really embraced as a "real" Canadian. I am a hyphenated Canadian, a South Asian-Canadian.

When I think back on my journey as a resident of Canada for forty-seven years, I have mostly positive feelings about the changes I have undergone. I am very happy here. I feel free to dress as I please, associate with people I love and admire, continue to engage in learning. I move around with great safety. I lead a pleasant and productive life and share my expertise and resources whenever I can. I can't say how those forty-seven years would have translated if I had remained in India. When I do visit India I find I am not as comfortable and not as free as I am here, especially as I age. The one thing I have never changed is how I eat. It's curry almost every day!

Sheila Nirmala Kumari (Denetto) was born in Bangalore, India, in 1943. Before coming to Canada in 1965 she had three years of post-secondary education, two of which were spent in teacher training. She obtained an MEd in Canada. Sheila worked as an elementary school teacher in Canada for twenty-five years. She has two children and three grandchildren, all born in Canada. She is an artist and exhibits her work at local shows. She enjoys writing and engaging in a variety of writing projects. Sheila also does volunteer work with refugees and seniors.

ON BECOMING A FILIPINO CANADIAN

Dr. Ruby L. de Guzman Formoso

I was born in San Jose City, Philippines, and moved to Manila with my family at the age of two. I lived in a modest apartment with my parents and was the youngest of seven children. Most of my siblings were already married and lived separately from us, except for an older sister, with whom I shared a bedroom. My father was a building contractor and built several homes in upscale areas. Ironically, he was not able to build one for himself because there were several of us he had to support through school. My oldest sister, who was in Canada, and my only brother, a doctor and the oldest sibling, supported me. They helped pay my tuition fees for medical school.

I was twenty-five years old, newly graduated from medical school at the University of Santo Tomas, and was engaged to be married to my schoolmate when I left the Philippines to come to Canada in September 1972. I travelled with my parents. Even though they had visas to leave before I did, they waited for me to make sure I would be safe in my travels. I arrived in Ottawa with a job waiting for me as a medical intern at Ottawa General Hospital. Shortly after my arrival, my fiancé arrived and we got married. We had three beautiful children in the span of five years.

My life in Canada has been wonderful – not that it's been easy. I had to work as a resident, rotating in various hospitals, taking night calls every three days, while also taking care of my children. Fortunately, my parents were staying with us, so they helped look after our children, which was a traditional practice among Filipinos here in Canada.

Looking back to my own childhood, I remember that some of my father's rules had a significant impact on my life. My father did not let me ride a bike. He said that riding a bike was for boys – it was not feminine. He did not allow me to learn how to swim for fear that I would drown, or roller-skate for fear I would break my leg. Thus, here in Canada, I could not go biking or swimming with my children. I was not interested in camping – I never did that back home. Camping was for Boy Scouts. Even though I was a Girl

Scout, I was not allowed to join this activity. I feel a sense of loss in my connection with my children because I could not spend time doing these activities with them.

I came here with a landed immigrant visa. Fortunately my schooling had been at one of the universities recognized in Canada. Most of my challenges were about language and cultural barriers. Though I had used English as a medium of instruction and learning from elementary school up through university, I was short on the colloquial expressions used in everyday conversations. Many times I found myself not fitting into group conversations with Canadians. As well, for some time, I carried a colonial mentality that placed all Westerners on a higher pedestal. I deferred to them as my superiors. In my home country, we were expected to respect our elders and teachers. So I refrained from disagreements or expressing my opinions. It was only later, after doing personal development work, that I gained enough self-confidence and self-esteem to break away from my tradition. I then began to speak more confidently with others, both peers and superiors.

As a Filipino woman, I am used to giving in a bit more, or giving up things I love for the sake of something important. For instance, when I was studying for my pathology exam, I chose to leave my family to do a locum in Fredericton, New Brunswick, for four months, with the hope that the experience would broaden my knowledge and give me confidence to pass my test. I sacrificed myself, living separately from my supportive husband and my young children. It was a very sad time of my life. The memory still brings me tears. But this pain of separation strengthened me and helped me to pass my exam and land a job as a pathologist at the Riverside Hospital in Ottawa.

However, while I was working as a pathologist, my inner desire to become a psychiatrist blossomed. I deliberated for two years whether to give up my current career to pursue my new passion. Finally a message came to me and said, "You can become sixty-five one day and if you do not follow your heart, you will up end up regretting your life." With that message inside my heart, I gave up pathology to pursue a new path.

It is customary for Filipino parents in their old age to stay with their adult children. I happen to be the one my parents chose, perhaps because I was the youngest. They were with me all my life. My father was extremely protective of me, even as an adult. I often felt he was treating me like a child. However, my parents were a great help to me. But it got difficult over time because they were getting older and becoming sick. My father died from a heart attack, and my mother followed, also dying from a heart attack three years later.

Through my grief, I felt that this was a defining moment in my life. I had lived my entire life with my parents, but now – even though I was missing them – I had this sense of autonomy – that I was the head of my family and not under my parents' authority.

In 1985, I took the Christopher Leadership course for public speaking, a Christian-based training program that helps develop leadership for those wishing to serve their communities. This ten-week course was my inspiration for getting involved in the Filipino community. I enjoyed being part of the community. I felt a great sense of belonging and began to feel a sense of being home away from home.

Through these years of growth, I developed my identity as a Filipino community leader. I had the honour and pleasure to welcome former President Fidel Ramos during his visit to Ottawa in 1994. I have also emerged as a psychiatrist with an interest in spiritual healing and development. In my advanced years, I saw how important kindness and compassion were to patients. I am grateful to have witnessed and shared the pain that many patients endure. I value how strong and brave they are. I see how much pain people can suffer, and I experience a sense of fulfillment when the light at the end of the tunnel shines.

I have a passion for studying. My personal development work gave me balance and a good sense of myself. When I am with my Filipino friends, I leave my medical identity in the office.

As I reach the later phase of my life, it is my wish to be strong in body and mind and to continue to be useful in society, offering help to those in need. I am indebted to everyone with whom I have crossed paths, in good times and bad. They have made this life possible for me. I am grateful to be here in Canada.

Dr. Ruby L. de Guzman Formoso started her career as an anatomical pathologist in Ottawa. In 1992 she began practicing community-based spiritual psychiatry integrating mindfulness, energy healing, spiritual healing, and neuro-linguistic programming. From 1985–89 she was the vice president, president, and adviser of the Filipino-Canadian Association of the Ottawa Valley. She served as chairperson for the Philippine Independence Committee of the Ottawa Valley, 1994–97; the Philippine Heritage Language School, 1986–89; the Philippine Pastoral Group, 1993–97; and is now chairperson for the Philippine Heritage Foundation of Canada and co-chairperson for the San Lorenzo Ruiz Filipino Catholic Mission. In 2002 she received the Banaag Presidential Award for Most Outstanding Filipino Canadian. She has three children and seven grandchildren.

DOES RACE MATTER?
FROM NEW DELHI TO OTTAWA

Peruvemba S. Jaya

MY IMMIGRATION PATH

When I think of my personal and professional journey, from India to North America, various words and thoughts, all jumbled, spring up – racism, ethnicity, woman, woman of colour, Indian, East Indian. All these words, and the accompanying emotions, word pictures, and images they conjure up, were completely alien to me back in India. I had never had to interrogate or consciously think about my place and location in a social space. I was Indian in India and was comfortable being that, and in some ways was not aware of anything more than that. Never having experienced living in any other country before moving to North America, questions about gender, ethnicity, race, place, voice, and my relationship to all of these were things that I had not really reflected upon.

The journey to the West happened rather accidentally, or seren-dipitously, as a result of a series of events, personal and professional, which propelled me to make some major changes in my life. I moved to Rhode Island to pursue graduate studies. After that I spent a year in Arkansas and then moved to Canada in 2001 to St. John's, Newfoundland, and Memorial University. This journey made me come to terms with my own identity. A process of introspection, combined with experience and the interactions I have had with the people whom I have encountered, finally saw me come to terms with my own self.

My parents and my only sibling (my younger brother) have been the biggest influence in my life and in shaping who I am today. Both my father and mother had an outlook on life that was grounded in honesty and ethical values. They instilled in me a sense of fairness, justice, and an urge to speak up when necessary and not to take things lying down. In reflecting on my childhood, I might add that my father and mother, as well as my brother, were feminist in their orientation and thought processes.

It is very difficult to write about what happened in 2006. For a long time I was in denial about the incident. I was happy to have found in Newfoundland a faculty position with a reasonable teaching load and a good research environment. I was comfortable and, from 2001 to 2006, felt settled. But one ugly day shook my sense of comfort and rattled me in a way I had not imagined. In my naiveté, in the five years I had been in Newfoundland I had thought I was accepted as a part of society, that I was not the "Other." I had felt I was a part of the university, as well as of the city and community, because of my participation and contribution to the economic life of the province and St. John's. Coming to Canada after graduate school in the US, and joining Memorial in a faculty position, I had thought that all the years of struggle as a graduate student in North America were over, and that I would be able to have a better life. On the outside, Canada seemed like a multicultural society, accepting of immigrants and their lifestyles. To think that racism in such a blatant way would be targeted at me, and could be possible in a place that I had come to think of, albeit slowly and reluctantly, as home, was extremely shocking – unthinkable.

It was the summer of 2006. I had completed five years at Memorial in the faculty of business. I had just received a faculty position at the University of Ottawa, after an interview for the position earlier that year. I had enjoyed my stay in Memorial and St. John's. I had built a life for myself there. I was glad to have found a better career fit in the Ottawa position, but I would be leaving with very fond memories of the lovely people of Newfoundland and the many friends I had made.

I was home one afternoon and decided to take a trip to the grocery store. I lived in an apartment complex and the parking lot was an open one, attached to the complex and accessible to all tenants and to anyone passing by. I was just about to get in my car when I saw something like black squiggles on the front the car. I went to look and was shocked and shaken. The "N word" was scrawled across the front of my red car with black paint. I did not know how to react or what to do. I went back inside, and by then my upstairs neighbours – a family of Romanian immigrants – saw me and asked me to come up and talk to them. They were very kind, offered me a cup of tea, and talked to me for a long time. The husband offered to take pictures of the car, which I readily agreed to. He suggested that I should not take this lightly and should call the Royal Newfoundland Constabulary (RNC) and file a complaint. I was really in a daze and feeling very confused. The very next day, I was to go to Ottawa on a house-hunting trip prior to my move. So I did not do anything.

I think it had not sunk in, the enormity of it. I was in denial. The seriousness of what had happened, that indeed it was a hate crime, was not clear to me at first. The next day I left for Ottawa and spent two days house hunting and was happy to find a suitable apartment in downtown Ottawa.

After I returned, I was able to sit down in my apartment and process what had happened. My neighbour's words echoed in my ears: "You should report it to the Royal Newfoundland Constabulary. You should make it public, and you should complain about it."

It suddenly and slowly dawned on me that I should not take this lying down. I should report it, file a complaint, regardless of what might happen after that. So I called the RNC and narrated my incident. Two officers came to my home and took my complaint. They wrote it down and gave me a patient and courteous hearing. Yet I felt they were not taking what I said very seriously. I was not sure they would do much about it. As a parting shot, one of the policemen said: "I guess it is likely a prank of some kids who do not know any better." That comment rankled me a lot.

I found I was deeply shocked, saddened, and offended by the incident. The more I thought about the reaction of the police, the angrier I felt. In hindsight I realized this was a good thing since it provided a catalyst to action.

I waited for a couple of days. For the first time I felt, perhaps irrationally, unsafe in my own home. My sense of personal safety had been disturbed to the core. After a few days I realized that the RNC was not going to do anything. I kept things to myself and stewed. But as time passed, I felt more and more angry. I decided to tell my family and a few close friends and colleagues in St. John's. The more I talked about it, the more I realized that I should make it public. I started by sending emails to everyone I knew in the university, both immediate colleagues and others in the wider university community. I decided to call the media. This set in motion a series of events and a flurry of activity. The incident was reported in the local news and in the university paper. I did an interview with the local television channel, as well as one for a radio station.

Very soon after that, I received emails of support from people all across the campus expressing sympathy. A meeting was arranged by the Women's Studies Council at the university, of which I was a member. I was both surprised and heartened by the response. Apart from the huge number of emails pouring in, community members organized events and discussions.

What started off as an incident that affected only me soon became a catalyst for a community-wide discussion. I think it sparked a sense of shame and outrage among fair-minded native Newfoundlanders, as well as the others who were attuned and sensitive to racism. It inspired discussion about the realities of the homogeneous social fabric of the province.

In the end, I was touched by the overwhelming support I received from the university and some of the wider community. Paradoxically, in my immediate neighbourhood, I sensed a shut down – embarrassment perhaps – and avoidance.

This incident helped me realize and understand the reality of racism by actually having experienced it. Until then, race and racism existed as academic concepts in my head, ones that I had intellectualized. But no amount of theorizing and reading about racism could have opened my eyes to its debilitating effect as this experience did. Experiencing it has been a valuable lesson.

Peruvemba S. Jaya, PhD, is an associate professor in the Department of Communication, University of Ottawa. Born and raised in India, Jaya came to Canada after earning a PhD in business administration from the University of Rhode Island, specializing in organizational behaviour and international management, and spending a year teaching in a small college town in Arkansas. Her research interests include intercultural/cross-cultural communication, organizational and interpersonal communication, gender, diversity, and multiculturalism issues, qualitative research methodologies, ethnic media and identity, globalization, and postcolonial theory. She is passionate about immigrants' issues, including immigrant women's integration and the challenges they face. She is affiliated with the Institute of Women's Studies at the University of Ottawa.

Section III
IDENTITY: WOMEN'S JOURNEYS TO BECOMING AND BELONGING

INTRODUCTION

Ikram Ahmed Jama

It will not take much insight to recognize that people who are most exercised about the issue of identity in terms of political and personal power relations are all people who have been repressed and marginalized...They are...people without names of their own choosing. (Bannerji, 1995:20)

The Whole Me

She looks at me with pity in her smile
Looks at me with blame in her eyes
Eyes that say how you could travel with eight
children alone? Why did you have so many children?

I look at her with eyes that say, my dear lady
Do not attempt to define me
I have lived through the residues of colonialism
I have lived through the invisible hand of
Neocolonialism
I have lived through the turbulence of nominal
independence
I have lived through the silencing of dictatorship and
the catastrophe of war
I have buried a child and miscarried quite a few
I said goodbye to loved ones, homeland and many dreams
I have lived, laughed and cried many a time   ‹ HK
Through it all I defied definition   *Hope*
                                                                  2011

So don't attempt to define me, to place me in one
category or another

Through life I have learned an important wisdom
That no matter what, one must carry on
So don't try to define me
For I am neither Victim, nor Victorious.

Ikram Ahmed Jama, April 18, 2002

As the passages above confirm, the concept of "identity" is complicated and complex. It is an essential part of who we are and how
others see us. However, identity is not fixed, but is influenced by the
context in which a person exists. It is continually evolving, being
redefined and negotiated through interactions and relationships
with others. Despite attempts to fix it as a constant, and present it as
stereotypes, identity remains fluid – influenced by culture, religion,
language, and other shared practices that connect the person to a
group, while also differentiating them from others.

As the stories in this section reveal, migration – leaving one's
original homeland – is laden with hopes, dreams of a better life,
sacrifices, losses, and a certain level of social demotion. Central to
the migration experience are challenges to one's identity and sense
of belonging. Adult immigrants come with already-formed cultural
and religious identities, and a sense of who they are. However,
during the process of resettlement within an established society,
they experience the loss of family connections, familiar places and
lifestyle, social networks, and the sense of belonging they may have
felt in their original homelands. Once grounded in a familiar culture,
language, and way of life, as immigrants they now are confronted
by a series of questions: What to keep from the old culture? What
to adopt from the new? Should they assimilate to the new culture,
which means leaving the old one behind? Should they reject the
new culture? Or, should they integrate by keeping some of the old
culture and adopting some of the new?

For the children of immigrants, referred to as second- and
third-generation, negotiating between the dominant culture and
that of their parents is central to their experiences, as is carving out

spaces for themselves as persons with dual identities. Factors such as family structure, self-knowledge, community support and social networks, employment, economic opportunities, a person's ability to cope with change, and the host society's acceptance of cultural diversity further complicate and impact identity negotiations.

The authors in this section are women who have experienced identity negotiation as first-generation immigrants (those who migrated as adults or were brought to Canada as children), or second- and third-generations (those who were born in Canada to immigrant parents). While each woman's journey is marked by her particular circumstance, there are common themes that connect these different stories. The writers in this section share with us their journeys of finding belonging, embracing multiple identities, balancing cultures of home and peers, rediscovering their parents' cultural and religious identities, as well as becoming a "minority" and encountering processes and incidents of racialization. They share their visions for themselves and their communities and exemplify how, through engagement and activism, they are changing the landscapes they inhabit and are contributing to positive social changes.

The challenges posed by migration are accompanied by opportunities for self-reflection, re-examination of views and values previously held, discarding practices that conflict with one's individual values, and rediscovering cultural and religious practices in order to make sense of and cope with the journey of finding "yourself." In their stories, the authors share with us what is it is like to live in "the spaces in between" or to "find middle ground" as a hyphenated Canadian.

Identity formation for immigrant youth, or those born to immigrant parents, involves juggling multiple identities and developing strategies for survival. Some strive to acquire skills that allow them to fit into the dominant culture. Some choose to resist pressures to conform.

The search for belonging and finding one's place is an ongoing process for immigrants of colour, including those who are second and third generation. Linguistic ability often is used as a marker by those from one's culture of origin, as well as by Canadian society, to establish legitimate membership in a particular group.

Several of the writers share how they reconnected with their original culture and sometimes used it as a protective blanket to deal with discrimination and "othering."

Through these stories we also come to appreciate that culture is not just embraced blindly, but re-examined and critically analyzed. The stories reflect women's struggles not only with the dominant culture, but with their original cultures as well. In this process of identity negotiation, these women were able to challenge inequities within their original cultures.

While these experiences speak to the difficulties in juggling and negotiating multiple identities, of occupying the "spaces in between" and not having the comfort and privileges that come with belonging to the dominant culture, they also demonstrate the strength of these women, not only in developing strategies for survival, but also in carving a space that affirms who they are.

The authors share with us their personal encounters with being the "Other" and how they navigated the process of racialization and the marginalizations that come with it. For instance, migrating to a country like Canada, with its history of white European settlers and subsequent colonization of the Aboriginal peoples, immigrants of colour become part of a racial hierarchy based on the norms of "whiteness." Racialized immigrants often get ensnared in this complex and contested history in which marginalization and exclusion become a shared experience. They are branded with new identifiers such as "people of colour" or "visible minority," or with labels imposed on them by all levels of the state and society, labels that they are often powerless to contest. As a consequence, perceptions of racialized immigrants as perpetual foreigners are ingrained into belief systems of dominant groups, enduring to negatively impact the lived experiences of subsequent generations.

Experiences of exclusion at school – and rarely encountering educators who reflect their identity – are shared by many immigrants of colour and their children. Some immigrant women comment on cultural or religious identifiers besides skin colour. "Othering" can arise from wearing the hijab, for instance.

While the experiences of racialization and discrimination described in these stories are often painful, the authors seem determined to create positive change from their lived realities as women of colour with immigrant backgrounds. They share with us their engagement in their communities and their contributions to creating "empowering spaces" for other women of colour, and their commitment to making lives better for themselves and for the next generations.

The authors in this section share their stories of struggle, loss, courage, resilience, and commitment. They reveal how they negotiate their place, their identities, and their visions for the future of Canada. Through their talents and contributions, they also illustrate the extent to which the landscape of Canada is changing. Their stories are now woven into the Canadian quilt, inspiring all those who are trying to find their place of belonging.

BEING HYPHENATED

Patrice Yamada

I am a third-generation hyphenated Canadian, born in 1953. My parents were both *Nisei* and migrated to Manitoba from the forced relocation of Japanese Canadians during the Second World War. For most of my life, I have resided on the Prairies, growing up in Winnipeg.

The challenges I encountered growing up were similar to those of my peers. Although our family was the only visible minority in a predominantly French/Métis/Ukrainian community, I always thought of myself as white. My brain processed mainstream images and I was always surprised when others asked me, "Where do you come from? You speak English so well." I still answer "south St. Vital," as if an obtuse answer will cease any further discourse about my different-ness.

In my semi-rural community, I lived a sheltered existence. Due to my parents' experiences arising from the war, our primary values were "assimilate or…" The Japanese community really did not exist and families dispersed into many different locales in the province. I learned about my heritage, but it was always with a twinge of quiet apology. To actually come out and proclaim my ancestry was to risk reprisal and another potential hate crime. The fear and racial paranoia of World War II were woven into my protective mechanisms. I quickly realized that racial tolerance held a very narrow spectrum, and that you could become the enemy in the blink of an eye.

Once in school, I acquired skills that allowed me to fit in to the dominant culture. I learned to observe and be quiet – to watch the dynamics and then imitate what was acceptable. I learned that being good at something allowed me safe passage through the white culture. I was a good student and used my intellect to deal with the challenges presented to me. There were few opportunities to celebrate my heritage with other Japanese Canadians because there were so few people of colour in our midst.

I can only recall a few instances of outright discrimination. In grade school, I was called "Jap" or "Chink" by strangers – as if the lack of "facial" discrimination on the part of my tormentors could be discerned. My peers accepted me and, more often than not, referred to my size as a tease, "Pattress the mattress." I felt very accepted and safe. The only place where there was a real mean intent was in our church. My family had converted to Christianity two generations ago. In the same pattern of assimilation, my parents opted to attend a mainstream United Church, rather than go to the Japanese congregation downtown. In this religious community, I encountered overt discrimination. One boy in my Sunday school class harassed and bullied me about my ethnic background. His behaviour was fully condoned and accepted by the adults supervising us. It is ironic that ethnic tolerance was not championed in a Christian setting. It demonstrated to me that tolerance and acceptance are a thin veneer once outside the safe niche of home/immediate community.

When my mother and I went to Japan to rediscover our roots, I realized that the dream of the culture is really ours. Japan is so westernized. Our notions of cultural traditions are not necessarily celebrated in day-to-day life. As hyphenated Canadians, we have the tourist view of our culture. We cling to an ideal that is historic, but it is a history that has been adapted to the chase for capitalism.

I became aware of culture and repression while in high school. By that time, I was bussed to an urban school, which was almost entirely Caucasian. There again, I used my coping strategies to blend – I excelled at my studies and took a course in American history. I became aware of the civil rights movement in the US and give credit to my female teacher who opened my eyes to the rights that belong to all individuals.

One of my classmates was an older student who appeared to be isolated – Elijah Harper (NDP MLA). I always felt empathy for him, as he appeared to not fit in to the larger dynamic. I think he had a "crush" on one of my friends, but given the prejudices about "Indians," this never amounted to anything. I admired him – he seemed to carry himself and his culture without any apology to the dominant group. He taught me lifelong lessons about tolerance and self-worth – dignity in the face of overwhelming adversity.

My career was definitely a choice, although at the time it appeared to be mired in gender-based oppression. I studied at university and obtained two degrees in nursing. I credit my profession with opening many doors by exposing me to life experiences I would never have encountered in any other field of endeavour. Due to the nature of working with ill individuals, I was forced to interact with and develop ideas about ethics, leadership, and the common good. My personality today is in large measure due to the risks I took to understand my patients' pain, grief, and chaos.

In the health care arena, I was exposed firsthand to layers of oppression. It was very clear that the food chain started at the level of MD and that male-dominated patriarchy was the modus operandi. What was also enlightening was that within the female-dominated profession, of which I was a part, there were covert ways of gaining power and advantage. Whether through shunning or withholding information, power was wielded, not always to the benefit of the patients. The notion of "patient-centred care" was not widespread, and it became a personal battle to advocate for the rights of ill people or their families. As a registered nurse, I saw infringements of human rights, not just the rights of women. Whether it was a female physician ostracizing a female nurse, or a surgeon trivializing a First Nations woman's beadwork, injustices played out in front of my eyes. This was a great education for me – it sensitized me to the rights of all human beings regardless of their race, gender, or creed.

In the sixties, my best friend became intrigued by the feminist movement. I think she saw me as a late bloomer, since my choice to enter a "female profession" was met with some disdain. She dyed her hair to look like Gloria Steinem, and I was subjected to many diatribes about the general state of the female nation. I was turned off by the trendy role models and retreated to the quiet waters of my profession. I was marginalized by doing so, since there were very few feminists in my workplace. However, I always felt autonomous and enfranchised. I felt free to make choices and exercise my rights. With those rights came obligations, and I am cognizant that I am accountable for my actions.

I married a wonderful man whose country of origin is India. Since both of us had established careers when we married, we decided to retain our own surnames. Although that was common among the late baby boomers, it is rarer now. I am still a "Ms.," but the title is a little jaded.

I am now retired and can look back on my life and career with gratitude. In terms of my profession, I believe I influenced others to do the right thing through role modelling and a respectful management style. I was glad to have achieved a professional goal for myself – to be the kind of boss who was participatory, patient-centred, and fair.

I volunteer with an inner city school, tutoring First Nations adults to achieve their high school equivalency. I am again challenged to maintain human rights and see beyond the stereotypes to achieve something really positive. We have many challenges in my city and I feel empowered to make a difference, one student at a time.

I have developed my own insights about the human condition. There is no justice, only acceptance and forgiveness. Being positive means seeing the cup as half-full. Living through bad situations heightens your appreciation of the good times.

I live in hope that some balance will be achieved for future generations. I worry that the efforts of feminists in the sixties were wasted and that gender roles have become more rigid and stereotyped. I continue to hope that women will exercise choice and that respect and tolerance will always be the mainstay of our mantra.

Patrice Yamada was born in 1953 in Winnipeg, Manitoba, and grew up in a satellite community south of the city. She feels fortunate to have her nuclear family reside in Winnipeg. Her undergraduate degree (BN) was undertaken at the University of Manitoba and her graduate degree (MSN) at the University of British Columbia. Her work life was spent as a registered nurse, teacher, and manager in cardiothoracic, medicine/intensive and long-term care. Patrice retired from nursing in 2010. She is looking forward to attending university classes, continuing her lifelong learning journey, and volunteering at the Canadian Museum for Human Rights.

THE SPACES IN BETWEEN

Leila Bdeir

Immigration is the one word that says it all to me. There is nothing in my life and in the life of my family that is not connected to the fact that we left Beirut, Lebanon, in 1976 to flee the civil war that had begun there a few months earlier. Since then, everything good and bad that has happened to my family has been qualified by the immigrant experience.

As with many people born to immigrant parents, difference quickly became a familiar theme in my life. My earliest memories of our language, music, food, and Islamic customs include the intimate knowledge of their contrast to the lives of those around us, and that they distinguished my parents from other adults, and myself from other children. There was my parents' less-than-tentative grasp of the French language in a primarily French environment. Nothing demonstrated this more than a visit to any government office or parent-teacher meeting. There was also their suspicion of the outside world. Things like my playing outside, sleeping over at friends' houses, and eating poutine were all rejected outright, and they came to symbolize the numerous distinctions between our culture and Canadian culture. As I look back now, it is obvious that the family's strategy for preserving its identity relied heavily on its efforts to distinguish itself from the host society as much as possible and even to take pride in this distinction.

In Quebec back then, immigrants and their children were known as "allophones." This was a category reserved for those who were not English and not French. Some of us had gone through the *classes d'accueil* (welcome classes for immigrant children) at school where we had the opportunity to work on our French language skills. The governing Parti Québécois wanted to preserve the French language and culture, so they passed a series of laws making French the official language of instruction in Quebec for most immigrants or children of immigrants. As a result of what came to be known as Bill 101, many children of immigrants in Quebec are now at ease in both official languages, and usually also speak a third one. One thing is for sure: Even today, I can recognize a "Bill 101 kid" a mile away! Their conversations are rarely conducted in a single language and can sound like this: "Ben là, what is that!?" or "My God, je n'en reviens pas!!" or simply "Yallah!" To the untrained ear, this sounds strange, but to us it makes perfect sense.

What did it mean for me growing up in this context? How was a young person supposed to reconcile such different messages regarding "the good life"? On the one hand, there is the need to belong to one's family, on the other, there is the desire to be accepted by one's peers and teachers in school. As a child, this meant first understanding that I could not belong to either world completely. After this, the most important and defining lesson has been to learn, to quote a friend, "to live in the spaces in between." It is hard to describe exactly, but I would say I learned to create alternative spaces for myself, where different parts of who I was could coexist more comfortably. The kind of language I speak with many of my peers is a good metaphor for the general life experiences we had of learning very early how to navigate through the different spaces of culture, language, religion, family, social, and, eventually, political expectations.

With many of the first Bill 101 generation, I shared the usual sheltered childhood, in that our parents tended to be stricter than those of "native" Canadians. It was a real relief to find Raquel, Khoî, Melanie, and Shanaz at school or in the neighbourhood, because only they seemed to understand that you were not allowed out past a certain time, or that boys were not allowed to come over to play. Everyone else looked at you as if you were from outer space, as if there were something inherently bizarre about you and the way your family lived. While putting on a brave face, this raised questions such as, Could they be right? And, Why were your actions so controlled in your household while other children seemed to bathe in a pool of freedom and merriment?

However, many wonderful things came with this childhood – not least, the funny stories that resulted at the interface of my family's otherness and the outside world. There was the time my dad tried to negotiate the price of a jacket at a famous European chain store, like he was in a *souk* in Beirut, only to be told by the saleslady that she really could not cut him a deal. Or the innumerable times

I fell for my cold-obsessed mom's promise that if I just finished my dinner, I would finally be allowed to wear a dress to school – only to be handed my long pants to wear underneath the next morning!

My parents also supported me very much when I received a scholarship to attend a strict private girl's school. The five years I spent there were instrumental in helping me to acquire not only knowledge but also the skills I would need for the rest of my academic and professional life. I learned to work very hard at the Villa, as we called it. The nuns taught me about Shakespeare and Molière and the teachers took us to see plays at Stratford. I memorized Latin for three years and practised German for two. All this might not have been possible for the daughter of a working-class and poorly educated family had my parents not made the leap to come to Canada. But even at the Villa, I was not part of the mainstream. I attended the French section of the school where students were expected to function in French at all times. My friends were the daughters of other immigrants like myself. We all seemed to gravitate naturally toward English, so much so that we insisted on speaking English to each other – even in French class! We were all from different backgrounds. I was the only Arab Muslim girl. Yet we very quickly became known as "les Anglaises."

As I got older, the issues surrounding identity became more important to me along with the need to claim my own space. As a teen, it had already been made very clear to me that none of the frolicking enjoyed by young people on the popular American sitcoms was meant for me. The family's reasoning was that as Muslims, their daughters did not engage in dating and other such inappropriate behaviour. It did not matter that I attended a Catholic school and that nobody in my family had ever displayed the slightest interest in observing the Muslim religion. Girls' loyalty to the tribe meant strict obedience and chastity, and overlooking all the systemic inconsistencies that disproportionately affect women. It was left up to me to make sense of these contradictions, and to be able to explain them to my friends and society at large. I would continue to try to explain them for many years to come. On the other hand, the larger Canadian culture was making its own demands: be pretty, be thin, be sexy, be cool, and be sexually emancipated. This was how you would be successful, my friends and I were told. Never mind that none of the criteria for beauty faintly resembled me or the people I knew. It also did not seem to matter much to the outside world that the road leading to "mainstream" success carried with it a real departure from the kind of reality I came from and the path my parents expected me to follow.

So, which side was I going to choose? For many years, I tried very hard to straddle these two worlds. I tried to be fully of each place – to be the dutiful daughter who looked for ways to meet the family's expectations and to be the Canadian girl who lived life on her terms, detached from any and all cultural ties. Ultimately, I had to recognize that I could not and did not want to be fully and only one of these two people. Neither model made complete sense for or to me. So began the deliberate carving out of a life between these two worlds, instead of across them. As I worked through what it meant to be me, I started to take back parts of the identity from which I had tried so hard to distance myself, including my Muslim identity. I was not from an observant family so nobody had ever given me an Islamic education, or even taught me the fundamentals of basic practice. Religion in our household served to restrict and confine. It had also served the purpose of justifying behaviour that was harmful to the women around me. In my early twenties I had also become acquainted with political and feminist ideas, which appeared incompatible with religion. Then 9/11 happened and, as for many other Muslims, my "Muslimness" was foisted upon me by society. So I decided that as before, I would not let others dictate the parameters of my identity. I was going to decide what Islam was for me and what kind of Muslim woman I wanted to be.

I also decided that I no longer wanted to be forced to promote a single model of the "good" woman. As is the case in many communities, I had been expected to preserve and perpetuate a very male-centric culture. This meant that early on, various members of the family weighed in heavily on my life choices. A very specific and single model of womanhood was offered: marriage, family, and home life. The fact that our own family's life had not played out in a traditional way (due mostly to my mother's chronic and debilitating illness), and that there were very few other role models I could turn to, did not seem to matter much. However, because I had gone out of the fold and been exposed to other dimensions of the human experience, I decided to design my own model. I took the traditional model of an Arab woman and adjusted it to fit my life. This meant pursuing higher education despite the general consensus that my studies were *the* cause of my status (at the time) as a single woman. After my first degree in communications, I began doing activist work around the Palestinian question and the sanctions against Iraq and discovered a great interest in politics. This led me to complete a master's degree in political science and women's studies. The focus of my research was Lebanon, and the status of women there as an indicator of the country's democracy. Studying the political system of my native country felt like creating another space in between. I also eventually moved out of the family home, despite not being married. This did not go over well.

It is important to mention that I was blessed with guardian angels throughout this process. Both in elementary and high school, my English teachers took an interest in me and tried very hard to nourish my enthusiasm and to help me overcome obstacles. As I left university and took on my first "real job," the woman who became my boss at this international feminist think tank would later become a lifelong friend and mentor. All of these people helped me in different ways, but one of the key things they did was to tell me success was possible. They all recognized and respected my reality, and they championed my endeavours.

My activism and personal experiences eventually lead me to speak out against society's attempts at homogenizing immigrant women, particularly Arab and Muslim women. I continue to fight for the recognition of immigrant women as full-fledged citizens in our own right. Injecting the recognition of our diversity into public discourse has been a huge part of that process. Another extremely important cause for me has been to obtain recognition of alternative voices for women's emancipation within feminist discourse in the West generally, and more specifically in Quebec. It is amazing how difficult it is for the mainstream Western feminist establishment to believe that maybe its model of liberation does not apply to the specific needs of all women, regardless of where they are from. I believe the only way we can eliminate oppression within the struggle for women's rights, and create the space necessary for "Other" women to speak for themselves, is by looking for the spaces where our struggles overlap. So not everybody buys into the concept of Islamic feminism or loves the hijab. Does that mean we cannot work together on issues of violence, economic emancipation, or access to education? We want more women in power – how about helping non-white women rise up in their own communities? These are still more examples of "spaces in between."

Although the road to a more authentic life has not always been easy, it has been tremendously enriching. I discovered so many places in between, and the fascinating people who reside there. After several years of working in the field of international development, I now have the privilege of teaching humanities at Vanier College, a CEGEP whose demographics reflect Montreal's tremendous diversity. My experience informs the content of my courses. It also helps me to better understand the lives of my students and the issues they face. I am happy to witness how they are negotiating the spaces within which they live, and I hope I can be of some help to them.

Leila Bdeir teaches humanities and women's studies at Vanier College, in Montreal. She has been a social justice activist for many years and in the last ten years has focused her efforts on issues related to Islamophobia and Muslim women's rights. Her blog is called The Other Feminist and she is a founding member of the Collective of the Muslim Feminists of Quebec.

FINDING MIDDLE GROUND

Preeti Nayak

Someone once told me that our stories are the best we got. Our experiences are our ammo and our voices are the mediums for shaking the structures that suffocate and silence our message. I strongly believe our own autobiographies often serve as the most useful pedagogical tools. I never really understood what it meant to suggest that the personal is political until I became cognizant of the void of racialized, feminized spaces in my life. Only then did I begin to explore identity, representation, and self-understanding.

My name has always been a cornerstone in my exploration of culture and belonging in Canada. Since coming to Canada at the age of four, my earliest memories include having my name distorted and my hesitation to correct the speaker, often a figure of authority. In fact, I came to a point where I would introduce an anglicized version of myself for the vast majority of my childhood and adolescent years.

When I found myself in a predominantly white city and was asked the question of where I *"really* came from," I soon realized I didn't belong in that anglicized world. It boiled down to the matter of roots, and is a question I still struggle to answer. I live in a reality where my heritage is filtered down to iconic Bollywood images and Asian Heritage Month in school. I disassociate myself from these versions of my identity. I want to proclaim an identity that resonates, that captures my trajectory in the Canadian diaspora, its struggles and its successes. I am not a token immigrant. I am not just another hyphenated identity.

Sifting through such questions fostered a desire – no, an urgent need – for South Asian female mentorship. I needed someone to whom I did not need to preface myself in regards to culture, race, and the immigrant experience. I needed a space to feel understood, an antithesis to my regular confrontation of white, male privilege that dominated my post-secondary space especially, among other institutions.

Throughout my fourteen years of formal grade-school

education and four years of undergraduate university education, I can count the number of racialized educators I have had, with eight fingers. Two of them were elementary school teachers. Four of them were high school teachers. Two were university educators. Out of these eight, three of them were women of colour and only one of these three existed in my post-secondary life, for my first year of university. It saddens me to discover that finding a racialized female educator to look up to has evolved into a complicated math problem as opposed to an acceptable social reality.

My experience as a young adult woman of colour in Canada can be characterized by a sense of disorientation. White privilege exists, yet the space to talk about its prevalence does not. White privilege is being able to walk into a classroom confident that your educators and peers reflect your identity. It means I would not have to scan the demographic of a room full of students and exasperatedly admit that inevitably I am going to be the student whose name will be mispronounced. It means I would not have to be in a classroom where my culture or religion is showcased, exoticized, or ignored. It means I wouldn't have to scavenge for my history in the margins of my textbooks. Ultimately, it means I wouldn't have to worry if my cultural identity is handled critically and with care, and that my existence is not just peripheral.

The toughest part is finding the middle ground. I struggle with the cracks in my own South Asian community, which undeniably also perpetuates notions of classism, racism, shadism, sexism, heterosexism, and other sites of oppression. I need to navigate and confront these sites regularly and ensure that I feel grounded in my own identity while I do this. Between my community and myself often lies a difference in values, life outlooks, and existential goals. And this difference is a barrier that colours my life every single day.

I have come to realize this is an integral part of life for women of colour, a series of navigations to find an end point of belonging, solidarity, and resistance. These paths are transformative, mind boggling, and painful, among other things. The guidance we seek in carving these paths is often absent, making it a lonely and often alienating journey. So we tell our stories to accelerate and ease this process of navigation. We tell them to help our sisters, mothers, and daughters find their end points, and realize that in the process of becoming stronger women agents of change, we are creating empowering spaces for our undervalued daughters of colour who seek a more just and equitable future.

Preeti Nayak holds a BA from McMaster University and a MPhil in education from the University of Cambridge. She is interested in issues around diversity, equity, and inclusion in the context of teacher education and comparative education.

PORTRAIT OF THE JOURNALIST AS A YOUNG VM
Amira Elghawaby

My Dad warned me it would happen.

I wasn't a member of a visible minority for the first twenty-two years of my life. At least, I never saw myself as one. Then, one day, as I walked past a colleague in one of the country's largest newsrooms, I became a "VM."

My colleague was reading a letter tacked up on the staff bulletin board. The anonymous author was full of hate, aiming his racism toward another summer intern with an immigrant-sounding name. The colleague noticed me and shook her head in sympathy. "It must be so tough to deal with things like that," she offered, or something to that effect. I took a step closer, read the letter, and realized she thought I was the one being targeted because I was the one who was visibly different, having donned the hijab just a few weeks earlier. The other summer intern and the real target of the letter was an Afghan-Canadian woman with jet-black hair and blue eyes. Like me, she had grown up in Canada. Unlike me, she was not visibly different. She wore small T-shirts and short skirts and, I suppose, looked far more Canadian than I must have looked at that moment.

Until then, I, too, had been just another young woman in any crowd. It was the first time I realized that I had a new identity: "the Other." I didn't like it. Both I and the other intern had grown up in Canada and had a typically Western outlook on life. But I felt as though I had now become a stranger, one who was hated by some and pitied by others, just for my appearance. Suddenly, self-doubt erupted. I felt deficient, not good enough to work in Canada's largest newsroom – because even in the country's most diverse city, I was alien. Perhaps my being there was an accident, or some kind of affirmative action. "Poor thing," I imagined other staff to be thinking.

But I didn't need sympathy. Just like everyone else, I was grilled by both the city editor and the hiring manager and landed the job after proving myself. I was interviewed over the phone though, because I happened to be overseas on another gig. That made it easier to decide to don the veil a week before starting; they couldn't blame me for misrepresenting myself – "Hey, you weren't wearing that thing when we hired you!"

Sure, the city editor stared at me in tacit disapproval when we all eventually met face to face, sitting around a wide boardroom table, sunlight streaming in from beyond Toronto's jutting skyline. Everyone introduced themselves; I did so quietly, apprehensive. Perhaps that was mistaken for meekness. It was the young Aboriginal woman on my right who whispered knowingly, "Watch out for the quiet ones, they've usually got the most to give." I took that as a compliment.

Later, in the same newsroom, a well-known political columnist approached me and whispered conspiratorially, "You're the first one in here." The warm smile breaking out across his beautiful black face was meant to congratulate me, to celebrate this moment of victory for one more "VM" to make it into the mainstream. And I do admit to feeling grateful for his support. But, in retrospect, it was just a scarf on my head. Why was my presence so significant? And why was being there such an achievement for me in particular? I had gone to journalism school like the others. I had a collection of clippings to show for an enterprising few years. I had earned my place. Hadn't I?

I've heard so much about a glass ceiling, but I think there's a glass bubble that too few talk about. It's the bubble around workplaces that prevents those who seem apart from the mainstream from entering. These days, those people are usually the newcomers and obvious immigrants. I suppose I was just lumped into the group because I looked like one. Despite the reluctant admiration and novelty of my ability to successfully work as a city reporter while wearing the headscarf, there was an implicit "How did you get in here?" hanging in the air.

So it was little consolation when the assignment editor told me, by the end of the internship, that I had done "really well" and "had improved a lot." Deep down I felt he only came to realize that I had any skills at all because he had slowly started trusting me with more important stories. It's easy to impress when the expectations are low to negligible.

Surprisingly perhaps, my decision to wear the headscarf was born out of feminist readings in university, along with activist writing in the campus paper, and an inner admission that I couldn't very well worship God if I kept partying all night. It was an option available to me because I did believe in Islam, and considered the headscarf as a way to hold myself back from all the temptations around me. It was also a way to transcend the beauty myth and focus on a spiritual dimension I had neglected for too long.

But my father, like many Muslim and immigrant fathers, knew about the glass bubble. His generation had fought their way into it with cultivated skills and education that were in high demand. Once inside, though, they knew that one had to look, sound, and act like those who dominated it. Why would I choose to make myself stick out *negatively*, especially when I was already fortunate enough to be without an accent: to look, sound, and act pretty much like members of that exclusive club? I had an instant ticket to a good job and a good life. Why make problems with a little ol' scarf on my head that carried so many unsavoury connotations?

Of course, being stubborn, I refused to acknowledge his point. I clung to the cliché that here in Canada I could look and dress however I wanted and still be respected. My friends at university totally supported me, after all. They asked thoughtful questions and were happy to hang out with me in public. My TV professor dispelled the skepticism of my well-dressed blonde and mascara-eyed classmates when he told me I looked elegant after hosting one of our class newscasts. "See, Dad," I'd say, "I'll still find a job and be successful."

To some extent, I did find both work and success. But I also struggled. It was okay being noticed for important achievements, but it was excruciating to be scrutinized once Islam hit the media big-time, post-9/11. I was in another newsroom by then and instantly felt the weight of the faith on my shoulders. While I was again grateful for the opportunity to help dispel the misconceptions that abounded, I also found it exhausting and even downright depressing to encounter so much ignorance and suspicion, especially beyond the newsroom.

People asked a lot of questions and that was okay. But periodically, people would make snide comments, or even act threateningly toward me. There was the typical "You don't have to wear that thing here," or "Why don't you go back to where you came from?" Sometimes, I'd respond angrily, even try to convince the critic that I do belong here; that I've lived here all my life and I have just as much a right to be here as they do. Sometimes I'd just pretend not to see things like the middle finger thrust in the air in my direction, or visibly react to the truck swerving toward me while its driver yells something I mercifully can't distinguish.

Yes, Canada is a multicultural place, with diversity visible everywhere. But is there really a place for it when it makes people uncomfortable? Is there a place for diversity that moves beyond celebrations and food and into an area of alternative thought on everything from philosophy, to gender relations, to politics? What happens when visible minorities seem to be everywhere, or in this case, when differing takes on women's fashion is on display on practically every street? Is that when things become threatening? Is that when hate letters became inevitable – precursors to those chilling comments now found below any online article that even mentions Muslims or Islam?

I'm still stubborn enough to believe I can prove my dad wrong on his assumption that too much diversity hinders success in this country. And if I do, you'll be sure to see the evidence at a workplace – or newsroom – near you.

Amira Elghawaby obtained a combined honours degree in journalism and law from Carleton University in 2001. Since then, she has worked as both a full-time and freelance journalist, writing and producing stories for a variety of media including The Globe and Mail, *the* Toronto Star, *the* Ottawa Citizen, CBC Radio *and* New Canadian

Media. *In 2012, she joined the National Council of Canadian Muslims to advocate for the human rights and civil liberties of diverse communities.*

THOUGHT FOR FOOD (X-TENDAMIX)

Angelica LeMinh

The pendulum must swing back. I read recently that North Americans are most prone to creating and believing the hype of food trends because we have no established food culture that defines us. That is, we have no *one* food history that defines us, because we are nations built on the backs of so many immigrants who bring their recipes and eating habits to a steaming cauldron of high-paced excess and our collective meals are rapidly emerging as a levelling gruel. As a human outside of the non-white elite, working in the field of organic food, I attest to the truth of this statement on a daily basis. From raw cuisine that comes with an ironically hefty price tag, to the politics of soy-based meat "substitutes," organic lollipops, and gluten-free everything – including soap – one must tread carefully not to be overwhelmed by the whirlpool of food (mis)information.

I am a thirty-two-year-old second-generation Canadian woman. I came of age during the specific mix and moment of third-wave feminism aligning with nineties hip-hop. I live by certain truths that I never thought to question or separate from myself. The sense of assertiveness and personal accountability to the land, animals, and people of the world, the pledge not to waste time, energy, or materials, and the survival instinct to make the most of any opportunity and situation are the values that govern the framework of my life. This framework has been earned, tested, and integrated at every moment along the way.

As an only child raised by a single father, I did not learn how to properly fuel my body. I had to undo years of damage. But there's nothing like regenerating from the inside to heal a neck-to-toe's worth of sores, bursting with blood and pus, to cement the lesson in muscle memory. My father had a few signature dishes that I learned to cook through osmosis, though none of them belonged to the cultural heritage that he passed along to me, because that also came with the belief that cooking was "women's work." The most important thing he taught me in the kitchen was to leave room for the unexpected – measuring isn't necessary, recipes are guidelines, and substitutions are easy, permitted, even encouraged. Also, a glass Coke bottle (unopened, you need the liquid weight) is handy to keep around to grind roasted peanuts that always make a lovely garnish. He was really good at sourcing out the best Vietnamese restaurants and inviting himself to gatherings when the most elaborate meals would be cooked by other people. I later reconciled all of this by making salad rolls out of every conceivable filling, and a few inconceivable ones – the smoked turkey cold cuts were a bust.

Growing up with a mother-shaped mystery, I missed out on a lot of things that girls with mothers get. But I had the benefit of being taken in and loved by other people's mothers. There is a lot of research around the "formative years." Mine were spent with my mother and grandmother during their leisurely days of buying groceries as they needed them, having no reason to abandon the market culture of Malaysia. Two generations of women in my life could not come up with a reason why the four-year-old me couldn't have a cup of the free coffee that greeted us upon arrival. Thus they shopped carefree while I was occupied learning patience with my daily cup, dressed with cream and sugar, in the front window under the watchful eyes of the cashiers. My grandmother is a woman defined by her love of cooking, despite her lack of skill. She is a big woman who makes friends everywhere she goes. Even though she only spends half the year living in Canada, the grocers always have a box of the best oranges waiting for her if she happens to stop by. The space after church was always filled around a huge dim sum table, and once she learned your favourite dish, she would forever order four plates of it just for you, restricting anyone else from touching it, swatting protectively with her chopsticks. My memory of my mother gets sketchier as the years pass (now approaching twenty-eight). The only food-related memory I have of her is a few years after my parents' divorce, when she took me to McDonald's for apple pie and asked me what grade I was in. It was from other people's mothers that I learned to navigate the world, to be financially independent, and that my hand is nineteen centimetres wide (thus, I carry a permanent measuring tape and should use it before buying and building loft beds that then don't fit the apartment they were purchased for). I have also benefitted from peer-parenting the women around me.

I had to tell my father that I got my period at age eleven. He promptly gave me the maxipad samples that came in the mail and five dollars to ask my teacher to buy me what the other girls were using, because he didn't know. When I was twenty-five, an eighteen-year-old coworker taught me how to use tampons.

I spent a year in Vietnam, after I (barely) completed my undergrad in women's studies and film studies. I went from being the only child of a single father, to being the only child of the youngest of twelve children, of a man who was the eldest of nine. Basically, every person I met that year, save the month that I went travelling northwards from Saigon, was related to me somehow. I had not arrived equipped with the language or the mental capacity to process what that meant. It was the height of the bird flu crisis, and along with the global communist news and my aunt's running commentary on how good-looking (but short, so short!) Vladimir Putin is, I saw nightly footage of mass graves dug and filled with incinerated chicken corpses. The snitching sentiment was alive and well and people were receiving rewards for reporting their neighbours. So the same knife (razor blade jammed onto a wooden handle) that I used to unsuccessfully peel and cut a papaya the size of my leg was employed in slitting the throats of the two old chickens and one ancient rooster in the backyard, just in case. Nobody had the heart to dine on the family companions, and nobody wanted to eat meat that tough.

I was berated on a regular basis for not knowing all the things that Vietnamese girls and women should know, despite the fact that I was born in Canada, raised by my father, and was "returning" after twenty-five years. I was laughed at for not knowing how to do laundry because I didn't come off the plane with the embedded knowledge of going to the well to fetch water and squatting in the gutter to wash and wring my garments by hand. I was told that I laughed too loudly, like a man, and that I should work on it in order to get married. But I should get married, because married women look after their own families, and unmarried women have to look after everybody's families. It's the loneliest existence that one can experience while surrounded by people. There are a few spinsters in every generation of my family, and it's looking like I might inherit the torch.

As soon as I touched down in Japan, during my stopover, I noticed the difference in the air and the sterility of Western living. Back in Canada, I had a hard time adjusting to the North American understanding of wide open spaces and living inside, shut away. I missed the sensual (as in, experienced by the six senses) living out loud outside, with the ongoing onslaught of life. The refrigerator was a status symbol and would sit empty if not for the bottles of water and occasional fruit. Food did not need to be preserved because it was bought and cooked daily. Elaborate dishes were pre-pared with love and distributed around the neighbourhood in bowls that would eventually return filled with something else. I had a hard time reconciling that a country where many people were without money, but nobody was without means or motivation to share food, was somehow "developing" or "Third World," while the "civilized" ones were increasingly either stuffed or starved.

My father tried to give me the comforts of relating to my Canadian classmates by bonding with me every Sunday over the Big Breakfast at McDonald's. Until they stopped shortly after my sixth year, there were weekly photos of me with Grimace, Hamburglar, and Ronald. The birthday parties in the same restaurant marked the annual gatherings of Vietnamese faces that I didn't know, recruited there to celebrate me. To this day I find comfort in a hash brown and a bacon-and-egg McMuffin. I use it as a remedy to combat sickness in a toxic world. I believe that we can only be so healthy on the inside before we render ourselves easy targets to be eliminated by environmental realities. I also gravitate toward Asian grocery stores and stock up on preserved plums, rice crackers, grass jelly, and other flashes of my youth whenever I think too hard about the isolation I continue to experience from both sides of my family. I consume everything I buy at an alarming rate and then return to my usual dietary program.

When I was twenty-seven, my father asked me when I was

going to grow up and give up my dreams. I believe that we grow up when we refuse to give up our dreams. No writer is motivated by money to pick up a pen. Well, no reader is, anyway. No writer can honourably write without reading. And readers never starve, because thought for food is a renewable resource. What I've learned as a writer is to create the conditions that I need to write. For me, this means a secure roof over my head, food on my plate, and the time and mental space to read and imagine. I have been welcomed at many a table, and though I have become an expert in cooking for one, I am always ready to welcome another at the transportable home that I have built for myself through matching plates and candles. They say writing is a solitary profession, but it is one that I have found the most enriching at its social moments. Whether this means a roomful of people responding positively to an unexpected cover of a rap song, or one person reaching out with praise for a life-changing interview I conducted with a trailblazing poet, connection is the most valuable commodity.

Angelica LeMinh does not believe that just because you take the stage, anyone is obligated to listen to you. She does believe that if you choose to take the stage, you are most obligated to say something. She reads many books and has reached a personal best of level 26 in Word Mole, a game she plays on other peoples' Blackberries. She blogs inconsistently at metrotextual.wordpress.com and is quite belligerent at basketball games. She is grateful for every invitation to share her words, food, clothes, and music.

"WHERE ARE YOU REALLY FROM?"
DIVIDED SELVES AND THE SEARCH
FOR ORIGINS

Eve Haque

My classic immigrant story begins, as do many, in a taxi cab. Last week while I was coming back from visiting my parents in Ottawa, I took a taxi from the Toronto's island airport back home to my small downtown apartment. As I told the taxi driver my destination, he sighed loudly and I could tell he was disappointed that I wasn't going to be the long and lucrative ride to the outer reaches of the GTA that my skin colour, middle age, and big suitcase (full of my mother's frozen dhal and work-related books) had initially promised. Completely understandable given the long period of time cab drivers have to wait to pick up a fare, but for me – given the heaviness of the luggage, my physical tiredness, and lateness of the hour – strictly not my problem. That being said, I always felt a measure of liberal middle-class guilt, which induced my need to give a whopping big tip at the end of the ride to mitigate the paltriness of the distance, even if, by that time, it was too late to prevent the inevitable sigh.

As we inched through the thick weekend and construction-blocked traffic of the entertainment district, I waited for it as I caught the driver's repeated and quizzical glances in the rear-view mirror. And sure enough, it came. The question: Where are you from? No amount of pointed staring at the glowing bezel of my smart phone and poking at its various twinkling apps could forestall what had become a lifelong experience for me; although increasingly in multicultural Toronto, it came less from the careful liberal white friends I was surrounded by, but almost always from racialized – particularly South Asian – male taxi drivers, regardless of their age. And almost always I replied in the formula that had become rote for me – a formula I had developed in order to cut down on the inevitable and persistent exchanges I felt forced to engage in so as to get at the heart of their inquiry: exactly which country was I *really* from. But although this was often the end point of the white "friend/person's" inquiry about my "true" origins (confirming or adding to their store of certainties about me), in the taxi, this was instead a search for some sort of commonality, for an engagement that often went far past my own comfort limits for intimacy and sharing, and was always underpinned by my gendered concern of "What will you want from me?"

As soon as he was able to confirm that I was indeed another "Bangalee," he quickly switched into Bangla and I had to negotiate the tricky business that comes with age and education – whether to use "tumi" (informal) or "apni" (formal), an uncertainty about location and relation that was symptomatic of the question looming over us both: What were the terms of our relationship? As the ride continued, it all unfolded as it had so many times in the past: What did I do, where had I studied, where did I work, and, depending on the level of his "Westernized" delicacy, questions about my personal life – Married? Children? etc.? However, I am rarely a passive actor in these taxi dramas and often I use my entrée to ask the questions about migration that interest me and often inform my own academic work. And as is often the case, what emerges is more than I want to hear or bargained for. In this case, I heard the story of a Bangladeshi engineer, well educated at home, who went to work in Saudi Arabia with his wife because of the availability of jobs, and the birth there of his son who was severely disabled for life by a botched forceps delivery. With a clear indication that any legal action for recompense within that Saudi system would be prohibitively expensive and protracted, they sought migration to Canada with all the hopes and limitations that entailed. Once here, with his wife committed to the round-the-clock care his son required that effectively barred her from paid employment, the cab driver took on long twelve- to sixteen-hour daily shifts of taxi driving. As he put it, life was hard; the struggle was unceasing and hopes for the future were truncated without the promise of a socially and economically viable second generation.

Of course the counterpart of this exchange was that I tell him my story, which was compressed easily enough. Born in Ottawa, studied in Canada, and now employed as a professor at a local university. Missing in this telegraphic autobiography was the generational cost that my parents paid, through their lifelong under-employment, their subsequent bewilderment at living a life that was a perversion of the immigrant Horatio-Alger promise, and the foundering of their clichéd immigrant hopes for me and my sister. Inquiring into my sister's area of study (math) he seemed to cheer up, stating that he was proud that we had done so well in our lives in Canada, and as the taxi drew up to my front door, I was unwilling to burst his bubble by adding that persistent gendered racism in the academy had led to my sister's eventual abandonment of her search for an academic appointment, and that a daily struggle against institutional and thinly veiled personal racism eroded any sense of accomplishment I was supposed to feel. As I got out of the cab, all we could do was wish each other the best for our complicated futures, our moment of forced engagement ending over a hasty monetary transaction. Of course these encounters never leave me untouched, always inevitably jumpstarting a series of melancholic reflections and the inevitable question: Where am I really from?

Being born and brought up in Trudeau's post-Pearsonian Ottawa meant socialization into the thinly and politely concealed fears of a predominantly white, Anglo Ottawa about the encroaching differences that were permeating a long-held, comfortable but insular existence. The outcomes of the Royal Commission on Bilingualism and Biculturalism (1963–70) had the biggest impact on Ottawa as federal policies around francophone recognition and inclusion shifted dramatically with the declaration of Canada as an official English and French country. Even though the post-commission multiculturalism policy was Trudeau's almost off-hand sop to the "other ethnic groups," who had not been pleased with the entrenchment of a dual English-French white settler nationalism, the paradigmatic changes to immigration policy that were also taking place in this era meant an increasing influx of visible minority immigrants from the global South. These policy changes signalled the advent of significant racial demographic changes in Canada, but issues of racial exclusion remained politely and resolutely outside of mainstream discourse, even as white settler nationalist sentiment continued to strengthen across the country.

Issues of racial exclusion remained sidelined in these early days of identity-based political organizing. But women were definitely fighting for their recognition and equality – a movement kicked off in this era with the Royal Commission on the Status of Women (1967) and the eventual formation of the National Action Committee on the Status of Women (1971), among other feminist advocacy organizations. While the plight of white women remained the focus of the feminist struggle in this early period, my growing involvement in feminist activism paralleled the increasing call to include indigenous and racialized women's experiences as part of the feminist agenda in the late 1980s and early 1990s. Although these actions also marked the heyday of identity politics, they opened up necessary spaces for those of us who had always felt the inadequacy of feminist organizing, but had no language for naming our unease. As Himani Bannerji (1995) has written so well, those who are most exercised about identity are those who have been marginalized, those who have had their histories erased and who have remained non-named. Although difficult and often frustrating, it is out of these struggles by women of colour that a valorized immigrant identity emerged and somehow became the paradigmatic figure for our identification. Even my overqualified cab driver fit into a recognizable subset of this coloured immigrant figure against which all of us with non-white skin here are defined. As I continue to celebrate the work of noted novelists, writers, and poets such Dionne Brand and Shani Mootoo, I realize that their stories have become the round hole into which my square peg won't fit, the dominant narrative of diasporic longing and difficult belonging for all women of colour in Canada. Even as our skin colour marks us as always from elsewhere, those of us from nowhere but here are always left with our awkward, long-winded explanations of where we *really* come from.

If, particularly as women of South Asian descent, we have moved out of invisibility into the recognizable figure of the immigrant woman, in a post-9/11 era, we have gained even more visibility as the veiled victims of Islamic fundamentalist patriarchal oppression, and our emancipation has become the justification for new iterations of empire and colonialism. What remains constant in these figurations is our consistent identification as always from and of elsewhere. In a post-9/11 era, this identification is made even more complex for those of us who are counted now as "homegrown" – a racialized fifth column caught between terror and tragedy. This fear of the homegrown yet always alien figure can be seen in such acts of state racism such as Project Samosa (2010) – an RCMP-led operation designed to ferret out "homegrown terrorism" in Ottawa – but also in the Islamaphobic representations of South Asian domestic violence as the tragedy of "honour killings." Sensational media coverage and commentary on cases such as the murder of Mississauga teen Aqsa Parvez (2007) and the trial (2011–12) for the murder of the Shafia sisters were uniformly framed as the tragedy of clashing cultures, rather than as outcomes of a patriarchal violence authorized through the inadequacies of the racist structures of Canadian social services. In these representations, the tragedy becomes primarily about how these young women are lethally caught between the backwardness of their familial cultures and the liberal possibilities of their adopted society; it is a stark binaristic framing – no matter the arbitrariness of this dividing line – that leaves us as the "homegrown" with only the limited possibility of reactive identifications, always caught between here and there as split and divided selves, unsure not only of where we are really from but also, then, where we might belong.

Even as we resist these limitations on our possible subjectivities, our daily encounters often serve only to remind us of a supposed lack of coherence and a split in ourselves, thereby constraining even our imagination and vocabularies of identity and self. In this way, not only does the white settler hegemony remind us daily of our provisional belonging – belonging always marked by the ambivalence that arises out of inclusion into a nationalist project underwritten by land theft and genocide – but often the imposition of a homogenized and dominant notion of cultural community also leaves us without a script to narrate ourselves and our lives across our various encounters. Ultimately, it means that my taxi rides are going to continue to be tricky negotiations across gender, generation, migration histories, and trajectories that will require some measure of dissembling and dissimulation in order to mask my feelings of ambivalence for seeking common ground and full engagement. Even as these encounters may continue to provoke melancholic reflection, they also remain a sharp and useful reminder that it is not necessarily a lack within either of us that constrains our ability to find common ground, but rather it is the history and practices of colony and empire – both past and present – which frame both the limits of our encounter and our struggle to find self, meaning, and community as human beings in passing, wherever we may be from.

Eve Haque is an associate professor at York University, who started out in community radio in the 1980s, worked with the DisAbled Women's Network of Ontario, the National Organization of Visible & Minority Women, and served on the Ottawa Advisory Committee on Equity and Diversity. She has served as co-chair of the Equity Committee at the Canadian Association of University Teachers, and is a member of the Race Equity Caucus at York. Her research traces the regulation of racialized migrants in a white settler society through such mechanisms as immigrant language training programs, as well as through the representation of violence against women in specific racialized communities. She has published widely, including Multiculturalism within a Bilingual Framework: Language, Race and Belonging in Canada *(UTP, 2012).*

MY MOTHER

Sara O.

Dear Elizabeth O – My Mother,

This is your twenty-four-year-old daughter, Sara. I have completed a joint honours BA and recently graduated with an LLB. I am almost a lawyer. My dear Mother, today and always, I want to thank you for your courage, strength, perseverance, humility, and selflessness. Because of you, I am the woman that I am, and I will be the lawyer that I plan to be.

I do not tell you enough how much I admire you – your silent suffering, humble working-class wisdom, resilience, and inscrutable ability to accept and triumph against the individual and systemic racism, sexism, and classism in Canadian society. My mother, you are first and foremost a devoted, magnanimous mother, an industrious, reliable, honest worker, a conscientious daughter, caring sister, concerned aunty, faithful friend, and a Christian soul. You assume these multiple roles, expressing few words of lament. My mother, you are a woman among women – you are the spiritual, intellectual, and concrete embodiment of what women of colour who were denied opportunities in Canadian society can give to their children, especially their daughters. I respect and greatly honour your tenacity, humility, and triumphs.

As a child, I witnessed your incessant, hushed struggles. It is what immigrants must go through to survive in Canadian society. As your daughter, and because of these struggles, I reached out to you. Oh, how I wanted to help, I wanted to make it better, but what could I do? Alas, I was the child and you, the mother. Then! I finally figured out how to make it better – a commitment to obtain an education. It is the zenith of upward mobility in any society. I committed and attended, but it is your achievement. From you, who had minimum formal schooling, albeit maximum education in the school of women's lives, I learned that adversity only makes you stronger, insults increase your determination, and hard work is your manual for success.

My mother, in this letter I want to communicate my observation of you and your social strategies of survival. Mind you, I may not know everything about you, especially the first twenty-three years of your life, for most of which you were a resident in a small village in Ghana. However, what I do know speaks to the souls of other women who have experienced similar ongoing marital violence and alienation in their lives.

The narrative commences in 1987, the year of your arrival in Toronto, covered in the identity of a refugee, seeking an opportunity to escape the abject poverty of your native village in Kumasi, Ghana. In the presence of my father, Daniel O, accompanied by your first-born, you disembarked onto the cold concrete of the airport. To many members of your native village, you are the lucky one – you escaped poverty and moved on to a better life. A life that stretched back to Ghana, for you were expected to share your good fortune, expressed in regular Western Union transactions.

What many people did not know was that behind closed doors your lived reality was plagued, fraught with a steady dose of physical abuse from your husband, the father of your children. You, my mother, a woman of such strength, sustained these abuses in silence! You, like many others, believed that you were his private property to abuse as he wished, and how he saw fit. No one outside the home saw the physical and emotional scars, but Ellen, your firstborn did, and like most children, she kept your secret but shared it with me. Ellen once asked me, "Don't you remember what he used to do to Mommy?" I replied, "I don't know. I was too young to remember." Ellen continued, "He used to beat Mommy really bad, with anything he could get his hands on; he even used to beat her with his guitars, breaking them on her body." Ellen was the star witness to this private treatment a husband gave to his wife. It ended when Ellen was eight years old.

My dear mother, what was it like to be beaten like a beast of burden by a man you were intimate with, the father of your children? I cannot begin to imagine what it did to your sense of self, your self-esteem, and your ability to think for yourself! Indeed, it was a new country, no friends, new language, weather you had never experienced. I can only imagine the piercing cold winters stinging your melanin-infused skin and the icy paths you had to learn to walk on, both in a physical and spiritual sense – as someone with minimum education, having to learn English, to find a job. What courage! What determination! What spirit! And you succeeded! I am a testament to your success.

You found a job in a car-parts factory as you simultaneously endured the horror lurking, waiting to pounce in your home. You were firm about one ideal: "There is no way that I came to Canada, a refugee seeking a better life, and will apply for welfare – absolutely not. I have health and strength and I am going to find work. In my life, at a very early age, I was introduced to hard, manual labour. I helped my family survive, and I worked. Even though I was denied an education, I sold homemade candy to school children. So sitting at home in Canada and receiving a meagre government cheque is not for me. I have health and strength."

I was born June 21, 1988. My earliest memory is of the day we moved into our new apartment in the west side of Toronto, Chalkfarm, with its heavy presence of police. Ellen recounted to me how, as the abuse became more violent, you fled for your life and for ours. In fear and with no idea of how you would survive, you went to a shelter. What courage! In a place with no family support, you had the audacity and resolution to leave your abusive husband! I know you did it for us, and I thank you for that.

Since I cannot remember the first four years of my life, the reality of repressed memories still haunts me. I can only imagine the pain and suffering you went through. The sleepless nights, where you debated with yourself whether to leave or stay. The frightening extent and culmination of the final incident that determined your decision to leave, a very abusive yet familiar space. These are all memories that you and Ellen have, memories you will take with you to your grave. It is your very own private reoccurring nightmare; you are the star of it. Mommy, I am so sorry you had to go through that, and I am especially sorry that the effects of such abuse linger until this day.

Mommy you are a workaholic. Every single morning, you woke up at 4:00 a.m. and travelled two hours to your factory job. I couldn't be more proud of you. The fact that you never let your physical, emotional, or spiritual ailments deter you from the factory is a testament to the strength of women all over the world to survive, despite and against the odds.

About a year after you terminated the relationship with my father, you got involved with a man who came into your life – and like a Trojan horse, he manipulated and used you for the sole purpose of getting you to marry his brother, so his brother could obtain landed immigrant status in Canada. Upon his brother's receiving his paper, this low-down, rotten scoundrel left you pregnant. Now there were four mouths to feed. In the intervening years, you steadfastly worked and supported your children and yourself. Mommy, how did you do it?

Shortly after your divorce, your ex-husband, my father, returned to Ghana. I was six years old. We were all sitting in our living room when we received a call from someone in Ghana. The message, "The man named Daniel O is deceased. He succumbed to an illness." For two years after the telephone call, you saved money so we could all go to Ghana to properly lament the death of my father, your ex-husband. As an eight-year-old, I had never seen you cry. In Ghana, in the presence of your family, your sobs were uncontrollable as you wailed for your deceased ex-husband. I did not know what to do. But your family members knew how to respond to your anguish. They held you close and encouraged you to cry, empty the bucket of hurt, disappointment, and pain you had secreted in your psyche.

I remember thinking, Why is she crying for this man? Why, after everything he did to you, did you still care and love him so deeply? I understand now that I am older. You are a truly loving spirit that only wants the best for people. So there is no question in my mind that the death of Daniel O was just as devastating as it would have been if you two had remained a married couple.

Thank you for taking me home to Ghana, where for the first time I got to meet my aunts, uncles, and beautiful grandparents. Meeting my family gave me a sense of identity and fulfillment. I know it was not easy for you financially, emotionally, and spiritually, but with the help of God, you made it happen. Mommy you are truly a blessed person.

Growing up, things were hard at times, going to school among children of hockey players, basketball players, lawyers, doctors, and other professionals. I always knew I was different. I did not understand why, but I did know that I had a strong mother, a good mother. As I continue to shed the layers of ignorance, my appreciation and admiration for you grow even stronger. You did your best to give us what we wanted, even when you did not have for yourself, and even when you did not know how your paycheque would cover the bills. Thank you. Your humility taught us well, and it is for that reason I give you my utmost respect, honour, and undying gratitude.

Despite all the trials and tribulations of providing the best for your children, you zealously continued your job. You moved us out of an impoverished area, with high street crime, to an apartment in a wealthy neighbourhood. I think this was one of the best decisions you ever made, for by age sixteen, most of Ellen's friends from our old neighbourhood were pregnant.

As life moved on, you finally encountered a good man. You were the happiest I have ever seen you. We loved him and you loved him. He was good to all of us, and he helped you tremendously. He carried some of the weight, allowing you to continue the finishing touches on the home you built for your family in Ghana. For years he was there for us, for you; and you were there for him.

The year of the millennium – a leap year, when tragedy is likely to occur – tragedy did strike. The Grim Reaper once again moved into our personal space. The Grim Reaper visited and plucked your best friend in Canada, the godmother of my little sister Sabina, from you. Aunty Augustina departed this world. This was the catalyst that unravelled your compact psyche of painful emotions. I believe it was an accumulation of all the suppressed pain you harboured within.

The symptoms manifested in your personal relationship. First you pushed the man who had shown you and your children so much kindness away. Ultimately, your treatment of him forced him to abandon you and your children. No one understood the reasons for your strange, erratic behaviour. After all, immigrants do not have psychological problems. We work and spend time with our families; this is how we deal with psychological problems. We do not give in; we do not break down.

But an ugly and deeply troubling illness – depression – picked you. My brave Mother, you continued to work. Upon your return home each day you succumbed to the demands of this new demon – you retired to bed at five o'clock. You struggled in your role as our mother. You managed to cook infrequently, but you were severely detached from who you are – the strong woman we had known as our mother. For eight long years we witnessed this, not knowing what to do. A friend or two tried to help, but for the most part, it felt like no one could do anything. Ellen had an extensive, busy social life, all-absorbing. I felt alone and scared. I thought I had lost you forever. Often, I cried myself to sleep, praying for God to help us through this. I could not take it anymore.

Your condition worsened, and you began to show signs of mental illness. Like most people who suffer from depression, you did not think you were sick, but we all knew you had lost faith and your sense of self. Repeatedly, I pleaded with doctors to do something. I remember going to a Ghanaian doctor. I broke down in his office crying uncontrollably, begging him to help me. Unfortunately, it was a legal issue. All of them said that nothing could be done to force an individual into care unless you got legal permission from a justice of the peace. What was I to do? I was nineteen years old, attending university full-time, working twenty-eight hours a week, and I had to make the decision of whether or not I would override my mother's rights. Would the justice of the peace believe me? Was I strong enough to reverse our roles? Now it was my time to demonstrate love, patience, and care. It was my responsibility to look after you, Mommy, and I did it. I, your daughter, Sara O, committed you to an institution inside the hospital, so that you could receive the help you so desperately needed.

I believe the stigma attached to mental illness in the Ghanaian community was killing you slowly. It was difficult for us all to deal with, but I had to do what I had to do to make sure you were okay. When I went to court to speak to the justice of the peace, the guilt I felt was indescribable and unforgettable. I was all alone, experiencing a mixture of emotions, feeling simultaneously sad and strong. I told myself I was not betraying you, I was doing the right thing, and that this act was going to help you recover.

I never lost faith. After hearing my submissions, the justice of the peace granted me the order. The hospital stay was the best thing we could have done for you. For two months you remained in the hospital. Tests determined that you suffered from a severe form of psychiatric depression and needed to be heavily medicated. But upon your discharge and return to the apartment, we saw your radiant smile. For the first time in years, your true self peeked out and we knew we had done the right thing. I even took some money I had stashed away for my education to refurnish our apartment for your return, and that surprise, I know, contributed to your exuberance.

It has been five years since you came home from the hospital. Although you are not 100 percent back to the woman we all knew, you have made significant progress. We are so proud of you for always maintaining your strength and working so hard. That experience has strengthened my faith and love for God, and my maturity level has reached remarkable heights. My humility, strength, and wisdom come from you, and for that reason, I cannot stop saying how much I love and thank you for being who you are. You are everything to me. Thank you for your courage, which has commanded me on this path. I want to do well for you; I want you to know that the pain and suffering you endured was not in vain. The countless sacrifices you have made, and continue to make, are witnessed by God and your family.

We love you Elizabeth O. You are the definition of a heroine, the invisible, marginalized feminist that we rarely read about – someone who never gave up. It is because of my faith and love for you that I succeeded in law school and progressed during the years of my education. As I complete this story, I vow today that this suffering will end with this generation, and your future descendants will always be conscious of your legacy. Thank you, Mommy. I deeply love you and respect you.

Sara O. is a twenty-four-year-old African Canadian who is a lawyer. She has completed a joint honours degree in criminology and political science, and recently completed an LLB. She is the daughter of a remarkable woman who, barely knowing how to read and write, has an extraordinary story. Sara has written her story as a letter to her mother, who has endured and overcome adversity in Canadian society. Having become a lawyer, Sara wants to credit her mother for this achievement.

CONVERSATIONS ABOUT BECOMING A MINORITY

Hodan S. Mohamed

"You're all liars!"

I don't recall exactly when I first became a "visible" minority. But I recall when the process of becoming one began. This was when I first arrived at the Canadian border in Fort Erie, wearing a pair of bleached blue jeans, slightly ripped at the front in the style of the eighties, a black leather jacket bought in Cairo, and carrying a small duffel bag with all my worldly possessions. It was well past midnight when I entered the building, having hitchhiked the distance between the American and Canadian borders. A group of Somali women and children were huddled in a corner of the waiting area. They looked wide-eyed and exhausted. I, too, was tired, having travelled all day and most of the night, but I looked, or so I thought, less out of place than they did. I was young, modern, and spoke English. They did not speak English or French and looked distinctly foreign in their Somali dress and hijabs. They had to wait all night for the Somali-speaking interpreter to arrive in the morning.

Most Somalis will say they have no idea why they chose Canada. A few individuals already in the country as students or diplomats probably told their relatives and friends about life in Canada. Everyone else probably knew somebody who knew someone who was in Canada. In this sense, we weren't unlike the first settlers who came because they were lost, and soon their wives joined them because they were lonely, and their relatives and friends thereafter came to escape something, or find something better. We wanted peace, safety, work, schools, and freedom. We all thought Canada would offer us these things, but not sure how, or why. Some only wanted to get away from the insecurity; some thought they'd find Shangri-La; some thought they'd be gone for a short while. In any case, we didn't have too many choices. War generally reduces one's choices: leave or face death. We were the lucky ones who left; we left many more behind to face death, or the threat of it anyway.

Not having suffered terrible things up to that point in my young life – things such as loss, hunger, disease, or disability – the unravelling of my beloved country, which until then had given me a sense of belonging and a firm sense of my place in the world, presented an opportunity for freedom from my family's close supervision. I was allowed to leave alone with the promise that I wouldn't violate their trust. I had been given, even as a child, a tremendous amount of personal freedom, and I had earned their trust, which served me well when it was time to leave for North America.

The white officer on duty the night I arrived at the border looked frustrated and tired. Having a bunch of people with small children sitting in the waiting area all night would have tested the patience of anyone. He said as much when he discovered I could speak English. He said that he did not believe we were genuine refugees. How could refugees from Africa make their way to the Canada-US border? That was not an entirely unreasonable question. But I hadn't thought about how Canadians would react to our arrival in their country. In the conversation that followed, he said, "You're all liars." I didn't react, just stood in stunned silence. I didn't respond. I didn't know how.

"Why don't you go back to where you came from..."

Three years had elapsed since my arrival in my new country. I felt instantly at home and safe in Canada, but then I had always felt at home in the other places that I had lived in or visited, even places as overwhelming as New Delhi or Cairo. I wasn't particularly given to feeling strange, and a generally positive disposition helped foster a sense of adventure and optimism. I was particularly pleased with my first full-time real job in downtown Ottawa, working as a cashier in a grocery store. I earned more money than I'd ever had, and I could help support my mother and relatives who had now become refugees in Kenya. My father and my brother weren't so fortunate and had fallen to the marauding militiamen terrorizing the countryside just before the government fled the country.

I especially liked this job because it was in the Byward Market where during the summer months happy, attractive customers strolled in to buy their groceries. Musicians played in the streets and buskers gave street performances, while people gathered around to enjoy the free spectacles. The energy from the street made the mundane task of ringing the cash register bearable. I also liked the job for another reason – its proximity to the ByTowne cinema. I have always loved films and had watched hundreds of Hindi, Egyptian, and American films by that time. The discovery of the ByTowne meant that on a given week I would "visit" a new country. It was the cure for my homesickness; it's where I found possibilities for the future. I loved sitting in the dark theatre, always in the same seat with my Glosette raisins and a cup of tea, waiting to be transported to a far-off place. I couldn't have imagined so many good films would come out of Iran.

One Sunday evening when I was working in the grocery store, an attractive black woman – of middle age, fair skin, and light-coloured eyes – came to the cash lineup. I was still serving a couple who had run back to grab an item they had forgotten while I continued to ring the rest of their produce. There seemed no rush to serve the lady as she leisurely walked to the cash area, so I waited for the couple to return to finish their order and to serve her next. We tend to read people's body language, to gauge their reactions to our words or actions, and I hadn't noticed any impatience on the lady's part; or perhaps I misread her. Either way, once served, as she was leaving, with no one else in the store she looked at me and said, "Why don't you go back to where you came from," adding for good measure, "nobody wants you here, anyway."

If the white border patrol officer's "You're all liars" came across as a spontaneous rant, the remarks of this attractive black woman struck me as deliberate and rehearsed. The words caught me off guard. The impact was instant. I carried that hurt for many years. It dawned on me, perhaps for the first time, that the boundaries within which I was going to exist were already conscribed, and things were more complicated than I had imagined. I took notice and became cautious. The safe spaces for me were not entirely clear. Once again I was silenced, this time by hurt, even as I murmured something incomprehensible after the departing lady.

"Is that what you consider yourself?"
Many more years went by. I had finished university, trained in video production, and got wonderful opportunities to learn about the fascinating but tedious world of film/video making. I was charmed that despite the many struggles along the way, I could at least fulfill my curiosity about how documentaries and films are produced. Some of these opportunities took me across the border to Washington, DC, and a new life for a number of years. By this time, I had come to accept a few labels as an inevitable part of my reality. I had come to accept my minority status, my black identity, and my refugee label.

I had made peace and set out to empower myself to acquire new fighting words from the experiences of North American blacks, Aboriginal peoples, and from racialized immigrant and feminist activists. I took it for granted – after more than a decade of living in North America and having successfully internalized my new identity as a black woman and a minority on this continent, and having learned to identify with the everyday struggles of black communities – that my "blackness" would come to be questioned and that there should be a different box within employment statistical forms I ought to check. But this is what happened. I had just landed a job in Washington, and my new employer, a woman of Irish descent, wondered why I checked "black" as my "race." Looking up from the form, she said, "Is that what you consider yourself?" I responded, "Are there any other options?" – which was greeted with silence.

"Do they really do that to girls?"

It seems events of the homeland do follow us. When the homeland is successful, confident, then the immigrant can bask in that glow. When the homeland suffers, so do we. And my homeland was dying even though I was thriving, albeit optimistically, in my new home. My once-beautiful country and people were on the path to rapid destruction. Everybody knew who we were: our distinct features, once a source of pride, now singled us out. We had become fodder for hungry news media whose gaze on our former homeland and our struggles to plant roots in our new homeland made daily living difficult. These were the days when pity for the destitute and dying children of Baydhabo turned to the horrors of Black Hawk Down and the debacle of the Canadian Airborne Regiment.

If I could ignore the events unfolding in the old country, it was difficult, as a young woman still enamoured with her independence, to ignore the interest our presence generated as the newest arrivals to Canada. The attention was sometimes benign, occasionally compassionate. Yet, at other times, it felt like an assault. It might have been my own sensitivity to these events – a feeling that was widely shared by other young Somalis at the time. When a beautiful Somali fashion model emerged to tell the world, "Yes, I am beautiful, a supermodel, but I've a secret," the safe spaces shrunk even more.

The secret that supermodel Waris Dirie exposed to the world in her infamous book, *Desert Flower,* was her experience of female genital cutting (variously known as FGM or female circumcision). At once, we came under the scrutiny of not just the media, but of lawmakers who sought measures to criminalize the practice. FGM, it was argued, was child abuse carried out by ignorant women who did not know the harm they inflicted on their girl-children. Girls had to be protected from their mothers. Those of us who were the daughters of such ignorant women, and who resisted and spoke for proper dialogue to raise awareness and bridge cultural differences in a humane way, were branded defensive. Perhaps we, too, had no sense to understand what was good for our children and community.

I never doubted the harm that the practice inflicted on girls and women. And yet, as a group that had lost so much and that had no settled community to advocate on its behalf, the sensation created by Waris's exposé (which also emboldened other women to come forth) had unforeseen consequences on the same girls the campaign sought to protect. One incident in particular stands out for me. The incident involved my young niece who one day came home upset because her teacher had invited her in front of the class to share "her experience" of FGM with her classmates. Embarrassed, she denied knowing what the teacher was talking about. At the time it seemed inconceivable that a grade nine student would be asked to speak about such intimate details in front of classmates. But it seems even more improbable that total strangers would feel emboldened to pose a similar question to a total stranger. Yet this does happen. Once in a while, a total stranger feels the need to ask: "I mean, not you, but do they really do that to girls?"

I remember these "conversations" in my earliest encounters as either baffling or hurtful. I only understood much later that a process of racialization and othering was at play, a process that would have adverse consequences for our next generation of children, our male children in particular. I also came to understand that for some of us, the path to citizenship – those periods of initiation that everyone rattles off without once asking "What does it actually mean to experience that?" – was a period fraught with tension. It felt as though there was nowhere to fit in: the battles had been fought, lines had been drawn, and we, Somalis, who were latecomers and carrying unwanted baggage, could not seamlessly fit with any group. And so the conversations, often hurtful, that make it possible for us to carve spaces in our new Canadian homeland, continue. Like others before us, we will look back at these early years in Canada as periods of trials and triumphs – as an important journey in becoming an integral part of the Canadian mosaic.

A doctoral candidate in population health at the University of Ottawa, Hodan is a social justice advocate, a dilettante, and a striving Muslim whose ancestors hail from the rugged plains of the Somali peninsula. Hodan is the recipient of the 2012 Queen Elizabeth II Diamond Jubilee Medal for Community Service. She calls Ottawa home.

SPEAKING THROUGH SILENCE
Silmi Abdullah

Recently, I accompanied my boss to court for a hearing. Our client was a Muslim and of Arab descent. As soon as I walked in, the female judge asked me, "Are you the interpreter?" By no means was I offended to be called the interpreter. But it was interesting that despite three university degrees and nine years of post-secondary education, my hijab and brown skin had, in the judge's mind, eliminated the possibility of my being the law student/lawyer-to-be. The automatic association with an ethnicity completely different from mine was also noteworthy. This was of course, not the first time I had experienced this.

In my early years of university, I had strangers ask me whether I was waiting for my husband, as they spotted me on the street while I was really waiting for my friends for an evening out. My employer from my summer call centre job asked me what the point of going to university was when I was going to get married, have kids, and quit work anyway. Ever since I arrived in Canada in 1998, and particularly after 9/11, I have repeatedly had narratives of early marriage, oppression, violence, and male misogyny imposed upon my body. My outward appearance continues to render me an empty receptacle, a blank slate for assumptions, prejudices, and myths.

This is a fate that Muslim women are confronted with all too often. We become involuntary tragic heroines of scripts written by others, and often what we call our "own stories" are simply tales of our efforts to negate those scripts, to justify our identities, to explain who we are NOT rather than who we are. For many years, I did the same. Comments that attempted to categorize me, label me, and attack me through stereotypes about my faith angered me. I would try to think of ways to combat such remarks the next time someone made them to me. I would craft arguments so that I could convince others that I was not oppressed, that my hijab was my own spiritual choice, and that my parents never treated me differently than my brother, until I realized the futility of such an exhausting exercise. When I understood the power of actions, and its ability to (mis) represent an entire faith followed by billions of people worldwide, I realized it was time for me to stop speaking. If suicide bombs and honour killings had the power to wrongly symbolize my faith, I realized that the only way I could effectively represent my religion was through actions – through compassion, kindness, love, and generosity – by embodying the values that I have known to be the true markers of my faith. This was also incredibly important for re-asserting my dignity and self-worth as an individual, and as a woman. So, as the activist within me grows more and more passionate, I become increasingly silent, and it is through this silence that I reclaim my identity and rewrite MY story.

Growing up, "freedom," "feminism," "progress," and "modernity" were not terms that I was overtly conscious of. This is because my family instilled in me incredible pride of being a woman at a very young age. These were values that were so deeply engraved within me through my religious, traditional, and familial teachings that I never felt the need to actively declare their presence in my work and my aspirations. These were not unachievable goals that I dreamt of, but rather tools that I already had by virtue of my upbringing, which I was expected to use throughout my life as a way of self-development. Ironically, it was when I came to Canada that terms like "feminism" and "modernity" seemed burdensome, simply because Eurocentric definitions of such terms were imposed on me. When I began to succumb to such impositions, which triggered in me the need to apologize for who I was, that is what eventually began to feel like the death of *my* freedom, *my* feminism, and *my* womanhood.

I have become tired of participating in the clichéd academic and popular debates of whether Muslim women are oppressed or not, whether their husbands and brothers are violent, whether the hijab is mandatory or a cultural product, whether Muslim women are brainwashed into thinking that hijab liberates them, etc. By doing so, I simply do a disservice to my faith, and to myself as an individual. By trying to explain defensively that the hijab is not oppressive, that I am a "moderate" and "progressive" Muslim, I give validity to a particular definition of "liberation" and "modernity," and the notion that the definition is exclusive and universal. As others try to figure out whether to place me in the category of feminist or Muslim, traditional or modern, it is futile for me to explain to them that I am not traditional, but modern, that "despite" being a Muslim, I am a feminist. It perpetuates the myth that religiosity, conservative dressing, and expressions of faith are incompatible with feminism, that they are foreign practices, and that I must practice my faith less, hence, more moderately to be in sync with Canadian values. In the process, I also end up demonizing those Muslims who are more devout and practising than I am. By participating in debates that discuss arbitrary constructions of tradition and modernity in polarizing terms, and trying to identify with one of the two, I reinforce the idea that these must be mutually exclusive dichotomies. I do nothing but keep myself trapped within the walls of this rhetorical space. Subconsciously, I continue to enslave myself in the name of feminism and liberty, disallowing others from appreciating me as a human being, the essence of whom extends beyond a piece of cloth. I fail to share the many unique aspects of myself and my identity that I am proud of.

· · · · · · · · ·

When I first arrived in Canada on a serene fall evening in 1998, I was thrilled to build new and lasting friendships, achieve professional success, and contribute positively to Canadian society. At school, I was warmly welcomed by my teachers and students. But I was disappointed by the lack of any real effort to know about me, the myriad experiences of my childhood that I cherished and was so excited to share with people in a new country. Except for a handful of people, most were so preoccupied with the shock of hearing me speak English without an accent and feeling sorry for my hijab that there was hardly any time to hear about my family, the unique amalgamation of my rich Bangladeshi heritage and diasporic upbringing in Saudi Arabia. I longed to tell people about my beautiful country, Bangladesh, my loving parents and extended family, my exciting anecdotes of travelling around the world. As people assumed and expressed pity for my "restricted" life in the Middle East, I hardly found the chance to tell them about the wonderful friends that I had left behind, the picnics, the exquisite food, nocturnal shopping sprees through illuminated Eid bazaars in the city, the majestic drives through the golden deserts, and the many wonderful moments of my life spent in that part of the world. Conversations seemed burdensome; the humanizing elements that form the basis of a relationship were largely missing. It took me years to realize why that was the case.

Now, it is only through my actions that I strive to explain that I am a feminist *because* I am a Muslim, I am educated and open-minded *because* I come from a 1400-year-old religious tradition of education, intellectualism, and tolerance. I am only able to achieve that when I live and breathe my faith, by practising it unapologetically. This is what invites and inspires others to know my faith, as it is more unsettling to see a kind, friendly, and educated woman in apparently oppressive attire, rather than an angry, reactive individual who isolates herself through defensive arguments each time her faith is attacked by racist attitudes. It disturbs the prejudicial notion of Islam as a violent, oppressive, and anti-feminist religion more effectively. My liberation, and my feminism, therefore, lies in defying and rising above others' definitions of such terms. By simply living the legacy of compassion, of peace, of love, and of kindness that has been established by my Prophet and passed down through the teachings of my family, I attempt to be an ambassador of my Islamic faith, and my familial teachings. I try to set an example through which I assert my dignity and pride as a woman, a Muslim woman.

This is not to say, however, that I equate compassion and silence with an attitude of escapism, or a practice of refraining from debate. As an emerging lawyer, silently accepting injustice is contrary to my values and my responsibilities. When groups, including but not limited to Muslims, are oppressed and marginalized with the support of discriminatory law and policies, it is my entitlement and my responsibility to use our human rights laws to advocate passionately for the rights of the marginalized. What I refuse to do in the process is to apologize for who I am or encourage others to apologize for who they are. I have been blessed to have many wonderful friends, mentors, and teachers in Canada, who have been an incredible system of support throughout my academic, professional, and personal journey. I have always been fortunate to work with organizations, with colleagues who celebrate diversity and recognize the plurality of feminism. It is because of those individuals that I have always found the courage to be vocal about my beliefs, and to pursue what I passionately believe in. For those who do fall within the trap of racist propaganda, I am hopeful that through my commitment to build friendships across borders, to serve the community with compassion and love, my values and actions will eventually appear as natural extensions of my faith, rather than the irreconcilable contradictions that they are too often made to be.

Silmi Abdullah is a lawyer based in Toronto. She was born in Bangladesh and spent her childhood years in Saudi Arabia. She immigrated to Canada with her family in 1998. As a Canadian, she takes great pride in her diverse background and experiences and is always seeking to build bridges across cultures and communities.

RIDING THE WAVES OF LIFE
Yumi Kotani

I grew up in a small town in southern Kyoto, Japan. I spent my entire childhood there, living with my parents and brothers. At age eighteen, I won a scholarship to go on an exchange program in the US, where I lived with a host family and attended a local high school in rural Ohio. I returned to Kyoto briefly to finish high school, and at age twenty, I left my home again, this time as an international student at the University of British Columbia. I wasn't necessarily planning on staying in Canada after graduation, but over the years I have become a highly engaged member of Canadian society. I am here for the long haul, as my personal and professional life is grounded on this side of the Pacific. Since my arrival in Canada, I have worked and studied in BC, Ontario, North Carolina, and now back in Ontario.

Ever since I spent that year in Ohio, my language – or my linguistic ability in English and Japanese – has become the single most common topic of conversation in my interactions with people. I received comments from people I knew back home, from Canadians or Americans I meet here, and from other Japanese expats/émigrés I encounter in North America. I suspect that part of the reason for this is that I learned English and North American culture more quickly compared to many in a similar situation to mine. But I think there's more to it than that.

Most comments about my English, typically from English speakers in North America, usually go like this: "But your English is so perfect! You don't even have an accent! I was so certain you were born here!" or "I can't believe you're not from here!" This is followed by questions about how long I have been in Canada, at what age I came, how long I have been speaking English, when/where/how I started learning it, and so on.

In contrast to these almost compulsive compliments about my English, the comments I receive from Japanese speakers about my Japanese usually go this way: "Oh your Japanese is terrible! Are you sure you're *really* Japanese?" or "You're so not Japanese! You've become a *gaijin*!" – a derogatory term for "foreigners," meaning "outside person" or "person on the outside." I should note that my Japanese isn't *actually* all that terrible.

What most people don't realize when making these comments, however casually, is the extent and depth of the struggles I have gone through over the years with both English and Japanese. The transition I had to make from a small town in Kyoto to a migrant life that spanned the Pacific hasn't been easy. It has taken a tremendous effort on my part in terms of language acquisition, cultural adaptation, and social and economic integration to get to where I am now. And even after more than a decade, this process is still ongoing.

· · · · · · · · ·

The first wave of criticisms about my declining Japanese started when I returned from that exciting exchange in Ohio, back to my family and high school in Kyoto. I had expected that going back home would be much easier than the process of settlement I had just gone through in Ohio, but I was wrong. I found myself scrambling to get my Japanese back up to speed. I found this process of reverse culture shock and re-adaptation even harder, if only because I was caught off guard by the experience.

In a sense, my nineteen-year-old self was still on cultural euphoria from that thrilling and mind-blowing experience of living in a new country for the first time in my life. I had just exposed myself to a whole new language, culture, and town. I didn't want this excitement to fade away, although I was feeling distraught about how quickly my English was slipping away.

I did not want my English to disappear because, at the time, I wanted to work in international development. I had read in a Japanese career magazine that I absolutely needed a master's degree from an English-speaking and/or "Western" university to do so. This was partly why I chose to go on the exchange program in the first place, to start that process. Now that this path was more within my reach, I decided to pursue undergraduate education overseas.

But for my old friends and family, adapting to the "new" outward-bound Yumi was shocking and unexpected. To them, I must have seemed like a different person from the one they thought was coming back. This probably felt like a loss of the Yumi they had known, loved, and were so looking forward to seeing again. Being caught off guard, they clung onto the "pre-Ohio" Japanese Yumi. Their sense of loss and grief was expressed through critical comments about my declining linguistic ability in Japanese. Their comments were not only about my language but were linked to my (ostensibly) declining worth or status as a "real" Japanese. I was often mocked for not having the Japanese "common sense" and was characterized as socially inept or just plain incompetent. The initially benign jokes turned into shaming about how I was "too Western(ized)," no longer Japanese, betraying my roots, and forgetting who I really was. In their eyes, I had become a cultural outsider, and had somehow lost my ethnic identity as a Japanese.

· · · · · · · · ·

I went through yet another period of frantic cultural adjustment as an international student in Vancouver. My conversational English was okay for everyday interactions, but it wasn't good enough for university. I also kept failing ESL tests my first year there. I was not at all equipped with the vast amount of cultural and historical knowledge that Canadian students and professors shared, and I found myself lost in classroom materials and discussions. The campus culture wasn't particularly welcoming for international students either. I remember receiving many comments about how we were taking university resources and seats away from Canadian students, and that people like me "really shouldn't be here." (I later found out this was untrue, as the university actively pursued international student fees as a revenue-generation strategy; hence we were not a "drain" on the system, as many assumed.)

In short, during these first years, I was desperately trying to learn English and to fit in to a new campus and society, where I *was* a real foreigner. I had the Canadian language, culture, university, and labour market to worry about, just like my peers back home did – with the distinct culture and intricacies of the Japanese university and labour market. In addition, like other young people starting university life, this was also a period of personal and intellectual growth. In my case, it coincided with the dramatic cultural/linguistic transformation I was going through. All these factors probably amplified the perception of my loved ones back home that I was becoming less and less the small-town girl they knew (given that as a girl, I was never encouraged or expected to have a career of my own) and also that I was becoming less ready to fit the mould of a "Japanese adult" or "Japanese woman."

· · · · · · · · ·

Today I am much less affected by these comments (which I still receive), as I understand where they are coming from. I also now know that these words don't *actually* reflect my declining value as Japanese, or as a person. In looking back, I can also understand why these words had such a confusing and devastating impact on me at the time.

I can now see a certain undercurrent to these comments about my language – both Japanese and English, based on the subtle but exclusionary assumptions about who can belong where. That is, the incessant comments about my language skills often carried implicit assessments about whether I could belong in each society and to what degree. Underpinning these was the assumption about who has the authority to appraise and decide who gets to belong and where. I have noticed this happening on both sides of the ocean, with linguistic ability used as an indicator, or condition, for belonging as a full and legitimate member of a particular society.

For example, compliments about my English have become almost commonplace as people I meet in Canada and the US find out that I'm not from here. Years ago, I had expected that the more time I spent here speaking English, the less of these comments I would get, especially about how "shocked" and "blown away" people felt by it. After twelve years of living and working here, and having completed graduate education in English, these comments have become a normal part of my life. Of course I still have small challenges in everyday interactions, for example in following conversations involving many people, or learning how to seize an "appropriate" moment to chime in. But compared to where I was twelve years ago, I certainly feel much more integrated and comfortable living here.

However, I am perplexed that the frequency and intensity of praise about "how good my English is" seem to increase with time, including at work, in social gatherings with friends and relatives, and even with complete strangers on the bus, the street, at coffee shops, public libraries, hair salons, dentists, and elsewhere.

For the most part, these comments and questions come from people's genuine intrigue with the way I picked up the language, and are intended to be complimentary to me. Therefore, I don't mind these interchanges *if* the conversation stays focused on the genuine wonders of the language acquisition process. However, these innocent conversations can quickly become uncomfortable – for example, when people *compare* me with other immigrants, who, in their mind, don't speak as "proper" Canadians. Often enough, the Canadian speaker directly compares my English to that of another foreign-born person in the same room or conversation, as though it were perfectly normal to rate or rank us that way. Worse is when they do this as though they've just granted me a special status above these "other" immigrants, and expect me to feel happy and honoured about it. In some cases people actually congratulate me for being "different from *those* immigrants" – because apparently *I* made it into this special club and *they* didn't, and that's evidently a cause for celebration.

When the conversation steers this way, it's no longer about the wonders of human languages, but about the social boundaries of who's in/out and who's above/below whom. When the conversation takes on this tone, it feels like some sort of "test" administered by the everyday judges of Canadian identity. I now know I will be required to explain how and why I managed to qualify for this status every time it is given to me. I know the individuals engaging in this conversation with me aren't thinking this way, and it's usually well-intentioned – but this process is extremely routinized, even down to the exact wording people use.

This is an inconsistent process, however, and the result varies depending on who is running the test that day. For example, some people – often immigrants who have been here much longer than me – suddenly start insisting that they can hear a "foreign accent" in my speech halfway through a conversation. I have noticed, however, that such insistence comes *after* they've learned that I'm not from here. At this point it takes on a patronizing tone, and the subject shifts exclusively to my suddenly discovered foreign accent, and the fact that *they* can hear it because *they* know English for real. It's as though they've just found the evidence that marks me an outsider, and now it's their duty to examine it more carefully. As the *true* insider, they have the qualified ears to detect the slightest signs of foreignness.

Again, I don't mind this conversation if the point of talking about my accent stays on the genuine intrigue about how humans learn languages, and how we pick up different accents as we move to and from different parts of the globe. (Because tell me, who does not pick up accents of some kind based on where we've lived or who we are surrounded by?) I enjoy such conversations about language and accents, as long as it's not really about placing one kind of accent *above* or *below* another.

Fortunately, exclusionary exchanges about my accent don't happen very often, but they can't be brushed off as isolated incidents. I think some of these comments about my ostensibly distinct foreign accent are a form of microaggression, or lateral violence from those who have experienced – and perhaps internalized – the subtle rules of in/exclusion and hierarchy in this society.

I know being excluded and being put down is hurtful for any

person, as it diminishes our sense of identity and self-worth. I also know we often take out our pain and frustrations on someone else, usually those socially constructed as below us in the pecking order. Unfortunately, but understandably, this is one common way we – as social beings who need affirmation from others – try to fix our diminished sense of dignity. I also understand that I sometimes become the target of it. Even with that awareness, however, I still feel the sting when this occurs (because exclusion sucks) and I may feel angry after the fact. But now that I have re-nurtured my sense of self in my own right, and am much less dependent on others' approval, I am much less shaken by these exchanges.

· · · · · · · · ·

But the process of adaptation, integration, exclusion, is a big, long, cyclical process – just when I think I'm over it, it comes back. Just as I became more settled in to my professional and family life in Canada, after finishing university, the "second wave" of criticism about my Japanese came, this time from fellow Japanese expats/émigrés in North America. This wave was almost identical in content and wording as the first wave from those close to me back home, but the mocking seemed stronger and more spiteful in tone. The belittling comments about my "terrible Japanese" turned almost immediately into their negative (and authoritative) appraisals about my diminishing status and worth as a Japanese person. They deemed me to be socially clueless and useless.

These comments were often so harsh that my sense of identity started to feel shaken again. I even started avoiding using Japanese in front of others. Reflecting back, I now see that these harsh comments came mostly from people who were living in Canada or the US temporarily, for study or work. They were coming from people who were having a particularly hard time with language and cultural barriers in this new environment that was hostile to them. Knowing this, I always made a point to reach out to them and played the role of the informal "settlement support worker" for all the new folks who weren't familiar with their way around their new country/city. I know what it's like to be there and I can share some of what I know to help ease that process.

Moreover, the most disparaging comments about my "terrible Japanese" usually came after their Canadian/American friends or colleagues extensively complimented my English in their presence or directly (though nonchalantly) compared their "poor English" to my "perfect English" and how "so Japanese they still were" and how "successfully Canadian Yumi was." In other words, these came as a backlash or lateral violence directed toward me. Such treatment, of course, created a sense of slight for them, especially when they were already feeling vulnerable.

These interchanges put me in a very uncomfortable position, thrust right in the middle of two distinct but intertwined circles of social in/exclusion and hierarchy. As a result, instead of feeling proud of my hard work, I started to develop a sense of guilt about all the compliments I got about my English, along with a growing insecurity about my (*supposedly* disastrous) Japanese.

· · · · · · · · ·

After this second wave of criticism, I worked on using Japanese more often, so that I could be fully bilingual and "bicultural" in my language/culture of origin and in my new home base in Canada. Initially, I started this to stave off the verbal attacks, but over time, this has helped me feel much more connected and whole in my now hybrid cultural identity, developed from all the places I've lived. It feels nurturing to be connected to my cultural roots as a regular part of my life in Canada, instead of having it cordoned off in the back of my mind, or avoiding using it for fear of being mocked.

Moreover, in my more recent visits to Japan, I notice that I receive more blatant dirty looks and hostile remarks from strangers in public spaces – but only when I am with my non-Japanese partner, or speaking English with him in public. (Mind you, we get these dirty looks in Canada and the US from time to time, too, presumably directed at our "interracial" relationship.) These overtly hostile encounters help me see that the increasingly critical comments about my "bad Japanese" and "good English" are in part an expression of the ethnocentric and xenophobic nationalism that has picked up in Japan in recent years – especially during its prolonged economic recession. This is mixed with the century-long racial complex of modern Japan, which views the West as its superior. These are contradictory ideas that don't really make sense together, but are projected onto me anyway. In short, so many of these comments about me "not being Japanese" are not really personal after all.

In hindsight, I feel silly for having been so self-conscious over the years about my supposedly dubious Japanese identity, especially when a group of my childhood friends from Kyoto were incredulous that others would make such comments about me. They told me that I had not changed *at all* in their eyes, and simply laughed away what they saw as an absurd allegation.

· · · · · · · · ·

It took me many cycles to *finally* realize just how much these experiences of everyday microaggressions and put-downs have affected me over the years. It took me a long time to find ways to heal from their impact and rebuild my strength and resilience to bounce back. Now that I see all of this from a healthy distance, the answer seems so simple: Don't let these things get to you. But at the time, it wasn't that easy.

As I overcome one challenge, there always seems to be another one, not only in the areas of language and culture but on so many other fronts related to how other people perceive me (as young, Asian, female, small, etc.). If I am really honest with myself, all these things that creep up in my everyday life still shake me up sometimes, and I still get angry, sad, scared, or discouraged. However, time and again, I have also shown myself and others just how much strength, courage, passion, humility, and deep human compassion I can pull out of myself despite the trying circumstances. I do it to elevate others so they don't have to go through this, and more and more, I've started to see the importance of doing it for my own sake, too.

· · · · · · · · ·

A few weeks ago, our family friend's ten-year-old son asked me what I wanted to be when I grew up. Without stopping for a second I answered, "I've already become what I wanted to be." I told him

I work in a field called "social inclusion and diversity." I explained that I do this work because I want to help shape our society, so that nobody has to be excluded or put down, so that everyone can become who they want to become, and contribute to society in their own way.

The fact that this was my first and honest response to this question made me feel accomplished and whole. This conversation made me appreciate how proud and fulfilled I feel about the contributions I have made, and continue to make – through my work, civic engagement, and personal relationships with friends and family – on both sides of the Pacific.

My line of work can be daunting and discouraging at times, but it reminds me of the joy of turning the experiences of pain – my own and others' – into fuel for envisioning and creating a more vibrant and inclusive society for all of us. I now realize that despite the many low points in my life, since I left my little town in southern Kyoto, I have now come to a place where I can stay grounded in who I am through my own values, passions, and actions, regardless of what kinds of labels or boxes others may try to slot me into.

Originally from Kyoto, Japan, Yumi has enjoyed life in BC, Ontario, Ohio, and North Carolina. She holds a master's in political economy from Carleton University, specializing in urban municipal politics, and a bachelor's in interdisciplinary studies from the University of British Columbia, focused on various forms of inequality. Yumi's career has spanned across sectoral boundaries, bringing together stakeholders from the public, private, non-profit, and higher education sectors to create inclusive and equitable communities and workplaces for everyone. Currently she manages Equity Ottawa, a cross-sectoral initiative to support the capacity development in equity and inclusion among local public and non-profit organizations. She also leads Advancing Immigrant Women, another inter-sectoral project aimed at women's career advancement into leadership roles within the banking/finance sector in Ottawa and beyond.

INVISIBLE VISIBILITY

Jacqueline Lawrence

Before my twelve-year-old self boarded Air Jamaica on August 11, 1974, I was seen, known, and identified by my family and their values. I was known and I knew myself to be the daughter, granddaughter, and niece of the Watsons and the Lawrences, and cousin to the Codners and Campbells. I knew myself to be Jamaican with my family living the national motto, "Out of Many One People," with Arawak (Taino), African, European, and East Indian blood running through our veins. I knew the joy of service as I sharpened HB pencils, matched tables and chairs, and laid out notebooks for the adult literacy class in the church basement, beside my grandmother as she lived and modelled the belief that "to whom much is given, much is expected."

Five years ago, I was reminded of the power of this identification process. I was working on a community project in southwestern Jamaica. One day, while in a market and unbeknownst to me, someone from the northwestern side of the island where I was born saw me and shared with my father's family that they saw a Lawrence face at Linstead market, but they didn't know the name. This question got to my father who lives in New York. Within two weeks, my father called to ask if I had visited Jamaica recently. When I replied "yes," he said he knew it must have been me and that the person did not know me because I had not lived on the island for years. Despite this, he actually did recognize me. This immediate recognition can put a damper on one's social life. However, I always felt safe, appreciated, and valued because people knew my name.

When I landed at Toronto International Airport, I knew I was landing in a foreign place.

However, I did not know I was landing in a place where the first and sometimes only aspect of me that someone would see and use to identify me is that I am of African descent. I did not know that my visibly black face would be the only identified pattern to let me and everyone else know I am not like the others: I am not Canadian. This "I am not" label began a journey of duelling worlds: the world of invisible and visible differences; the world of the Canadian and the immigrant; the world of belonging or not. I did not know that at times I would feel like a foreigner in each world. I did not know that, for a while, I would become a foreigner to and within myself. And, I did not know that this journey would be the access to meeting the "Other" that I did not know was within me.

invisible visibility

in the sea
of invisibility
I visibly stand
erect
alone

in the sea
of visibility
I invisibly roam
freely
willingly
freely

This shift from declaring to myself "I am the daughter, granddaughter, niece, and cousin of..." to defining myself by the contrasting "I am not" label was the start of a period of unpacking and distinguishing invisible visibility. At home, I was reminded that I am not like Canadians. As a result, my only instruction to navigate this new landscape and to ensure success was for me to be ten times better than Canadians. During my first day of school, I thought this was going to be an easy task because my grade six classmates did not display a high degree of intelligence when, shortly after I was introduced, one of them asked if in Jamaica we swung from trees. Later that day, during recess, without asking permission, another classmate pulled my Afro puffs, or pom-poms, as he called them. At school, and during my early working years, when I was the only black face among many white colleagues, I felt I was on display. I felt I was in a fish bowl and people wanted to feed me who they thought I was before getting to know me. Or they wanted me to play some caricature of who they thought I was based on something they had read, heard, or seen on TV about black people. On my first day of school, I began to want to make myself invisible.

I later discovered that this ten-times-better rule was more difficult than I had thought – because it applied to every single thing I did. This was especially interesting when my actions were earmarked as signs or examples of my race. For example, to show frustration, upset, or, even worse, anger over anything was the worst thing I could do. Any show of ordinary human emotion, in situations where my voice was being silenced, was magnified as atypical of my race. I did not miss the irony that in Jamaica there were high expectations of good behaviour to show that I was brought up properly, but in Canada, my good behaviour was seen as an exception, to be noticed with statements such as, "You are not like most Jamaicans I know" and "I don't see colour." As well, while I knew I was being judged by my race, if I were to bring attention to the unfairness of this when it arose, it was often interpreted as playing the race card.

While there may have been no malintent during these exchanges, the impact was the same; there was a feeling of shame. The message received was that this round hole needed to become like the square peg to be accepted. And if you cannot do this, you are not good enough, not smart enough, not beautiful enough, not valuable enough, not loveable enough… This sense of shame cannot be fully understood without understanding the messages that are attached to persons who are different and unfamiliar. This includes different being held as a deficit, a dysfunction, or a deficiency. Being marked as different, I began to speak as little as possible. I began to fear making mistakes. I began to question everything I did or was scheduled to do. And I began doing my best to avoid drawing attention to myself instead of focusing on being my best. This began my shift to pursuing perfection instead of excellence. It was a path I danced along for many years. I captured this dance in a poem.

The Steps

Out of step
Out of time
I am going to the left

You are going to the right
I am going slow
You are going fast
I move to the beat
You are in between
And you jump to the lead

Leading is your privilege
So you were taught
And you were an apt student
Now ready to teach
So you tell me
(not in so many words)
I'm doing it wrong
And you tell me
(not in so many words)
This is the right way to be
And I trip
And I stumble
And bite the insides of my lower lip
As my toes become your dance floor
And you hold on tighter
Squeezing me
Bringing me closer
Directing me to paste on a smile as bright as yours
To show that everything is all right

And I wrestle with my feet
To not run the other way
To seek that beat again, that beat within
I speak my heart's desire
(not in so many words)
Asking you to stop – face to face
Was not what I was taught
And I was an apt student
Now ready to teach
I surrender to follow
To keep the peace

And you believe I have changed
the beat playing in my head
And now you have me to do your will
While I listen for the song to end

There were times I just did not have the energy to dance these steps in order to stay under the radar. During those times, I simply lived what people thought of me. I became the angry black woman. And, I became the black person who only wanted to be around other black people, to feed my soul.

THE WORLD OF CANADIAN AND THE IMMIGRANT

Marianne Williamson, an internationally acclaimed spiritual teacher, activist, lecturer, and author, says "relationships are assignments." In 1990, I decided to accept my migration process as an assignment that is given by life in a classroom instead of a battlefield. I thought this would align my mother's migration dream of a better life for me, while I generated and lived my own dreams. An essential part of this assignment was the ongoing excavation of shame, doubt, worry and fear about pleasing others at the expense of myself. If I had not begun to do this work, I would have missed a critical lesson that was delivered to me while I walked in Centretown, Ottawa on a hot and humid July day. My African print wrap skirt was blowing in the breeze, doing its job, keeping me cool when my stride was momentarily interrupted by an outstretched hand. This experience is captured in the poem below:

Welcome to Canada

a quarter miss…
a quarter miss…

I shook my head,
walked past his
outstretched hand
first at Rideau
then at Somerset
he looked me up

looked me down
then scornfully said
"Well, welcome to Canada!"

I walked away
with his chorus in my steps
a quarter sir...
a quarter miss...
a quarter sir...
a quarter miss...

This was a major turning point in my life. It happened the way that turning points often do: unexpectedly and quickly. In less than twenty seconds, this panhandler held up a mirror to reflect the stark naked truth about the power dynamics of systemic racism in Canada. It is utterly absurd. It makes no sense. And – it is real.

This man, begging for 25 cents, did not get what he asked for. He believed he could talk to me in a scornful and demeaning way, simply because of the colour of my skin. It doesn't matter how long I live in Canada, it doesn't matter that I carry a Canadian passport, some Canadians will, consciously or unconsciously, only open a space for me to be who and what they wish me to be, but never fully open a space of welcome for me to be all of who I am. The day was a turning point for me because, in that moment, I got clear that those who think like this no longer deserve the energy I was pouring out to convince them of their flawed thinking. It was no longer important for me to convince anyone of anything. Instead, I restated my willingness to be engaged with anyone who is ready and willing to be in a transformative conversation.

Around the same time, a friend shared that she was asked by a caller at her work for services for "normal" people. My friend went on to share the caller's definition of normal that is captured in the piece that follows:

Normal People

said she couldn't get help
because she wasn't immigrant or black

said she wanted help for normal people
normal people like her

"and who are those?" I asked
"those like me who are Irish and white"

The timing of these two events opened the possibility for me to explore who and what is normal within the twenty-first-century construct of a Canadian. This new normal was very different from the one I had conceived in Jamaica, and even the one I had experienced upon landing in Toronto many years ago. This new normal included a growing number of Canadians whose parents migrated from the Caribbean, Africa, Asia, South America, and the Middle East over the last thirty to fifty years. This new normal also included a sense of loss for those whose parents or grandparents migrated to Canada prior to the 1960s. This loss was rooted in the belief that if services or programs were developed to serve an expanding diverse client base, others would no longer be served. And finally, this new normal wants to hold on to the status quo that normal equals being white.

And what's even more absurd, we still do not share or discuss these experiences in polite or public conversations. This silence continues to perpetuate the myth that racism does not exist in Canada. As Bob Marley reminds us: *"who feels it knows it."*

THE WORLD OF BELONGING OR NOT

A few years ago, I was attending a retreat in Thunder Bay and an Aboriginal elder shared that "the relationship between a man and a woman is like the wings of an eagle, when one wing is clipped the other cannot fly." I have come to transpose the message of this experience to all types of relationships.

This experience expanded my desire to look at what I have brought into my relationship with Canada as an immigrant. I got clear that while the separation that comes with migration may appear to leave behind all that is familiar, knowledge and skills are within us, and those can be shared. This also helped me to further distinguish between fitting in and finding a space of belonging that I discovered during my first year of university. During that year, there were many students from the Caribbean attending Carleton

University. I immediately felt at home. I knew this world. I knew the food. I knew the music. I knew the humour. I knew the nuances of class and race. I knew in this space I would be lifted up. I knew in this space I was nurtured, safe, valued, and respected. I was reminded that there is an inner power that comes with knowing your history and culture. And there were also life skills such as patience, perseverance, and reliance that are transferable anywhere I go in the world. I was reconnected to my cultural foundation in a new way. And in doing so, I began to stand on strong roots that continue to hold me up as I grow and expand internally and externally. Over time, I became adept at developing my own checklist of expanded spaces where I could build trust, feel welcomed, be heard, have respectful boundaries, be able to bring my wounded wings to be mended, just in time to continue my flight to my highest self.

LESSONS FROM MY JOURNEY

Sometimes you begin a journey and you end up right back where you started. One of the things I have learned is that you never go back to the beginning as the same person. You come back with new information, revelations, and insights that shift how you look at what has always been there, and what is to come. My migration has taken me on the longest journey I have taken to date in my life – the journey from my head to my heart. On this journey I have fallen in love with Jamaica at a deeper level. On this journey, I have a new depth of love for my family, especially the tools they have given me to live life. On this journey, I have fallen in love with all of Canada's landscapes. And in the process, the greatest gift for me is that by holding all of who I am, I believe and trust my voice and my dreams. Here are some of the lessons I have learned along the way:

I believe in striving for excellence instead of perfection.
I believe we are custodians not owners of this world, including our lives.
I believe we need more bravery than bravado.
I believe in forgiving instead of forgetting.
I believe in compassion not condemnation.
I believe in humility not humiliation.
I believe in building bridges not walls between us.

I believe if we co-operated more, we would compromise less.

I believe your life is your testimony; your job title is just a title.

I believe you can describe me; however, you cannot define me.

I believe I can encounter you and not fully experience you.

I believe in commitment not containment.

I believe in passion not possession.

I believe too many of us are in entanglements and we call them relationships.

I believe when people feel threatened or small, they try to live large – especially in their minds.

I believe too often we are willing to pull up our sleeves and engage in the battlefield of life, yet we miss the opportunity to learn from life's daily classroom.

I believe in standing up for the smallest person – especially when there is nothing in it for me.

I believe reverence is a silent rebellion.

I believe in a relationship with God, not religion.

I believe in the sacred not the scared, that's how we get scarred.

I believe God intentionally created the diversity of the heavens and the earth, the diversity of plant and animal life, and the diversity of people so that we know that we cannot make this journey alone.

I believe in love. I believe that's all we are here to do – to give and to receive love.

I believe you cannot love unless you are willing to be vulnerable, and you cannot be vulnerable unless you are willing to surrender your ways.

I believe dying teaches us how to live.

I believe Mama (my grandmother) has been ahead of me and with me in every step of every journey I have taken in the last fifteen years.

I believe I am capable of being all these and more as I continue my longest and daily journey from my head to my heart.

A diversity strategist by day, poet by night, Jacqueline Lawrence's mission is to heal hearts through words. As a published poet and author, she enjoys the journey to dance with curiosity, vulnerability, and paradox, to mine possibilities and sacred wisdom. She's very excited about her forthcoming book, Invisible Visibility: On Being Black, Fat, and a Woman.

WHAT IS TO GIVE LIGHT
MUST ENDURE BURNING...

Sonia Lala

A few days before Christmas of 2010, in the back of a dusty trinket shop in Jaipur, India, an allegedly world-renowned palm reader named Vishnu grasped my outstretched hand from across a desk. *Your parents possess two powerful but opposing energies. You have torn yourself to pieces constantly trying to align with one, then the other. Your body is preoccupied with managing the fragments of who you are, but your spirit is always somewhere else. Decide who you want to be, call your spirit back to you, and occupy your life!* Ten minutes later I stumbled backward out the door, trying to escape the piercing blue stare that had dissected me so masterfully. Nine days later, I stood quietly on a beach in Goa in the silvery dawn, with a man I had just met. "I have never been in someone's company and felt so completely alone," he said. His name was Ameya and, from our first conversation to the final moments of our journey as a couple three and a half years later, he only ever spoke to me in deep truths.

I had enjoyed a relatively pleasant childhood in Toronto among a close-knit community of Bengalis who had migrated from Kolkata in the 1960s. I was treasured as the perfect sequel to a firstborn son and was given an easily pronounceable European name. In many tangible ways, my brother and I were incredibly fortunate. We had access to music, dance, and language classes. We were well fed and clothed, and reasonably well travelled. We had our own rooms, lovingly decorated and filled with comforts. We spoke English without accents and generally grew up in an era in which pop culture had made India hip and fascinating. Our parents were liked and respected. They set a good example of hard work without complaint and generosity toward others.

Unlike what most people would assume about the typical Indian family structure, Bengali women are known for their dominant personalities. Our family was no different. My father was a well-educated, hard-working man who held positions of authority, both professionally and within the community. But in our household he, along with my brother and I, were merely vestigial extensions of my mother. We lived in a mini-dictatorship of four.

As far back as I can remember, my mother was a force of nature. A wiry woman with boundless energy, high cheekbones, and large, flashing eyes, the emotions she triggered deep within me were as complex and volatile as her moods. Her laugh would make my heart sing with joy and I'd feel as though anything in the world were possible. In the very next instant, the beautiful sloping planes of her face would harden, filling me with a dread I couldn't explain.

I knew my mother had spent her childhood below the poverty line. She would tell us how she would cajole a local vendor to loan her school books she couldn't afford, so she could painstakingly hand copy them by night before returning them in pristine condition by morning. She told us how her mother, a child bride who was widowed shortly after having her eighth child, single-handedly raised and educated them with only sugar water in their bellies some days. My grandmother had famously declared that her three daughters would be married to a doctor, an engineer, and an accountant, from oldest to youngest. And they were.

My admiration for my mother was tremendous. Her extreme drive, assertiveness, and ambition were qualities I believed had empowered her to raise herself from one standard of life to an entirely different one. I tried to emulate her, certain it was the path to a life I too could be proud of someday. Sometimes in the middle of a heated argument, my dad would tell me he worried that I was becoming a bit too much like her but not necessarily in a good way. I had adopted her strong opinions and was often quick to judge people and situations as good/bad and right/wrong using the framework she had developed, without questioning its validity.

Although I'd always felt more of an unspoken kinship with my father, it was my mother's high standards I wanted to live up to. I recognized that my mother's reverence for education derived from the reality that, given the strict societal class system and extremely polarized economic conditions in India in the 1940s and 1950s, it had been her only available life raft. With so many people fighting for so few opportunities, being the best was imperative.

I learned very early that the surest way to make my mother happy was to strive for perfection, in and out of school. I remember that for Mother's Day the year I was twelve, I packaged up every single glowing report card, certificate of merit, badge, and ribbon I could find and presented them to her as a walk down memory lane. I had hoped it would make her feel proud of me and of herself. It was the most personal gift I could think of to give.

In my high school years, meeting her standards became more challenging. It was increasingly clear that as an ideal Bengali woman, my two most important duties were to procure an impressive university degree and then, with that, procure an impressive husband. My worth would be more or less collapsed down to my academic pedigree, which would cease to matter after marriage, as I would then be defined by the academic and professional success of my spouse.

The list of attributes that qualified as "impressive" seemed to grow longer with each passing day. The rules I had to follow in order to achieve these things became more prescriptive. And still I persevered, dreaming about that magical day that my mother and I could celebrate my successful completion of these duties together. I retook classes in which I got less than 90 percent. I practiced endlessly at the piano, progressing through the Royal Conservatory levels at breakneck speed. I began my day at 6:30 a.m. and ended it past midnight, sandwiching a full school day between sports and music and dance classes. I sat in my designated study area for the mandated period of time each evening. Falling asleep at my desk, I would surreptitiously use the reflection in the metal clip on my pen to check the clock behind me, so I wouldn't get caught turning my head and be penalized for slacking off.

Life felt extreme most of the time, but because she was my mother, I trusted that she was motivated by love – the fiercest, most devoted and protective kind of love imaginable. It became deeply imprinted on me that you show someone you love them by presenting them with a road map for their success and happiness, and that the more you love someone, the more forcibly you shove them toward realizing their highest potential.

Developing a dominant, unyielding personality helped me survive a degree in engineering physics. It was a discipline known for its rigour. The department took pride in its punishing curriculum that "separated the men from the boys." I was one of three women in my year. It was an environment I had grown used to since, partly due to the availability of the gifted program, where I had been the only girl in my elementary school class for many years, and one of just two girls in my high school class. Later I went on to become one of three women in my graduate program in clinical engineering, and the only female in the first group I joined as a new graduate.

Because most of my formative years had been spent immersed in masculine energy, it was a continuous struggle for me to adopt the restraint and feminine charms my mother was certain I needed to attract the right kind of man. I was reprimanded for laughing or talking above a certain volume. I was instructed on how (not!) to dress, sit, leave an answering machine message, dance, or pose for a photo. I was told to abandon my passion for playing soccer, hockey, and percussion instruments, activities that may have suggested I was wild at heart and difficult to handle. One by one, the pieces of me that were joyful, authentic, and unique had to be put away in a box so that I could be who somebody else needed me to be. I couldn't reconcile what was being asked of me with the fiery, unchained woman who was doing the asking.

The mechanics of magically transitioning myself from monk-like scholar into marriage material completely baffled me. I knew nothing of love or how to conduct myself in a relationship. Those were not conversations I could have with my parents. I made secret, halfhearted attempts at dating people throughout my twenties, and even experienced major infatuations and heartbreaks in the process. But somehow I always sabotaged the relationships before they developed into anything noteworthy, knowing they didn't fit what was expected of me.

It was understood that I would marry a Bengali boy, three to four years older, with either an MD or a PhD in engineering. Matters such as height, complexion, family history, and country of residence were factors, but only secondarily so. Personality and core compatibility didn't even make the list. Because I had been labelled by educators as gifted, trained in piano and Indian classical music and dance, studied engineering, came from a long line of decorated professionals, and was comfortably pleasant to look at, it was assumed that only the best suitors would be in the running. As I stretched out the conventionally acceptable period of being unmarried to its fullest, people in the Bengali community began to speculate upon what kind of groom my family and I were holding out for.

The day I told my mother about Ameya was the day she felt like her worst nightmare was coming true. He was Marathi, had studied sociology, and was younger than me. Using her hierarchical framework, this was all she needed to know before deciding that I had ruined my life and deliberately betrayed her in the worst possible way. Love hadn't made me delusional about who my mother was, or hopeful that she could change. But it made me despair that despite being the daughter of immigrants, the only prejudice I'd encountered came from within my own culture.

I had warned Ameya from the very start that there was little hope of ever gaining my mother's acceptance. He understood and respected Bengali values and, in the throes of blossoming love, was confident he could handle it when the day came to cross that bridge. Every time I panicked and tried to end the relationship, he never once asked, convinced, or told me to stay. He simply requested that I identify the root of what I was truly afraid of. And every time I stood on that threshold poised to flee, I wondered how I could possibly walk away from the only person who had ever made me feel so completely understood and perfect in my own skin.

For three and a half years, we struggled and sacrificed for each other and for our own growth. He busied himself with the logistics of getting accepted to a top-tier Canadian MBA program, understanding that establishing himself here professionally would greatly improve our chances of a future together. I busied myself with the thing I had spent my entire adult life avoiding – fighting my mother for the right to be whoever I was, and to love whomever I loved.

My mother tried to threaten, guilt, shame, and bribe me into leaving the relationship. Up until the very day Ameya told me he couldn't be with me anymore, her efforts were relentless. I spent more than three years caught in a miserable limbo, feeling utterly compelled to continue learning about romantic love, yet grieving for the loss of my mother's love in a horrifically unfair trade-off. The demands I began to make of Ameya evolved from simply wanting a better life for him, to needing to ensure he would give me the kind of life that was worth losing my mother for.

He remained loving and committed until one day it became

more painful for him to be with me than without me. Looking back I can see so clearly how often he had pleaded with me – to release the fears and constraints I placed upon myself, to realize that they belonged to someone else, and that in letting them go, I could feel joy again. To flex and yield with whatever life brought my way; to trust in his love and the spaces in our togetherness. To trust my ability to choose what I needed for myself.

But it was the incessant monologue of my mother's voice – at times in reality, at times in my own head – that influenced the state of mind in which I woke up or fell asleep every day. When Ameya left, I knew how hard it had become for him to love someone who had abandoned herself and become a slave to other people's rules. How lonely it felt to be with someone who was always sifting through memories of the past or frenetically trying to predict and avoid future outcomes. Just as lonely, I imagine, as he'd felt that day on the beach in Goa.

I recently discovered that my mother's family had actually been quite affluent at one time, but had suddenly lost their wealth in events following her father's death. I can now understand why, in the face of life-altering events, neither predictable nor controllable, my mother set out to derive an algorithm that might foresee and circumvent potential threats. Her stringent code of conduct derived from the raw data she had meticulously collected and analyzed from her own history. Teaching me this code was her way of ensuring I had at least the same modest amount of happiness and security that she had.

After her father's passing, duty – so revered in Indian house-holds – became imperative for the sheer survival of her family. Her duties to her mother and siblings included eventually capturing the interest of the family of a respectable accountant, for which she had been earmarked, and leaving her paternal home for her marital one. Carefully wrapping her fiery and dominant personality in yards of silk and artfully draping flowers over her imperfections became the only way forward in life. I came to see how much of her life – and by indoctrination, how much of mine – has been governed by fear of abandonment, loss, and rejection.

Ah, hindsight, what a gift and a curse – after the breakup I realized that I was well into a life-threatening identity crisis. Like a series of nesting dolls, I had become engulfed by the boundaries defining my mother's existence and, in turn, had engulfed Ameya by the boundaries defining my own. All in the name of love. We could have continued on painfully in that way, but his name was Ameya after all, which literally translates as "he who is boundless, without limits."

The universe had brought me a powerful messenger in the form of this once carefree boy from Mumbai who adored, explored, and challenged every aspect of my existence. He showed me that the world in which my mother's rules made sense doesn't really exist anymore. He taught me to stop running away from discomfort and, instead, to sit with it, asking the right questions. And the answers have revealed that I am a person – a person who is worth loving and cherishing as is, and who deserves to attract good things in life, not by following a laundry list of instructions but by knowing and valuing who she is.

Your mother is in pain. She is in a state of crisis and needs your help. These were the last words the palm reader said to me before I fled the room. How could I be the one to alleviate her suffering if I am also the cause of her suffering, I had wondered at times. I had tried to justify my life choices to her by appealing to her logic, crafting convincing arguments using fancy words and a loud voice. I know better now.

Ameya chose to release me by simply climbing out of my confines and into a life of unapologetic self-realization and acceptance. He showed me that I can do the same for my mother, climbing back out of her and quietly trusting that, like me, she will find her truest self within the hollow that was once occupied by someone else. There is still a chance for us both.

This isn't meant to be a song of despair or a scathing tell-all exposé. This is the most honest love letter I could ever write, to my mother and to Ameya. It's the most honest love letter I could write to myself. It's a Declaration of Personhood! There is no anger, no blame left to cast. I struck that match and burned in the flames for longer than I care to remember. All that remains is my purified spirit, glowing and grateful, ready to return to its home.

Sonia Lala grew up as part of a large Bengali community in Toronto, and studied and worked in Halifax, Vancouver, Ottawa, Palo Alto, and New Delhi. She completed a bachelor's of engineering physics at McMaster University and has a master's of clinical engineering from the University of British Columbia. After working for eleven years at the Canadian Nuclear Safety Commission in various roles, she is taking a year-long sabbatical to explore writing, industrial design, and music. She is passionate about helping people to live their most meaningful life, and hopes to eventually have a career designing products and creating conceptual art that empowers others to overcome phobias and personal constraints.

Section IV
EXPLORING FEMINISMS

INTRODUCTION
Yumi Kotani

The stories and essays in this section deal most directly with the theme of "feminism" – or more accurately, its plural form, "feminisms." In these stories, we recognize the *multiple* meanings this word holds for each of the women. They each tell a unique and powerful story of what feminism has meant for them, what they believe it should be, what they want it to be, and what they have made it be through their respective life paths.

At a first glance, these stories reflect in broad strokes the historical trajectory of the feminist movement – from the first wave, to second wave, to third wave – and perhaps an emerging fourth wave. And yet, a closer look at the women's life journeys – which they have taken in different parts of the globe over different time periods – defies any attempt at formulating a singular, or linear, or academic, or Western-centred narrative.

The sources of these women's exposure or introduction to feminism(s) are varied. Some recall "joining" the movement in Canada, either because they were born here or because they settled here between the 1970s and 2000s. Others trace their feminist roots to their upbringing "back home," drawing from their cultural traditions, religious teachings, local political struggles, or inspiration from their mothers, grandmothers, and other strong women in their lives. Some women were influenced by (Western) academic feminist theory during their university studies "back home" and in Canada. Finally, for some, their journeys to feminism(s) came through community-based activism around women's issues in their home countries, as well as in Canada.

These stories portray a strong tension between the experiences of racialized immigrant or refugee women in Canada,

< Abida Rahman
Beautiful Goddess
2014

and the principles and ideals espoused by Western feminism. For example, the women's stories reveal that for them feminism is not primarily about patriarchy and struggles for gender equality or women's rights. Instead, it is about critiquing and challenging historic and contemporary manifestations of Western colonialism, imperialism, slavery, and racism. Framed in this way, Western/white feminism is also critiqued, especially its tendency to remain impervious to the realities and perspectives of women from the global South.

This disconnect from the realities of women in the global South is reflected in how the different authors position themselves in relation to Western feminism, as well as in how they express their own variants of feminism. They draw important and inseparable links between their gender, culture, immigrant, or refugee status, as well as their religion, faith, or spirituality. Some of the women strongly embrace the word "feminism" while others find ways of "bridging" the gulf between Western feminism and their own. There are others who make a deliberate choice to work outside of the feminist orbit altogether (or the politics surrounding it), and don't use the language of feminism at all. Such choices are made, at times, to engage with substantive issues of equality in their own ways. Whatever their reasons for embracing or rejecting the terminology of feminist and feminism, the writers in this section demonstrate their profound commitment to, and beliefs in, the strength, creativity, capacities, and leadership of women, often because they have been influenced by such women in their own lives.

In many respects, the stories in this section show us that feminist theories have not kept pace with the many forms and variants of feminism that continue to develop, including hybrid forms being created and lived, especially by racialized women, whether they be recent immigrants and refugees, or part of the second generation.

The stories shared by women in this section make clear that racialized immigrant and refugee women are reshaping mainstream, white, Western feminism, expanding the previously restrictive boundaries of *what* it stands for, and *who* it pertains to. Some have done so by carving out their own space to organize within the Canadian feminist movement whose focus was predominantly on white women's issues.

In addition to academic and community-based activism,

professional choice is an area where many women have sought to define and live their own forms of feminism, while facing challenges for their choices from within their own communities.

"Feminism" for many of these women seems to be about being true to, and proud of, who you are, despite negative assumptions made about your gender, race, ethnicity, faith, immigration status, country of origin, or anything else. What matters to them is not necessarily the subscription to a movement with a name (i.e. "feminism"), but a commitment to their core values and how they live their personal and professional lives, including their commitment to equality, social justice, (human) rights, choice, respect, freedom, love, compassion, and solidarity with and for women.

ALIA'S STORY
Alia Hogben

Easy for the king in *Alice's Adventures in Wonderland* to say, "Begin at the beginning and go on till you come to the end: then stop." But where is the beginning for me and where the end, and more importantly, what transpires in between?

Hopefully answering the thought-provoking questions, which have been posed in the call out for this book will assist in understanding my beginning and direct me as to when I should stop.

What was significant and shaped me? Were there specific events and people who inspired and influenced me, or was there a defining moment in my life? What about the influence of the Canadian women's movement and feminisms? What are my hopes for future generations, such as my grandchildren?

What do I value and what continues to raise my hackles and my passion? Why do I not just "give up" when faced with what appear to be insurmountable challenges? The very simple but truthful response is that the alternative would be despair and silence.

I believe in the universality of human rights. I wish that we could go beyond the pettiness of whether these are Western values and joyfully accept that they are positive for all.

One of the fundamental values for me is the equality of all, which does not mean sameness or the eradication of differences. It is that individuals, regardless of gender, race, class, or caste, have opportunities and options, and that they are not restricted to prescribed roles. I would like altruism and consideration of the welfare of all to be guiding principles in politics and in all institutions. I find it demoralizing when the mean-spiritedness – present in all of us – is given legitimacy by government policies.

In my youth, I considered becoming a lawyer like my father. But I was drawn to social work, perhaps naively, as a means to practice my sense of social justice and compassion. If I were in any sense blessed, then I had the responsibility to help others achieve their well-being. As a social worker in Canada, my jobs have been in services for children, for those with disabilities, and for women who are abused. Though each group has some distinct needs, all have to deal with abuse, neglect, often poverty, and discrimination. These experiences taught me about diversity, about the lack of fairness and the disregard of the tragic lives lived by far too many.

My commitment to others is because of the ethos and values of my parents. My mother was a strong Indian Muslim woman who practised the teachings of her religion – Islam – and the cultural teachings of India. She was wonderfully generous to others. As a young married woman, she took in three homeless children whose father had killed his wife. She must have received a lot of criticism at the time, but it did not deter her. And when our family had barely escaped from war-torn Burma to India – with little material wealth and a husband who had to set up a new law practice – she opened her home to other refugees who walked the Burma Road to India.

I was influenced by my father, who was one of those who wanted freedom for India from Britain. I don't recall if he called himself a Socialist, but his actions were those of a person who believed in social justice.

I may have been too young to understand colonialism, but I was certainly old enough to be aware of the blatant racism, arrogance, and disregard for human rights that were the results of colonialism. As Franz Fanon noted, any form of superiority bred into a people leads to very bad results in the psyches of both the colonizer and the colonized.

We were raised to be proud of our heritage – Indian and Muslim – and now I believe that I can continue to be proud of both these elements within my Canadian identity. I have lived in Canada for fifty years and only recently recognized that I am a conglomerate of both the East and the West. It is only in Canada that I can acknowledge who I have become. Fortunately for me, I am of a generation that was not raised to believe that never the twain shall meet. This does not contradict the racism, prejudice, or lack of opportunities facing many of us minorities, but I believe we can stand up for our rights in Canada.

The Islam practised in my family was quite wonderful in its simplicity and its tolerance and openness to other faiths. The reason I continue to grapple with the issues facing Islam and Muslims is because I see some of the current teachings as perversions and contradictory to what my parents taught me. I know that my parents' interpretation was more closely aligned to the original message of the faith. Compassion, social justice, and the equality of individuals are integral to Islam and have to be the guiding principles of a Muslim's life.

When did I consciously become aware of feminism? As a Muslim, I was taught to value the equality of all humans. From there it naturally followed that women and girls are equal to males. This belief led me to question why women the world over are seen as inferior, as dependent on men, or as childlike and, therefore, requiring male guardianship and protection.

To me the fundamental fault of too many societies and communities lies in the acceptance of patriarchy as the norm – to such an extent that even women have absorbed the values of that system. The belief that patriarchy is somehow religiously mandated has further embedded patriarchal values within the family, society, and laws of many states.

The tidal wave in the last thirty years of literalism, patriarchy, and conservative religious interpretations that deny equality, tolerance, and social justice is overwhelming. Clearly, this is not limited to Muslims, though in Canada, despite progress in dismantling many aspects of patriarchy, more needs to be done. Sadly, many Muslim majority states have not moved beyond patriarchy, and some newer immigrants to Canada come with this baggage.

Feminism is the opposite of patriarchy. Feminism is a response to the abuses of that system. It is too bad that, in Canada, some women and girls shy away from this term because of the misperceptions and negative connotations that have accrued to feminism.

I appreciate the complexities of the discussion regarding Western versus universal feminism, and the ills of Western imperialism affecting women in developing countries, but I don't want to get stuck here. I think neo-imperialism and religious fanaticism, not feminism, must be fought by all who desire universal human rights for everyone, whether they be at home or elsewhere.

I am grateful to all the women who fought for women's rights. Feminism – the desire to gain rights for women – has been instrumental in allowing women like me to benefit from their years of struggle, in Canada and elsewhere.

I am fortunate to have been part of the Canadian Council of Muslim Women (CCMW) for several years. CCMW is a national organization founded thirty years ago. Its objectives are to create change within Muslim communities, while simultaneously addressing issues of discrimination, racism, and lack of opportunities. CCMW helps women participate as fully as possible in all aspects of Canadian life so they can be agents of change rather than passive recipients.

A task that we take very seriously is to provide an interpretation of Islam that is founded on compassion, equality, and social justice. We are not alone, as there are scholars and international networks pursuing the same objectives.

No matter what "good" I could have done as an individual, I can do so much more by joining a group of women whose goal is the empowerment and equality of women. It is not just one community-based civil society organization, but the collection of many organizations that can galvanize and create change. CCMW has created alliances with other women's organizations as well as with international networks such as Women Living Under Muslim Laws and MUSAWAH – Equality in family laws.

An example of how a group – of women and men – was able to create change was our successful struggle against the legalization of family religious laws in private, legally binding arbitration. We were encouraged by a statement attributed to Margaret Mead: "Never doubt that a small group of thoughtful, committed citizens can change the world. Indeed, it is the only thing that ever has." In following this principle, we were both exhausted and exhilarated when more than thirty organizations collaborated to change the laws so that religious family laws were not given legal authority anywhere in Canada.

Those who insist that religious laws should be accommodated base their argument on religious freedom and cultural relativism. However, to us at the CCMW, while religious freedom is an essential right, no right should supplant the equality right of women.

For me, the concept of multiculturalism is far better than the contrasting one of the melting pot. Multiculturalism allows us to create a Canadian identity that encompasses all the diverse parts of our individual identities. Though there are some valid demands for religious accommodation, there is a danger that in some situations this may lead to fragmentation and segregation among us as citizens.

My own family has become an example of multiculturalism. My husband's parents were immigrants from Scotland, my family is Indian via Burma, our children are a mixture of cultures and traditions. All this is possible in Canada.

My hope for future generations is that they can live in a democratic country which implements fundamental constitutional rights, such as human rights, tolerance, and co-operation. I hope that the state will ensure that each citizen has opportunities to organize and participate fully in the political, economic, and cultural life of society, that they have equal protection under the law, and that the rule of law is applied with compassion and justice. This requires not only good governance but also citizens who take seriously their responsibility to ensure this happens.

We are fortunate to live in a democratic country with democratic institutions. But every government or state needs to be monitored and held accountable. Majority rule must be coupled with individual and minority rights, including the rights of dissenters.

Among the measures to ensure government accountability, it is essential that there are well-organized and well-funded civil society organizations. It is naive to think that these can be funded by citizens only. These organizations require funding from the public purse. A government cannot deny funding because, after all, the money, along with power, belongs to the people. No government should be fearful of advocacy or activism aimed at accountability. However, any organization receiving state funds must abide by the core constitutional values of Canada. Inequalities, racism, and power imbalances will continue, but what is essential is commitment and funds to fight against these.

I hope that Canada continues to value diversity within the framework of a united country. I hope that my grandchildren, and all our children, will be treated well, developing a sense of what it means to be Canadian – one that encompasses all aspects of their identity.

As a Muslim, I pray that we move beyond literalism and narrow interpretations to focus on the fundamental message of the Quran, encapsulated in this verse:

"True piety does not consist in turning your faces toward the east or the west – but truly pious is the person who believes in God, the Last Day, and the angels, and the revelations, and the prophets; spends his substance – however much he himself may cherish it – upon his near of kin, and the orphans, and the needy, and the wayfarer, and the beggars, and for freeing of human beings from bondage; and is constant in prayer, and renders the purifying dues; and truly pious are they who keep their promise, and are patient in misfortune and hardship and in time of peril: it is they that have proved themselves true, and it is they who are conscious of God."

Alia Hogben is the executive director of the Canadian Council of Muslim Women, a national organization founded in 1982. She is a social worker and has taught at a community college. Currently she writes a regular column in the Kingston Whig Standard *on issues of faith and women. For her activism work, she has been awarded an honorary doctorate from Queen's University, and has been made a member of the Order of Canada.*

LAUGHTER, PAIN, TEARS, DANCING, SINGING, HEALING

Bibiana Nalwiindi-Nzakamulilo Seaborn

Feminism is a slogan I carry. It is about a cultural mix of women growing together, working toward our common project, and continuing to influence people's ways of seeing the world. We have to embrace women, not because of what they do for money, but because of what they bring to the movement.

Feminism has made a difference in my life. It has created true friends, nationally and internationally. I have learned that if someone is quiet in a meeting, it does not mean that person has nothing to say. Our world is so intimidating. Women are always censoring themselves. They may ask, "Do I have anything to contribute to this political debate?" They may think that all they have to talk about is how their own community is struggling with poverty, or how women celebrate the arrival of a baby in Zambia, for example. And yet, in feminism we should embrace all that, because that is who that person is, and that is what makes her unique and special.

Feminism has a culture of sharing, despite the differences among us. I take great pride in my ancestral upbringing. I do have something different and unique to share toward a common goal. Women need to just be themselves. Feminism takes time, energy, and effort – even just to stand up and use the word feminism can be a challenge. The more we say it, the more confident we become.

I come from a family of twelve children, but only eleven of us survived. Being the fifth born in such a large family was tough. There were never any leftovers. I am a proud Tonga African woman from Southern Zambia in Central Africa. Today I can add that I am a first-generation African-Canadian woman, living and working in Canada.

In Ottawa, where I live, I continue my oral traditions in different ways. For instance, storytelling is a tradition through which I talk about my life, who I am, and the many struggles I have faced. Feminism has helped me through these challenges, by using the methodologies I know best – storytelling, dancing, singing, and ululating. These are powerful ways of reclaiming hope for a better future and sharing my history so that it will not be forgotten.

Being a black African woman living and working in North America creates many challenges for me that I have to live out on a daily basis. One good change is that I no longer have to justify being who I am. Over the years I have become a stronger person, better able to withstand other people's inclinations of racism. I now deal with these through constructive education, so that others can learn that their actions or words directed at people from elsewhere had racist overtones. I am very happy and proud of my own growth and sensitivity, and that I am able to be in many different situations, among people from all over the world, and still value who I am.

I learned a number of things from the traditional songs I grew up with, which contain a lot of feminist teachings. In North America, we have always been seen as Western feminists. But when one asks what feminism is, one gets a whole lecture on what feminism is not

– and this creates a problem. One time, when I went back home to visit, I had this at the back of my mind. I thought this would be my opportunity to sit down with the elders and talk about what feminism is all about in their understanding.

The discussion resonated with what I was already putting in place. Through singing, gender issues were dealt with at the community level. Issues were talked about and solutions found and implemented so the community could continue living in harmony. For example, when women gather outside in the shade pounding maize to make flour, if one of the women is going through some difficulty, she will sing and pound at the same time. Others will try to figure out why she is singing that particular song. Then, when they go to collect firewood or laundry by the riverside, people might ask, "Why were you singing that song, because the words we heard were such, such, so there must be a problem?" She is then able to explain to them what is going on in her life. In this way, her issues get talked about by different people in a variety of circles. By the time there is a meeting to solve that problem, everybody already knows about it and can offer input on how to solve the problem.

I have extended these teachings and learning with my colleagues here in Canada, because we are also dealing with gender and equality issues in our communities, homes, faiths, or professional environments. At times people have questioned my feminism, and I have taken their questions as opportunities to tell my story, without getting into long complicated explanations about the differences between so-called African and Western feminisms. Women have a right to *be* who they are everywhere, and they should not be silenced or made to feel their opinions do not matter. We have to have a voice and speak up and support one another.

This is to say that there are differences when you look at people from Africa and the African diaspora. But the bottom line is that we are all people. Whether one is living in Canada, the Caribbean, or the United Kingdom, we are all dealing with the same structures that exploited us way, way back. The interrelatedness of feminist issues, and how these issues and struggles are being solved in different contexts, is an ongoing discovery about the richness of stories. We have to recognize that there will be difficulties as one goes along, but at least there will be a basic understanding of why Bibiana is speaking the way she does on this issue, and why Joyce is taking another line. The key is to respect and recognize that the context actually makes us do things differently, but the goal is the same. We all want to build a bright future for our children and have fullness of life for ourselves as we continue with our activism.

One of the most inspiring projects I worked on was with the World Council of Churches' Canada chapter called Urban Rural Mission Canada (URM). In this program, a cultural mix of people met in different regions of Canada and around the world. Our common project was storytelling, which brought to life all the struggles people were going through in their various communities. Guess what? Feminism was at the forefront of all our discussions and sharing, despite never naming it as feminism. The reflections were all about giving a voice and space to share our stories. In these spaces, the first question would not be "What do you do?" but "What story do you want you share?" This would create a forum to *just be* among women and men in the storytelling circle. I believe that we have to educate, inspire, and stay connected through our stories of joy, pain, laughter, tears, poverty, richness, and health issues, while remaining truthful to the challenges that feminism and feminists continue to face – even after all these decades!

Bibiana Nalwiindi-Nzakamulilo Seaborn is a Zambian-born Tonga woman of Southern Africa. Today she can add that she is a first-generation African-Canadian woman living and working in Canada, where she continues expressing her cultural values with determination and telling who she is despite the many struggles of life she has faced. Feminism has assisted her through these challenges, expressed through methodologies she knows best: storytelling, dancing, and singing.

WOMEN WEEP AND MEN ROAR:
THE TUMULT OF THE GENDER WARS

Ferrukh Faruqui

I write these words hesitantly on a snowy afternoon in December. Twilight is just beginning to fall, and with the approaching dusk, my thoughts turn melancholy. The bright day is drawing to a close, just as this fading year winds imperceptibly to its end, and nudges us to sift through the chronicles of this and past years.

Sometimes it seems that life is more and more tenuous. The days of quiet joy and unthinking security that marked childhood are receding so quickly from memory, and I find myself wondering whether those days were real. Childhood seems like a dim, scarcely remembered land visited long ago, and with each year that passes, it takes on the quality of fantasy, fairy tale, or longed-for lullaby, as hazy and elusive as a fragment of song.

As we grow older, it seems natural to look back on a life lived and muse on its sweetness, its vicissitudes, and the inevitable bitterness that cuts through each narrative. Those who peopled our journey from childhood to adulthood are the objects of speculation and wonder and sometimes frustration when we cannot pierce their armour or solve their mystery. But to my dismay, with every day that passes I find myself less able to make sense of the world, be it the larger backdrop of a globe that is in perpetual crisis and which we observe in real time, or the more intimate geography that we traverse daily.

I start each day with a sense of gladness at the blank canvas of time that, like a fresh snowfall carpeting an immaculately white field, beckons with its pristine beauty. The untrodden ways that wind through the edges of consciousness are similar in their seduction; we are charmed into believing in the potency of effort that could miraculously mend the world and make it the idyll we left behind before growing into cynicism.

I know that I turn back more and more to a different era, to 1970s Winnipeg, when life seemed so simple and happiness so assured. When I dream at night, the visions that fill my brain are those of an unassuming city that was often dull, and I smile know-ing that its very pokiness, its steadfast lack of glamour, was the key to the peace we felt there. Those were the times of uncomplicated affection and artless trust and oh, how I wish that those innocent times, unmarred by indifferent reality, could return!

My family was a traditional one, like so many others, with a loving, though stern, father, a less stern and more loving mother, and two siblings. My family was peculiar in the way common to other immigrant families in lonely prairie towns and white mid-dle-class suburbs where we hesitated sometimes to bring our friends home, mindful of the foreign language our parents spoke and the differences in food, manners, and dress.

As observant Muslims, we spent weekends learning the tenets of our faith and studying in detail the meaning of the Quran. The exegesis of the texts in plain English, explained in voluminous notes by Abdullah Yusuf Ali, induced, at least in me, a reassuringly rhythmic assurance of the value of girls and, indeed, there were for me no existential doubts linked to gender. Sometimes certain notorious *hadeeth*, or sayings ascribed to the Prophet, that were egregiously misogynistic troubled us, but when we asked as to their provenance, the responses were either glib or deliberately vague and the responder curiously unperturbed by the obvious inconsistency between clear Quranic verses and the putative words of the Prophet.

For Muslim girls, the lack of denunciation of these unjust pro-nouncements by several of the Prophet's companions can mean the beginning of a painful schism from both their faith and its more rig-orous adherents. For those determined enough to search the sacred texts and related literature for coherent answers, their disillusion-ment is complete – and its effects almost impossible to repair – when they happen upon such nonsensical primers as *Woman's Place in Islam* and the like that gleefully belittle the nature of women. No one sets out to become an apostate, but there are legions of women whose longing for inclusion in the sacred spaces and the community of believers has been repulsed, time and time again, by either com-placent mullahs or a self-righteous army of followers.

Wed faith to culture, and both the romanticized practices of the motherland left behind and the spurious claims of gender equality in the West become equally suspect. As the underpinnings of societal and gender roles become more prominent, the sense of outrage at the falsehoods we've been fed becomes overwhelming. My father was unquestioningly the head of the house, even when my mother was liberated from dependence by her profession. My brother was permitted freedoms we girls were not allowed, and the resentment this engendered, in me at least, was not easily soothed. Within a family, to question such differential attitudes is to challenge the status quo and the wisdom of collective society. My parents, especially my father, expected professional success of us all, but we could not help noticing that even with women intellectually superior to him, he felt himself, by virtue of his manhood, to be fundamentally wiser. His infuriating paternalism extended especially to practical matters such as driving. I remember motoring down from Dauphin, Manitoba, to visit, and the satisfaction of his shock when I appeared intact at the door, my car parked tellingly in the driveway.

Small acts of subversion became important to me. When I completed my residency, I chose to practice emergency and intensive care medicine, the most challenging field I could think of, to prove I was capable of taking on the most acute and critical cases and of running the hospital with only a small crew of mostly female nurses to back me up. There is nothing more exhilarating than running an emergency room and saving the lives of the gravely ill and wounded. These years were critical to my evolution as both physician and individual. I also chose to take on sexual assault calls, much to my father's consternation, and would drive in the blackness of the night to the inner-city emergency room to gently question the victim, who was invariably female, often Indigenous, and sometimes heartbreakingly elderly. I would proceed to collect the forensic evidence needed to prosecute the case. Even then I could be demoralized by the questions on the form – the queries regarding dress, sexual history, and the ingestion of intoxicants all seemed at some level irrelevant to the question of whether an assault had occurred.

One of my most gratifying experiences was appearing as a witness for the prosecution in court. Although rape has always been difficult to prove, I felt I was striking a stand for the victims of this scourge. When I was much older and learned of the cynical use of rape as an instrument of war, my shock was absolute. As jaded as we grow, we always believe in the invisible thin line between utter depravity and human decency. The lexicon of weaponry grows steadily more complex as nations race to outdo each other in technological innovation – the better to kill. But systematic rape is the ultimate weapon – primitive, brutal, and effective. It has the added advantage of ensuring silence, since the shame of violation, often in full view of family, guarantees impunity. Simple violence, destruction, and fear as elements of conflict, painful as they are, can be understood, but such cruelty, especially when perpetrated on the most vulnerable, destroys both victims and society. This is a cost of war that is seldom articulated.

Feminism was an abstract notion for much of my early life. As one of only thirty women in our 1987 graduating class of one hundred at the Faculty of Medicine, brains and a capacity for hard work and deferral of pleasures were really the only criteria needed to succeed in the mythical world of physicians. Most of our professors and teacher-clinicians were men, and I wasn't really aware of bias on the part of faculty. But no one warned us of the struggles that lay ahead. We were the lucky ones, you see – bright, ambitious women, poised to have it all.

The girl that I was and the girls I see around me still contend with the same insoluble problems. Most of these are tied to culture, and some cross all societies. The prospect of love, romance, and marriage all seem at times so farcical that I often secretly commiserate with my daughters, who, like many young women, are reluctant to entertain the traditional roles that we alternately bemoan and esteem.

Some essayists warn of the demise of the family as a cornerstone of Western society, and cite emerging trends such as childless couples and satisfied singletons of both genders who eschew the responsibilities of family life. Observers of social movements who note contemporary society's relentless devotion to career say that modern women simply don't have time to either bear or rear children, while other, less orthodox couplings find more novel and biologically defying ways to have a child.

And yet, having chosen to be a mother (which seemed the natural next step after marrying in the most traditional way possible), now, eighteen years later, if I had not already embraced the principles of feminism, I would have no other choice. For the world is hard on women, and women are hard on themselves. And hardest of all is to be a mother.

Motherhood, sacred across cultures, is exhausting, demoralizing, and thankless. It leads to the most profound sorrow and the deepest grief; no other role is so fraught with expectation, so hammered by demands of perfection, with its attendant self-sacrifice. The mother who dies in childbirth is not so much mourned as shrugged aside, as life goes on. We're assured that the physical strains of pregnancy and labour are a small price to pay for the commensurate rewards of maternity. Of the mothers themselves, so much is asked: they must be professional superstars, domestic goddesses, and gorgeous partners, and they must turn out extraordinary children.

This is the shameful reality of family life, even for women professionals who lead in boardrooms and operating theatres. Their lives, far from being easier, are tasked with ever-increasing responsibilities. The cult of the superwoman thrives in a culture that applauds her Herculean stamina. Too bad this so-called superwoman is too exhausted to care anymore and is either sobbing in her bedroom at day's end or blearily blaming herself for her weakness while seeking help in a pill at the doctor's office.

And so…And so I find myself in the middle years of a life that has played out against frantically evolving Western society, where women have made tremendous strides, yet have eschewed happiness.

More troubling still, our society has been transformed by the porous nature of cultural trends across the globe that have rendered incoherent previously traditional values. Overt sexualization – if not outright "pornographication" – of girls and women, even boys, is a reality of life, accessible by a click of the mouse. Commodification of the individual – the marketing of ourselves on social media and reality television – has made liars of us all. The relentless pursuit of physical perfection, the lying, cheating, and mendacity of society have perplexed most of us. The body count is high, even among those still standing.

The irony is that none of this is new. Across cultures and throughout history, humankind has evolved then declined into inevitable decay. We hurtle like Alice down the dark rabbit hole to a realm where time, space, and self are all out of kilter, where despair is writ large and humanity broken.

Men, no less than women, are puzzled. Confusion reigns supreme. Each of us craves power and fears losing it. But back in the earthly realm away from rarefied planes, women think and care and nurture and create, and they suffer and they die, and sometimes they love and are loved. Our desires are simple; our needs fundamental.

We crave respect and the love that's founded on that unyielding bedrock of respect. And so we can only go forward, to emerge from the rabbit hole of insanity and raise our arms to hold aloft our banners and continue our quixotic march to that mythical Holy Grail.

Ferrukh Faruqui is a first-generation immigrant from Pakistan, who grew up in Winnipeg. She is married and the mother of three grown children. A physician in active practice in Ottawa, whose passion for women's rights, education, and literature inform her community activism, she concentrates on empowering girls and women through her writing and her volunteer work. She finds solace in her Islamic faith, and in her free time enjoys all water sports and the outdoors.

LOST IN THE STRUGGLE: (RE)SURFACING THE BODY IN THEORIZING IMMIGRANT IDENTITIES

Jessica Pinto

As a minority immigrant woman and a temporary academic, I have learned, and have constantly been taught, that I have a place in this society, and by extension, a certain (amount of) space that I occupy. I have learned from (academic) feminists, in their efforts to understand and map out the overlapping consecrations of subjective experiences and objective impositions of place(s) and space(s), that I am somehow relegated to figurative manifestations of punctuations and typographical settings. In other words:

The multiplicity of my identities can (only) be expressed and experienced most accurately in hyphens and commas – I am a Canadian-Indian woman, with Indo-Portuguese ancestry, who is a postcolonial, Third-World feminist;

My thoughts and their articulations are unwittingly tied to an endless stream of parentheses that seek to convey the complexity of these places/spaces – I have (re)tried every (im)possible way to (re)think the (mis)representations of these (re)imagined identities that (dis)place my sense of self; and

I am constantly reminded through (feminist) theory and my own experiences that I hail from the margins – I am one with the seemingly blank space that defines the location of the centre, the norm, the illusive nexus of knowledge/privilege that those from the margins are expected to crave and hope to carve a place in.

I have been taught, through experiences with non-feminists and feminists alike, that I am to take up a certain (amount of) space both within wider systems of power and in interpersonal relationships. This space is defined, not by my own thoughts, ideas, and beliefs, but by the way people relate to me and interpellate me into intricate machinations of power. As an immigrant, I have been taught that this space must be porous to allow the outside in, but never the inside out. This has become especially apparent to me in several instances where my pronunciation has been corrected openly in an effort to help me learn the "correct" way to speak English. The fact that I fluently speak the language, historically imposed on my ancestors through centuries of colonization, and that this is indicative of my conformity to the norm, is not sufficient in allowing me access to the centre. I am still expected to accept these varied instances of sheer embarrassment as "learning" moments that would somehow allow me to crawl a hair's breadth closer to the centre of both wider society and feminist communities. However, and per-haps more importantly, my assimilation to the centre is based on the uni-directionality of this flow of "correctness." I am not allowed to correct the aforementioned pronunciation police on the correct way to say *basmati* and can only do so at the risk of coming off as the stuck-up minority purist (read: race-card puller) whose issues must be dismissed with little consideration.

It is such experiences that have caused me to pause and become aware of renderings of place(s)/space(s) that are more literal than figurative. I have come to realize that these literal renderings are manifested in the very corporeality of my being and that my location, whether in the margins or closer to the norm, is determined to a great extent by the space *of* my body and all its varied articulations and its influence on the space that my body and its articulations cause me to *occupy*. While the former refers to the very manifestations of my body – for instance, the colour of my skin, the way I pronounce words, my fatness, etcetera – the latter refers to how these manifestations influence my location in relation to the norm. My place(s)/space(s) then is(are) determined not only by the impositions of hyphens, commas, parentheses, and margins that lay out my identities, but also by the space that can be occupied by my physical, emotional, and mental selves/beings.

It is the constant circumvention of this rendering of space that forms the basis of my continued struggle with what Jessica Yee calls the academic industrial complex of feminism. In my interactions with feminism(s) within academic circles, I have constantly struggled to understand and (re)align, (re)(in)state and (re)position my overlapping experiences as a woman, a visible minority, and especially an immigrant. However, the theorizing of diverse gendered immigrant experiences, in feminist discourses at this level, tends to take place within the extremely reductionist parameters of identity politics that see identity as an amorphous concept. I have found this recent immutable focus on theorizing identity as a concept, rather than an experience of the body, to be sorely lacking in its ability to theorize the place(s)/space(s) I have come to occupy, particularly as an immigrant.

These limitations of identity-based theorizing become especially evident to me when most, if not all, of my experiences as an immigrant, a woman, and a minority are indelibly linked to my body and less so to concepts of identity. This link became particularly apparent to me in my very first experience as an immigrant, that of the invasive medical examination required by the Canadian immigration process. It is through this event that the palpable breach of my person and the excruciating feelings of powerlessness became inextricably linked with the experience of being an immigrant. Each subsequent experience I have had as an immigrant has only served to reinforce that it is my body, first and foremost, that is used to define my place(s)/space(s) and their interactions with the systems of power. It is the interpretations of my body and its articulations, preceding any knowing of my multifarious identities, that instantiate my position in the margins as the other that defines the norm, the centre. The very act of correcting my pronunciation – the way my tongue moulds words – instantly defines my place as the Other, positioned in the margins.

Academic feminists are no strangers to theorizing the body. Indeed, much feminist theory revolves around gendered bodies and their interactions with various structures and institutions. However, the theorizing of immigrant experiences tends to focus on identities as continuously evolving concepts that are constituted by an ever-increasing series of punctuations. The importance of such theorizing cannot be overstated. But I strenuously argue that attempts to understand and conceptualize minority immigrant women's experiences should begin from and be grounded in corporeality, and that only through an understanding of the treatment of the body can the subjective experiences of identity be truly captured and addressed.

Jessica Pinto is a doctoral student with the Department of Sociology and Anthropology at Carleton University, Ottawa. She has completed her undergraduate and MA degrees in criminology, sociology, and women studies, which has caused her to have a strong vested interest in feminist and women's issues emerging from the global South. Her current research focuses on examining the connection of fatness to conceptualizations of the Indian nation and the portrayal of fat female bodies in relation to the nation in Bollywood films.

REFLECTIONS AT A TRENDY CAFÉ

Lula Adam

I question if there is a place for me within the constructs of feminist theory – these theories that are written/thought up in the hallowed halls of academia. Is the voice of my experience being reflected in those women studies discussion groups?

As I write these few lines at a trendy coffee shop, I look up from my notebook and gaze at the posters on the bulletin board. All the images are of Caucasian faces except for the poster that is advertising the play *Othello*. On this poster, I see the lone black face of Shakespeare's Moor, Othello, who killed the innocent white Desdemona. What I see on the bulletin board is how I see feminism – all white with one or two non-white colours.

Being a Muslim black woman who wears the hijab, in my city, I am that random black face on the bulletin board in our local feminist sphere.

I sit at many a table where I am the "diversity factor." I am the one who brings up the topic of diversity and the need for it. Many a time I have stated that I cannot be the spokesperson for all the "Others" in our community – Others being members of cultures and religions that are not represented around the table.

Then a thought strikes – what would the conversations look like if I weren't there? Would there be a conversation on diversity? If that poster of Othello is removed, then who misses it? I, for one, would. It is my stamp that says I am here. It is the acknowledgement that "otherness" exists.

I was recently brought to tears while watching a film. I took note of this and am recounting it to you since it is a rare occurrence. This documentary tells the story of two middle-class American white women who lost their husbands in the tragic 9/11 plane crashes. These women did not want their lives to be simply an extension of their grief for the loss. They wanted to do something. They decided they wanted to help widows in Afghanistan, where, according to statistics mentioned in the film, there are more than one million widows.

I felt for these women and their loss, but my throat constricted and my tears flowed when the young Afghani women talked about their poverty, the hopelessness of their situation as widows, their hunger that continues for days. The tears continued to flow when they talked about burying children they had lost due to hunger.

As I watched the documentary it occurred to me that the two American women identified with the Afghani women as widows and as mothers, but not as women. Their lives are so far removed from the lives of the Afghani women that they cannot connect to their realties as women.

Many a time I feel that feminist theories as they stand are far removed from the lives of women of colour, or African women, or Muslim women. We are always being asked to fit within a framework that is built around the experience of privileged white women.

I see this when I hear the feminist discourse around the hijab. It is frustrating to hear women who fight for women's right to choose arrogantly and unapologetically dismiss the hijab as a symbol of oppression. According to them, I and other women who wear it must have been pushed into wearing it by our male relatives. The rhetoric is that no liberated, self-respecting woman would wear it. This unabashed ignorance and dismissal of my experience and those of other women who choose to wear the hijab is exasperating.

It seems that freedom of choice is only for women who want to take their clothes off – it does not extend to those who want to "cover up."

The frustration level increases when I attend meetings with feminists who question my feminism. My ideas and thoughts are questioned and/or challenged, based on the perception that I am speaking from a place of oppression. The thinking infers that since I am wearing the hijab, I am an oppressed Muslim woman who doesn't know she is oppressed and, as such, all my thinking is tainted.

Feminists continue to struggle to align their theory on what is feminist with women choosing to wear the hijab or the niqab.

I distinctly remember attending a committee meeting with women advocates and self-identified feminists and asking about a case that was being tried in Toronto. This was a case wherein a woman who wore a niqab was sexually assaulted. The woman wanted to keep her niqab on while testifying. It was interesting to experience the silence in the room. These are women who normally are quite vocal regarding women's right to choose, and many work as advocates. The response was that we should wait to see how a provincial Muslim women's group responded to this case, then we would draft our response.

This same group of women were outraged a year later when a Toronto police officer told a group of young women at York University that "women should avoid dressing like sluts in order not to be victimized." The backlash was tremendous. The same group of women was outraged that a woman could be told what she can and cannot wear. They had to do something, and many supported or participated in Ottawa's version of the "Slut Walk," a protest march that started in Toronto as a reaction to the officer's comment and quickly spread to the rest of the country.

The difference between the two incidents is that one was within the preset constructs of feminist theory while the other did not fit it. It was different!

There seems to be little desire to hear or reflect the voice of the Other. This leaves some of us Others disenchanted with feminism and feeling that it has little to offer us.

Many women's groups want to increase the diversity of their membership but are without a proper notion of what that means. There seems to be an expectation that the individuals have to conform to their idea of what a "feminist" looks like and sounds like. You, the "Other," have to change in order to belong. Many groups' idea of increasing diversity is to translate their brochures or posters, without an understanding of the culture and the women of the culture. They do not seem to realize that recruitment strategies need to be built on an understanding of the subculture whose attention one is seeking.

Many a time I find there is a lack of respect for the experience of women of colour. There is a lack of value placed on what we might be able to bring to the table. The feeling is always that we need to be helped. That is why the talk in many places is that the women of colour need to be "educated," helped," "defended," "advocated for," etc. Their culture, dignity, strength, and life journeys seem to be admired with words, but not respected. You often hear young women activists speak of how brave that African woman is or how they admire that Aboriginal woman, but the admiration does not translate into respect that grants the woman of colour any authority or influence.

As a worker in the field of domestic violence, I see the dire need for respecting women's experiences. Women who are fleeing abuse are at a very vulnerable point in their life's journey. If their life experience is not honoured, and they feel that they are being dismissed, they will not get the support they desperately need. They would rather live with the abuse than be denigrated by strangers.

This is why I stay in this field. To ensure that we do not move so far away from understanding women of colour that they are not supported. I have the privilege of sitting at many a table where policies, initiatives, or actions are discussed. I use my voice to ensure that a semblance of otherness is reflected in the conversation. I am a black, African, Muslim woman who wears the hijab, and I have a strong voice. I use my voice, despite the challenges, to create a space that fits me, without having to completely transform myself to fit in the existing parameters.

However, I am but one of few voices, a rare breed of diverse women who work in a field that is dominated by white feminism. Our presence is important so the voice of the "Other" is heard, but more women of diverse backgrounds need to join their voices to ours. The constructs of feminism that reflect the experience of one group of women needs to be expanded and modified to reflect the voices of many.

That is the work that is waiting to be done. Until then, I and the other women of colour will continue to speak loudly and thrust ourselves into the midst of the existing homogenous feminism, in pursuit of a more heterogeneous feminism.

Lula Adam is a woman who feels things passionately and enjoys the occasional cup of coffee at the local coffee shop. She has worked and volunteered in the field of violence against women for more than ten years.

RANDOM THOUGHTS ABOUT FEMINISM

Monia Mazigh

Growing up in Tunisia in the seventies and eighties, feminism had a very weird and changing connotation for me. In the mind of the little girl I was, and later the teenager, this word rhymed with politics, but not with all politics. It was associated with the Destourian Party, the ruling party that had been in power, without any contest, since the country got its independence from France in 1956.

I remember watching the evening news with my family. The anchor spent interminable amounts of time praising President Bourguiba, "the Supreme Combatant" and "Father of all Tunisians." We listened to what he said during some meetings, about how he worked hard to save the nation. And sometimes, saved for the end as a treat, we were shown how Bourguiba swam in his palace: once on his back and once on his tummy. Then, we were bombarded with multiple footages of ministers meeting with foreign politicians, inaugurating some random public offices, or cutting the ribbon for new infrastructure.

Usually among them were well-dressed women with nicely done hair, forcing huge smiles while visiting poor peasant women with sad faces, long, colourful traditional dresses, and their hair covered with small handkerchiefs. Beside them would be some sheep grazing, or chickens pecking, and they would of course be surrounded by herds of children. The women officials, often the president of the Women's Union or Minister of Women's Status, were seen encouraging the other women to go to the newest planned parenthood office in the village, to help them have fewer children.

For many years, these were the only "feminists" I knew of, and, to be honest, I simply detested them. I saw through their hypocrisy, opportunism, and arrogance. Maybe some of them were genuine, but for me, they were all fakes. I sympathized with the other women, the poor ones. They worked in the fields for long days; they took care of their children and raised animals to survive the hardship of life. Some of them went to sewing classes, or to learn how to read and write, in an effort to eradicate their illiteracy and get out of the crushing cycle of poverty. As we were watching, my father never had any good words to say about the Tunisian political regime, and I followed in his footsteps, criticizing all the TV propaganda that we were forced to swallow.

A few years later, when I went to high school and had a better understanding of things, I came to know that there were many Tunisian women in the opposition parties. Some of them had spent time in prison; others were quieter but still very active in the arts scene, literature, and politics. I didn't see these women on TV, but I read about them, sometimes in foreign papers, and I also got a chance to meet some of them.

My best friend's mom provided the new "feminist" image for me. She was a math teacher and a single mother bravely raising two daughters. She had sharp political opinions, and a little weakness for communism. She took me and her daughter to art exhibitions, conferences, and spectacles. She had a strong personality with a lot of human principles. The only glitch I could find with her was that she was an atheist, and I was a believer. We disagreed on this but agreed on everything else. Many other "feminists" I met were a little like her. Not necessarily atheists, but secular. For some time in Tunisia, to be accepted as a feminist, women had to show their "freedom" by smoking, having a job, speaking French, and sometimes rejecting religion, which was seen as the mother of all oppressions. Values of social justice, human rights, and freedom of religion were almost eclipsed from feminist agendas. For some this was partly by conviction, but for others, it was due to the general climate of lack of freedom under a police state.

In the 1990s, when I decided to wear the veil as part of my own personal reflection, I was automatically and blindly put on the side of the "peasant," the extremist, the ignorant. I could not even dream of being considered a feminist. I didn't mind much, as this time period coincided with my immigration to Canada. I was looking for freedom. I was eager to open my horizons!

Other models of feminism were waiting for me there in the North. There were women like the ones I knew growing up in Tunisia, but there were also many other sorts of women who lived their feminism in different forms. They were passionate about issues of child poverty, domestic violence, women's equity, gender equity, and women in politics. They had different approaches, different (or no) spiritualities, and different colours. Some of them didn't even like to be named feminists; they just wanted to be regarded as women. Simply women! The freedom of expression in the North allows many forms of feminisms to emerge. Women can live their feminism as they wish and as they feel.

Later, when my husband was arrested by the American authorities, imprisoned, and deported to Syria (his home country), where he was tortured and kept in an underground cell, I met more Canadian women from different horizons. Some were deeply religious; others called themselves humanists. I admired their principles, their courage, and, most of all, their commitment to women's issues. All of them shared one thing: they wanted to make this world better.

It was not always easy for me to be accepted or taken seriously with a veil on my head, even in Canada, and even with some staunch feminist activists. Denise Bombardier, a controversial public figure in Quebec and a strong feminist, once faced me in a panel discussion and said, "You might have all the best degrees in the world…. For me a veiled woman is an oppressed one!"

Ouch! Welcome to the land of free expression! I responded to the criticism and rebuke with the following questions: Who are we to judge others? Are some women better than others? Is their version of feminism more enlightened than others?

In Tunisia, I was judged by a class of feminists that concluded I didn't liberate myself enough from religion by embracing "modernity." In Canada, I was judged by some feminists who subconsciously kept alive the tenets of a post-colonialist era where oriental women were portrayed as passive creatures, submissive to their male relatives.

Today, a wind of change is blowing in North Africa and the Middle East. Veiled women walk in the street beside women with uncovered heads. Even though polarizing threats between secularism and Islamism are still present, it is reassuring for me to see diversity of opinions in the streets and on TV.

In Egypt, a big campaign was recently launched by women artists and activists to denounce sexual harassment, a widespread practice in the Arab countries affecting all women, veiled and unveiled alike. It means a lot for me to see women from different horizons join their voices together and denounce this scourge.

Our clothing can be different, our religions can be different, our approaches to feminism can be different, but solidarity, social justice, and women's rights must trump. Always.

Monia Mazigh is an academic, author, and human rights advocate. She was born and raised in Tunisia and immigrated to Canada in 1991. Mazigh was catapulted onto the public stage in 2002 when her husband, Maher Arar, was deported to Syria where he was tortured and held without charge for over a year. She campaigned tirelessly for his release. Mazigh holds a PhD *in finance from McGill University. In 2008, she published a memoir,* Hope and Despair, *about her pursuit of justice. In 2014, she published her first novel,* Mirrors and Mirages. *Her second novel is due in September 2015.*

LIVING FEMINISMS: REFLECTIONS FROM A FAMILY PORTRAIT

Patricia Hyacinth Harewood

There is a framed picture that hangs on my living room wall where I can see it whenever I am having breakfast or supper. It is a black-and-white photo, circa 1961, taken at the airport in Antigua. A West Indian woman with horn-rimmed glasses stands purposefully in a floral-printed dress, with a handbag hanging over her left arm, two of her daughters by her side. To her right is my fifteen-year-old mother in her homemade, carefully starched skirt and blouse. To the left is my thirteen-year-old Aunt Naomi, smiling wistfully in her tunic-like dress. The woman is my maternal grandmother – Inez Pigott. This triumvirate had the most influence over my understanding and articulation of how feminisms are lived. While only my mother would dare call herself a feminist, these women profoundly shaped my womanism as a first-generation black woman, born and raised in Ottawa.

We are the products of our upbringing – the racial, gendered, and class structures, the socio-political context of the time, the uprootings. I come from an immigrant family. My mother came to Canada from Antigua on scholarship in 1964 to obtain a BA in French and Spanish at the University of Western Ontario. There she met my father, who had come from Barbados in 1958 to study classics at the University of Toronto. The rest, as they say, is *herstory*.

My passion for feminist theories was first ignited by my brother, Adrian, who is a voracious and radical reader. He introduced me to the writings of Audre Lorde, bell hooks, Alice Walker, Angela Davis, Patricia Williams, Afua Cooper. With my interest sparked, I read Dionne Brand's *No Burden to Carry*; *This Bridge Called My Back: Writings by Radical Women of Colour*, edited by Cherrie Moraga and Gloria Anzaldua; *We're Rooted Here and They Can't Pull Us Up: Essays in African Canadian Women's History*, co-ordinated by Peggy Bristow; *Silenced: Caribbean Domestic Workers Talk with Makeda Silvera*, and many of the feminist works published by Sister Vision Press.

But my lived experience of feminism – the belief that women and girls have as much of a right to power and resources as men, and that a global struggle is required to end male violence and domination – came from my triumvirate, as well as from the teachers and mentors I have come across so far in life.

THE TRIUMVIRATE

My grandmother helped shape my ideas about feminism and women's place in the world in many ways. Here was a woman who raised ten children with my grandfather at a time when life in Antigua for the black population was too often poor, short, and brutish.

Antigua and Barbuda is a twin-island state of approximately 90,000 people located in the Eastern Caribbean. This is where my mother was born. Colonized by the British, it was once a lucrative sugar colony and relied on the labour of African slaves to achieve prosperity for the former British Empire. Now an independent nation, or what Antiguan-American writer Jamaica Kincaid calls "a small place," Antigua remains a largely mono-crop state, with tourism as its main crop.

My grandmother would have been one of the first generations of Afro descendants post-emancipation to live in relative freedom.

My mother considered it essential that we get to know her. So each summer, she sent me and my siblings, especially my sister, Anne, off to the Caribbean. We spent many happy summers in Antigua getting to know our grandparents and the rest of our extended family.

My grandmother was assertive, independent, and very intelligent, though she had very little formal education. She was a disciplinarian but also the one who kept the family together. Grandma Pigott was a strategist, a home economist, a savvy socialite, a crochet artist, and an active member of the Antigua Labour Party. She valued education and made immeasurable sacrifices to ensure that each of her children, girl or boy, graduated from high school. Given that opportunities for advancement were limited in Antigua, she encouraged her children to go abroad to work and study. When they returned, she was forever proud to boast of their accomplishments.

Not once did I hear her say that girls did not have a right to an education or that a woman's place was in the home – quite the contrary. Grandma always voiced her opinion, even when it differed from that of my grandfather, and it often did. Unlike the women of her generation, she insisted that when she died, she wanted to be buried in her pantsuit; women can wear pants too, she thought.

When we travelled to the Caribbean, it was my Aunt Naomi who looked after us. She lived with my grandparents and worked as a stenographer at Parliament. Always the family comedian, Aunt Naomi enjoyed telling off-colour jokes. She was "bold and barefaced," far from the stereotype of lady-like. She cared very little about what "society" thought of her. In fact, in a society in which most women her age were married with children, Aunt Naomi was neither. She remained on her own, running a business on the side, selling beauty products to supplement her modest government income. I often tagged along with her when she went to drop off products for clients.

In Aunt Naomi, I saw an example of an independent woman with her own career and her own money – the freedom to make choices as to how she wanted to live her life. Aunt Naomi had lived in Canada for a couple of years and worked as a public servant. She would often comment about how she preferred home, citing examples of what was better in Antigua – the food, the culture, the sense of community. "You can die alone in an apartment in Canada," she would say, "and nobody would know."

In providing these critiques, she helped me as a child to realize that there were many people in the so-called developing world who did not consider Canada or the US to be paradise. This realization would later contribute to my understanding that the feminisms of the so-called developed world could not be imposed on women in the South who knew the particularities of their environment best and could figure out the most sustainable solutions to their own problems. From Aunt Naomi's example, I learned that women must have the right to decide whether or not they wanted to marry, and that women could live rich and fulfilling lives *without* being married to men or having children.

It is difficult to summarize what I have learned from my own mother and what I continue to learn from her. Much like my grandmother, my mother has always walked her own path. I grew up seeing her raise five children with my father while always holding a full-time job. I saw her first as an English professor at Algonquin College, then as a communications consultant, and finally as a public servant. With a graduate degree in applied linguistics, and an undergraduate degree in French and Spanish, my mother excelled at anything she put her mind to. She can be intimidating because of her sharp intellect coupled with her deep pragmatism and artistry. Our house was filled with her artwork – cardboard toilet rolls turned into hanging xylophones, hangers and pantyhose transformed into human figures, homemade hats, bags, and clothes. She was always reading – anything and everything – and ready to have a conversation with us about it at the kitchen table. She read Marx's *Das Kapital* in her sixties, many of the works of global feminist theorists in her forties, and fiction by Canadian authors and writers from around the world.

From her example, I realized that education and economic independence were key to women's liberation and true equality. I understood that I could use my own creativity to develop and reflect an original aesthetic that represented me and my community. I also learned about the importance of getting involved in the community. As a columnist for *Contrast*, arguably Canada's most important black newspaper in the 1970s, my mom made her views known, shared her poetry, and engaged.

When her engagement changed due to her child-rearing responsibilities, she still remained involved in different ways. She participated in her union, volunteered for a community theatre organization, and practised solidarity. I remember hearing about an event she organized at home to support the late Mary Pitawanakwat, an Ojibway woman who was involved in a decade-long human rights battle against the federal government.

GROWING MY FEMINISM

Growing up with these *heroes*, it was not difficult for me to develop a womanist ethos. It was all around me. My belief that girls and women had equal rights to resources and power was further supported by my school environment. My parents sent me to Elmwood School in Rockcliffe. There I spent a decade during which, through sports, academics, and arts and culture, we received constant positive reinforcement about our place in the world. "Elmwood girls can and do achieve. Elmwood girls go on to make positive contributions to society," we were told. While there is no doubt that Elmwood catered to the privileged few and that even the history we were taught remained white, male-dominated, and Eurocentric, we still gained critical thinking skills. Equipped with these mantras, I began to articulate my own expression of feminism. In 1992, I wrote *Herstory*, which was later published in the *Ottawa Citizen*:

> *I will cremate your history*
> *And make my own*
> *In stone*
> *I'll carve my herstory*
> *And rectify the throne*
> *And though you laugh at my humanity*
> *Trod upon my spirituality*
> *I will not cast aside my role*
> *Nor will I dig a grave size hole and bury your past*
> *But I will birth a story that will last*

Fuelled by outrage, perhaps with what I had not been taught at school, I also wrote *Eve*:

I am Eve
That's short for evening or evil
Created by Adam man
I am woman
As in of the man
Bearing fruit and eating them
Like evil Eve in Eden
Am I heathen
Created by Adam man that
Called me woman?

My experiences at university refined my understanding of feminisms. At McGill University, I participated in the Shakti Women of Colour Collective, founded because the McGill Women's Union was not adequately addressing issues faced by women of colour and immigrant women. At the time that I was involved, the group was more of a social support network than an advocacy organization.

However, my groundings with my sisters in Shakti helped me to see the deep contradictions within the Canadian feminist movement. Through Shakti, I witnessed the racism, classism, and homophobia that created divisions among us. These experiences also cemented my lifelong commitment to advancing women's equality, in whichever format and with whatever tools were at my disposal, always keeping in mind Audre Lorde's words – that *the master's tools will never dismantle the master's house*.

I continue to be involved in women's organizations or women-led initiatives in Ottawa as a former focus group coordinator of the City of Ottawa project on Women's Access to Municipal Services (precursor of the City for All Women Initiative), a board member of MATCH International, a member of the steering committee of the Black Women's Civic Engagement Network, and a volunteer co-host of *Black on Black* on CHUO 89.1FM.

We hear, over and over again, that the feminist movement in Canada is dead. Some elder feminists are of the view that a new national feminist organization, similar to NAC, is needed so that we can effectively fight the federal government's attacks on human rights and women's organizations. Many younger feminists are of the view that the feminist movement has been transformed. They say that thanks to the Internet and social media, it is now more democratic, global, and interconnected with other movements (such as the environmental movement, Idle No More, and the Arab Spring) than ever before.

One thing is certain: access to affordable childcare, eliminating violence against women, fighting for pay equity, and demanding justice for the families of the more than five hundred murdered Aboriginal women are all critical issues that require our immediate attention. Now, more than ever, we will need to work in solidarity with others, across divisions of class, race, gender, sexual orientation, and so forth to achieve full equality.

The women who have most influenced my understanding and practice of feminism did not express their feminism in the same way. Their feminisms were expressed through their actions. I learned by sitting on their laps, looking over their shoulders, holding their hands, working and walking with them. And as I sit here in my living room, looking at this family photo, I am humbly reminded that I still have so much more to learn.

Patricia Hyacinth Harewood grew up in Ottawa and obtained a BA in geography and international development from McGill, and degrees in common and civil law from the University of Ottawa. She currently works on labour and human rights issues at the Public Service Alliance of Canada. Patricia is passionate about women's rights, and has worked in various capacities for women's organizations in Ottawa and Montreal, including the MATCH International Women's Fund, the National Association for Women and the Law, the Shakti Women of Colour Collective, and the research project on Women's Access to Municipal Services (precursor to the City for All Women Initiative).

CONFESSIONS OF A "NUANCED" FEMINIST

Veena Gokhale

"Why am I a feminist?" was the title of an op-ed piece I wrote in the early 1980s for the Indian men's magazine *Debonair*. (Branded at that time as a magazine for intelligent men, it also featured "artistic" female nudes!) I was then a journalist living in Bombay, India. I don't recall my exact words, but I remember it was an eloquent and forceful argument on behalf of feminism.

As an Indian woman, it was easy to become a feminist. Evidence of sexism and women's inequality and oppression was everywhere. The most blatant examples I recall from my teens were the headlines that slashed a leading national newspaper – *The Times of India* – from time to time stating "Tribal [or Low Caste] women raped." This could mean gang rape of a single woman or rape of multiple women in one village. There were caste and class factors – high caste men raped the women of low caste men as a way to teach these men a lesson. The reason could be that they perceived that these lower caste men had "stepped out of line." The infringements, if any, would have been slight. But it could well be just a brutal, feudal-style display of power, as portrayed by talented and socially conscious Indian film directors of the day.

Yet I did not come to feminism until I was in my early twenties. Born into a liberal, middle-class family, I spent the first ten years of my life with an Amazonian grandmother figure at home, in a small town in India. My mother was a doctor – and although they definitely did more of all household tasks than the men, the mostly Maharashtrian women in my immediate vicinity were voluble, played badminton and bridge, and sported a confident air. The men were upright breadwinners. I was never given the impression that I was in any way inferior to men. In fact, one of the women ran a children's club, where I recall singing a feminist song about the strength of Indian women!

My earliest experience of gender oppression came in the form of "eve teasing," a.k.a. sexual harassment, when I became a teen. I was drawn to the latest fashions, including miniskirts, Western pop music, junk food, and anything new and out of the ordinary. By then we lived in Calcutta, and I recall having my bottom painfully pinched as I was leaving a crowded cinema hall. It came as a total shock. I could not make any sense of this act.

Still, Calcutta was decency personified compared to Bombay, where I went to university in my late teens. And I hadn't even spent time in Delhi yet, where a simple walk down a street became a vivid illustration of the objectification of women.

By then, I was also reading about bride burning, female infanticide, and custodial rape in the newspapers, and developing a growing rage about the differentiated measures for almost everything that applied to men and women. Equally shocking for me was the everyday and commonplace shackling of women's freedoms. A study done by the Indian branch of an international NGO revealed, for example, that women had to get permission from their husbands and/or mother-in-laws to go buy food for the family at the local market. This act could be easily curtailed, and as a result, the women would be kept indoors.

The power and privilege of ordinary men – not to mention the "higher-ups" – were becoming more obvious to me. Some of my female friends shared stories about the preferential treatment given to their brothers. No wonder I lapped up feminist theory as easily as mother's milk when I finally came to it – I had already seen it all in practice!

One of my reasons for immigrating was to get away from the daily reminders of women's inequality, and the sexual harassment on the streets. Or at least that's what I realize in hindsight. It was tiring to be an angry young woman, always challenging sexist notions. I was doing just that up until my early thirties, when I finally left.

I want to make it clear that there was and is a strong feminist movement in India. There are strong social and environmental justice groups and movements too. Equity is an issue that always comes up in public debate, however fractious the debate may be. My direct link to the Indian feminist movement was through a women who was an editor, teacher, and friend of mine. I am in touch with her and she continues to inspire me, as do other activist Indian friends. By then I had volunteered at a distress helpline for women and children in Bombay and explored issues such as the use of sexist language in the media with a group of women journalists. I reported on the destructive Narmada Valley and Sardar Sarovar Dam Project. There my justice-oriented vision, which had included gender, class, and caste, expanded to include rural-urban inequalities, and the rights of other species and nature – the ultimate voiceless "victims" of human exploitation.

Growing up in a small town, with a garden just outside my door and open land in front of the row of houses, I had always felt very close to nature and experienced a bond with trees, flowers, water, sky, mountains, birds, and animals. I could not understand why these were seen as less valuable and consequential than humans. I still can't.

Flash forward to Toronto in the 1990s, where I pursued a master's in environmental studies. Now oppression based on race and sexuality also entered the picture for me, as did poverty and powerlessness resulting from globalization. Gay Pride Day and Toronto Days of Action – which were among the early anti-globalization protests – occurred at the same time as the Take Back the Night march for women. I loved the idea behind Take Back the Night – that the perpetrators of violence, a.k.a. certain men, needed to get off the streets after dark, instead of the women they attacked.

Immigration brought me recurring uncertainty in terms of employment, and accompanying financial anxiety. I became a migrant within Canada and internationally, trying to keep afloat by moving for either higher studies or work. Stripped of privileges that I once had in India, my alliance with the have-nots of various kinds grew stronger. My world was in flux and still remains unstable.

I live now in Montreal and my professional and financial struggles continue. I am not "integrated," whatever that means, nor am I a hostile alien here. I have some sympathy for Quebec nationalism, as well as for immigrants who feel they are not welcome here.

And over the twenty years of being in Canada, my perception on activism has changed. I believe as strongly in equality and justice for all living beings as ever before. I believe we must keep voicing our concerns, participating in struggles and movements, and, most importantly, living our values in daily life the best we can. I believe in celebrating victories, however small and partial. But I no longer hold the black-and-white worldview I used to have – that people who are left-wing, feminist, or green are necessarily in the right, while others are in the wrong. The world has shown itself to be infinitely more complex, with human behaviour, of individuals and groups, much more intransigent and contradictory.

It's not the goals of these movements that I find problematic, but the means. Often one cannot distinguish between the communication styles and tactics of the right and the left. Aggression and assumption, distrust and confrontation, seem to rule, despite the fact that most humans seem most comfortable on the middle ground. Are these middle-grounders not the people we want to take along – to address and try to convince, if not convert?

I think I developed this view because I worked in non-profit communications and found that these organizations were mostly reaching out to the converted, or at best to those already mostly convinced. Going out into communities was not always a priority. The method they seemed to favour – rational, wordy argument – was too limited. This is fine and necessary as one approach, but more creative means were needed to reach a more diverse audience.

Admittedly we do not have the right media, or the political and social environment that allows for dialogue and nuanced communication to cultivate new communities. There is also the constant pressure of time, time running out, with corporate, power-driven divides and environmental disasters – monsters pressing at our windows. We humans have become so afraid, so fearful of real contact and interaction with the proverbial "Other," even as migration, immigration, and mixed marriages/unions of all kinds proliferate. Or is that what pushes our panic button – because real shifts are in our midst?

Nothing is as impressive to me as the idea of truth and reconciliation processes, flawed and incredibly tough though they are. If oppressor and oppressed in the most extreme situations can dialogue post-conflict, or even post-genocide, then why can't the groups here? And I am not even talking about groups that are really facing in opposite directions, but merely groups that actually may share ends, if not means. As a society, we seem to have a knee-jerk "for-or-against" response, which is at best immature, and is often worse. Our talking, listening, and discussion skills seem low. This overarching tendency infects us all, including activists and activism.

But without at least tentative stabs at bridge building, we are doomed.

Perhaps I am drawn to the idea of trying out differential tactics because more than a decade ago I became a Buddhist. I agreed with the idea that the key "enemies" to realizing our human potential were passion, aggression, and ignorance. (Passion can be a driving force that achieves results, but it can also make you lose a holistic perspective, and that all-important quality – compassion.) These three are not separate entities, of course, but are intimately linked emotions that feed off each other.

And what of feminism, which I embraced with such force and hope in my early twenties?

I am still a feminist. I meet amazing young women and middle-aged and older women, and men too, who are all drawing from the rich and continuing legacy of feminism. At least in the international development context, feminism now includes looking at "masculinities." It now includes how these are constructed and how they come into play in social relations. That is, "women's lib" includes releasing men from constrictive roles. It always did. At the same time, in the North American context, reading about mounting anorexia, the use of plastic surgery and Botox, and bullying – cyber-based or otherwise – makes me wonder if feminism has somehow failed, or at least faltered.

I recently presented from a short story collection I published this year to two groups of pre-university students. In both classes, the boys were much more vocal. Later I asked the professor why this may be so. Her reply was that the girls don't want to be seen as too intelligent. That was horribly disappointing. But I am not entirely defeated, because there are always counter-examples. A couple of wonderful young women I know express their ideas on gender equality differently than I would. And that is fine. After all, I learned a while ago that feminism is about accepting individual differences, within certain parameters.

My activism today takes the form of trying to listen, observe, and participate. This may not be good enough, but I accept that this is where I am right now. I find writing short stories and a novel has helped me reflect and has addressed some of my confusion and concerns. I am also trying to get my work out there and use it as a basis for discussion. Fiction, after all, is rich in nuance and contradiction, much like human behaviour and life.

Born in Bombay, India, and immigrating to Canada in the early 1990s, Veena Gokhale has worked as a writer, editor, journalist, and informal educator. She has also done communications and project coordination for non-profit organizations. She is inspired by social justice, environmentalism, nature, and the arts. Her collection Bombay Wali *and other stories was released by Guernica Editions, Toronto, in 2013. Her novel, set against the backdrop of international development and land issues, is being considered by a publisher. Having lived in several cities, she now calls Montreal home.* Website: veenago.com

ODE TO MY SOMALI MOTHER
Ubah Hersi

The first time I really thought about the term *feminism* and how it relates to me was when I first started wearing my hijab – or more specifically, as a result of how others reacted to my hijab-wearing self. It was the early 1990s and there were not many young Canadian Muslim women wearing the hijab in Ottawa. When I compare that time to now, I realize, while many of the same stereotypes existed, there was more ignorance about the diversity of Muslim women then, especially about those who wore a hijab. In today's post-9/11 world, there is a whole generation of Canadians who grew up with hijab-wearing Muslim women and who know firsthand how wrong many of the stereotypes are.

However, back then, I often had to wade through Orientalist assumptions about Muslim women and the hijab. I came to understand, much later, that what for me had been a purely spiritual decision was seen by others as a means of subjugating myself, and/ or trying to buck the conventions of my Western environment. But during my first days as a *hijabia*, I really did not notice what was going on around me or how others were reacting to me, because I was in a bubble of spiritual awakening. In other words, I was focused inward, striving to connect with my creator on a personal level – to find my individual path.

Months later, when I visited my university's women's centre, a quiet place I had gone to many times before to do my reading homework, I was asked what I was doing there, as I clearly was not a feminist. At first I did not know what the woman was talking about; I knew she was neither a staff member nor a volunteer at the centre, and I did not understand who she was to question me. Moreover, I did not realize she was reacting to me as a Muslim and not as a black woman. She then asked why "we let ourselves be forced into wearing that thing on our heads." I was so blown away that I was stunned into silence. Until that moment, the only racism or stereotyping (whatever you want to call it) that I had faced as an immigrant/minority in Canada was due to my race – to being black. Walking away from the woman, I realized that my Muslim identity, not my skin colour, was the reason for her reaction. For some reason, I was now seen as somehow less of an autonomous woman because I was a Muslim. This was new for me, despite the fact that as an African immigrant growing up in Canada I had to deal with many stereotypes and racist assumptions. But being seen as somehow not my own woman – dependent – had never been an issue.

Although I come from a Somali Muslim family that fasted during Ramadan and prayed, and I was always upfront about my identity as a Muslim, I didn't realize until I wore my hijab that I had not truly been seen as Muslim by the outside world. Now, because of this piece of cloth, I was viewed by many as a voiceless, powerless woman who "allowed" herself to be subjugated. This stereotype of Muslim women as powerless beings, controlled by others, was something that always made me scratch my head in confusion, because this was far from my reality. Growing up, I was surrounded by strong Muslim women, and most of my Islamic knowledge came from women – my mother in particular.

It was strong Somali Muslim women, like my mother and aunt, who led by example, showing my sisters and me the need to challenge the limitations and boundaries the world would try to impose on us as girls. It was my mother who taught us to learn our *Deen* (faith/ religion), because if we did not, others would impose their often skewed, patriarchal interpretations. It was my mother who taught me the first of my many lessons on being a visible Muslim woman in Canada. When I told her I was going to wear the hijab fulltime, and not just when I went to the mosque or for prayer, she said I should make sure I was ready for it, and realize that once I started wearing it in public, I would no longer be seen as an individual, but would be representing the whole community. At the time I thought she meant that I would need to behave as a "good Muslim," because everything I did/said would reflect on all other Muslim women. I finally realized that she was also subtly warning me that what other Muslims (especially those wearing the hijab) said and did would reflect on me.

Looking back, I realize that the many cultural sayings, poems, and subtle lessons on being a Somali Muslim woman, which I took for granted through my formative years, were my mother's way of giving my sisters and me the tools we would need to challenge the stereotypes the world would impose on us. Lessons about the many strong Somali women who took part in colonial struggles, famous women poets who lyrically challenged injustices, and mothers who found quiet and clever ways to ensure their daughters were not denied their God-given rights by working to prevent the archaic practice of genital mutilation were among these tools.

Two decades later, these lessons have become my foundation as a feminist activist, working on issues of social justice and gender equality. That day, so long ago, when my feminism was challenged because I wore the hijab, seems like another lifetime. I look back now and realize that while my mother and aunt may not have taken public roles, such as marching for women's equality like their sisters in the West, they nevertheless passed on a cultural legacy that gave me the tools and confidence to challenge the many patriarchal boundaries I would face as a woman. Because of these strong women, I never felt there was anything I could not do as a woman, despite the stereotypical boxes the world would put me in. However, I also realized, so long ago, that unlike my mother and aunt, I grew up in a society that would always judge me on numerous levels. In my diverse Canadian society, I am not only a woman, but also a black woman, an immigrant black woman, a hijab-wearing Muslim immigrant black woman. These multiple identities ensure I have to deal with different barriers, and there will always be those who want to put me in one stereotypical box or another. In order for me to pass on the legacy I was given to younger generations of Muslim Canadian women, I need to combine the lessons of quiet strength I learned from my mother and aunt with the overt social activism of Canada's diverse feminist pioneers. I do this by being vocal and assertive in how I define myself – I'm a proud Muslim Somali Canadian Feminist.

Ubah Hersi is a Somali Canadian who has lived in Ottawa since 1979. She holds a bachelor's degree in political science from Carleton University, as well as a master's in gender and development from the University of Sussex in Brighton, England. She comes from a long line of strong African women who have helped shape and inform her academic and employment choices. From these women, Ubah learned the importance of gender equality, social justice, and individual responsibility in contributing positively to society.

LESSONS I LEARNED FROM MY MOTHER

Lucya Spencer

My mother, Ivy Imerna Daniel (née Samuel), was a special woman in my life. She was the last of four children born to the late Evelyn (Mother Sam) and Uriah Samuel. As the only girl, she held an important place in her family. Mother Sam was a striking, powerful woman, approximately six feet three inches tall with a heavy build, who worked as a psychiatric nurse at the mental institution in Antigua, West Indies. She commanded attention wherever she went, given her physique, her eloquence, and her ability to engage anyone in conversation.

Shortly after the death of Mother Sam's husband, her three sons left home, but Ivy remained with her mother, who instilled in her certain virtues, principles, and religious doctrines. Mother Sam was a strict disciplinarian and made sure that her daughter demonstrated what she deemed appropriate behaviours and lived up to the expectations of society at that time.

My mother was a gifted, talented, and fashionable woman who aspired to achieve many of her lifelong goals. She left an indelible mark on those with whom she interacted, especially her nine children. She had a dry sense of humour and was well respected by many in her community. In communicating with her children, friends, and young people, my mother often used particular statements, many of which helped shape the person I have become and the career path I have chosen in Canada. Some of these are presented in this story along with the lessons I learned over the years.

"Always strive to be a figure but never a zero."
How can one strive to be a figure? What is a figure? Does it mean one has to stand erect to strive to be a figure? These are just some of the questions we asked my mother whenever she made the statement. She would smile and proceed to tell a story about the realities of life.

My mother shared with us stories of young people who made wrong choices and, as a result, found themselves going down the wrong path. Some of them were from respectable families in the community, and their parents had held high hopes for their children.

One example she shared was of a family that had six children. Five of them followed career paths chosen by their parents – doctor, teacher, banker, airline pilot, and civil servant. The sixth chose his own path, associated with the wrong crowd, and eventually became the black sheep of the family, or what my mother referred to as "a zero."

Having listened to her many explanations and examples, I have grown to appreciate the time she took to share these stories and can only imagine that her desire was that none of her children would become "a zero."

My mother's words had a profound impact on all facets of my life. While I recognize that perfection is an elusive dream, I have always gone beyond the call of duty to fulfill any task I have agreed to undertake, and the results have spoken for themselves. Some of my efforts have been recognized by others through testimonials, awards, or just the common words "thank you" or "God bless you" – words I treasure deeply, as they cannot be equated with a monetary value.

I believe I have fulfilled my mother's wish of "striving to be a figure and never a zero."

"Learning to be industrious will not harm you."
I received my first lesson in feminism from my mother. She firmly believed in equal opportunity for all, regardless of gender. She was convinced that every child – boy or girl – should be able to help themselves at all times, and not become dependent on anyone to fulfill their needs. Once the first set of children became teenagers, my mother got rid of the house help and taught the boys and girls to perform household chores such as cooking, cleaning, and laundry.

In those days, while it was good to see all my siblings engage in household chores, I felt my mother was turning my brothers into "auntie men" – a term used to describe men with feminine character-istics. As my awareness has grown, I now see the term "auntie men" as derogatory and homophobic and I am able to see the positive results of my mother's efforts and their benefits to my brothers' families. All of my brothers are great cooks, and very helpful in their homes.

This experience has made me more sympathetic to the many women who have shared with me problems occurring in their homes, where there is a clear distinction between the role of the son versus the daughter, and the role of the mother versus the father.

In an effort not to disappoint these women who have conveyed to me their innermost concerns and problems, I have used the opportunity to help them problem-solve and find solutions that would reduce some of the tension in their homes. Helping them to see the issues through different lenses and highlighting the realities of the new country versus the home country have proven very beneficial. This opportunity to share what I have learned with others is emotionally and spiritually gratifying.

My advocacy work in Canada and internationally has also yielded many positive results. For instance, for more than twenty-five years, my involvement with organizations such as the National Organization of Immigrant Women of Canada and the Ontario Council of Agencies Serving Immigrants has enabled me to speak out on government policies or programs that were not achieving positive results for immigrants. This advocacy work has given me opportunities to meet with politicians at all levels to discuss program initiatives and policies, and to find solutions to some of the problems faced by immigrants, especially women and children.

I do not believe my mother realized that the valuable lessons she taught me during those early days would have such a positive impact on my life, and help shape my career path in Canada – to become a voice for the voiceless and an advocate for change.

"One can take the clothes from your back, but never what you have acquired through education."
As a young girl growing up, my mother had a passion for both formal and self-education. She was an avid reader. She read many books, first of which was her Bible and religious material and then other books on health, life, philosophy, and social sciences. She had a special interest in medicine, and her dream was to follow her mother into the health field. Her mother was her inspiration, but sadly, my mother never fulfilled that dream. The sudden death of her father and her newfound love – my father – contributed to her choosing a different course in life. Nevertheless, in spite of these

changes, she maintained a focus on education, and as she built her own family, she instilled the importance of education in all nine of her children.

Time for homework was a must in our home. Everyone was expected to spend at least two hours on school nights completing homework or reading educational material. As each child graduated from high school and gradually succeeded at university, my mother beamed with pride. One could see her joy and exhilaration as she attended the various graduation ceremonies.

Live your dream and hope for success was a valuable lesson I learned from my mother. One of my dreams was to acquire property, as I hated the confinement of apartment living. Coming from a place where one was not constricted by walls or space, I found it most uncomfortable to limit myself to a two-bedroom apartment, which was equivalent to one bedroom in the home I left behind in Antigua.

I worked two jobs, one in the evenings and on weekends as a hospital sitter, the other as manager of a social enterprise during the day. I even found time to enhance my education by taking a few courses at Algonquin College and Carleton University. I had a dream and I was determined not to lose sight of it.

In 1992, I purchased my first home – a town house. Four years later, I bought my current home – a four-bedroom home. Looking back on this journey through life, I can truly say I have followed my mother's advice about education. I have lived my dream and experienced the successes along the way.

"Patience is a virtue."
"How do you do it? How could you sit there and listen to those false accusations against you and not get angry?" "How can you exercise such self-control, grace, and dignity?" "You have a very calm demeanour. Where did you get all that patience?"

These questions are sometimes asked of me by friends and colleagues, even strangers, when they witness my patience in volatile situations. These questions take me back to my childhood days, as my mother was often asked the same questions. Her response was, "Why stress, when you are unable to change the situation or the person? Truth will always surface, no matter how long it takes."

I concur. On numerous occasions, I have witnessed the unveiling of truth and the humiliating blow it directed to those who thought wrong could triumph over right. Recently, during a discussion with managers/supervisors in one of the sectors where I work, I listened as they shared their frustrations and difficulties in their jobs. They raised issues about managing differences within their teams, and the energy that was required to handle conflicts that might have been prevented. One member of the group, realizing I had not engaged in the discussions, raised some of the complexities she thought I had to deal with, including cultural and linguistic issues.

I shared an experience I'd had with a consultant who was hired to deliver a specific program, and who after a while tried to assume the role of my supervisor, supported by some persons to whom I reported. She tried at every turn to undermine my efforts and dictate my role in the agency, but at no time was she able to ruffle my feathers. I bore her onslaught of criticisms and false accusations with a grin, knowing the truth would surface at some time, and that she would not last forever. Of course, she did not. Although it was a harrowing experience, there were lessons learned by others who observed what was going on. Some were apologetic for the consultant's actions, others realized that they were misguided and applauded me for staying true to myself throughout the ordeal.

"Every disappointment is a blessing in disguise."
In explaining this statement, my mother used her own story of wanting to pursue medicine. Though unsuccessful in this dream, she met my father, and they had nine wonderful children. Would she have had these children if she had pursued medicine? She is of the opinion that the children are the blessing that was in store for her.

She advised us to look for the blessings in every disappointment and I continue to do so every time I face a disappointing situation.

Conclusion
My mother was very proud of her children. She spoke of them repeatedly to anyone who would listen. My telephone conversations with her often focused on her children and grandchildren, their contributions to their communities, and the importance of reaching out to those less fortunate, who are trying to find their way in society.

My mother believed in helping others and nothing was too good for her to share.

In August 2013, I made a quick, unplanned trip to Antigua. I had the opportunity to sit and chat with my mother about life changes, about her childhood days, and places in the country owned by her grandparents, where she spent a lot of time. She asked to be taken on a trip to one of these places, known as McNish Mountain. She was very alert, very conversant, and even humorous. She died a few hours later, two weeks before her ninety-third birthday.

Reflecting on her strength, her tenacity, her determination, her dry sense of humour, her legacy of statements, I can truly say that she lived a fulfilling life. My desire is to keep her memory alive. I have experienced great joy in sharing my mother's legacy with my own daughter and many of the younger generation.

She was truly a special woman.

Lucya Spencer is the executive director of Immigrant Women Services Ottawa, and for the last thirty-two years she has demonstrated outstanding leadership in advancing issues that affect the lives of immigrant, visible minority, and refugee women. A tireless worker, Lucya currently serves as president of LASI/World Skills. Some of her previous involvements include past chair of the Ontario Government's Outstanding Achievement Award for Voluntarism – Selection Committee; guest editorial board – Canadian Women's Studies; president, Children's Aid Society of Ottawa; President, Ontario Council of Agencies Serving Immigrants and the National Organization of Immigrant and Visible Minority Women of Canada. Lucya has been the recipient of many testimonials and awards in recognition of her exceptional work related to immigrant women.

LESSONS IN MY GRANDMOTHER'S COURTYARD: CULTURE, FEMINISM, AND ME

Ikram Ahmed Jama

"A tree with a simple root structure won't survive the wind but a tree whose roots go deep into soil and is firmly anchored stands a far better chance." —MAYA ANGELOU

For the first five years of my life my regular companions and friends were women over the age of fifty. I was born at a time of change and optimism in Somalia. The years following independence brought increased opportunities in education, employment, and business, which resulted in individuals and families moving from their local communities to bigger cities. My parents decided to move to Mogadishu, the capital, where my father found better business prospects. For my mother, however, the move meant being away from the support of family. She was lonely and homesick, and struggling to get used to her new home. She was finding it hard to cope with four young children in a new city where she did not have any family connections. My maternal grandmother suggested that my mother send the youngest of the children to her until she got to know her new home. That child was me. The plan was for me to be with my grandmother for a few months. I stayed for more than four years.

In my grandmother's house, I was the cherished grandchild. I followed her everywhere. My grandmother, Hawa Ahmed Salaan, was widowed in her early fifties. She was a businesswoman and raised her youngest three children in the city of Hargeisa in northern Somalia. During most evenings of the week, five or more women would gather at our house and discuss the business of the day – mainly their children, their business adventures, the challenges of life they were facing – and offer support and solutions to each other. They also did creative projects together. Each month they would start weaving a carpet or make a *fijaan*, the traditional meat container given to daughters when they marry. They would sit in the yard after dinner and bring out the materials, starting where they left off the last time. And they would sing:

Gabadha soo galbiyaay guud xariiray gayaankeedii baa helayeey

Here comes the bride with the lovely hair who found her mate

I sat in these gatherings, soaking up everything, and thought this was how the world lived. My grandmother was the second wife of my maternal grandfather. He was a wealthy businessman in what was then (during colonial rule) British Somaliland. My grandmother was about seventeen when he married her and brought her from the Ethiopian-controlled Somali territories. She had grown up as a nomad in a very established family. My grandmother never went to school, not even religious school, because she was a girl, and the priority for a girl at that time was to learn how to care for livestock – sheep and goats – preserve food, and weave all the materials a nomadic household would need. In other words, her schooling was done by her mother and other women in the family.

After she married my grandfather, she moved to the city and had to learn how to be an urban wife. She had seven children, made a name for herself in her new home, and became a much-respected woman among her husband's kin. My grandfather married another woman after her and, unlike many women who showed displeasure when their husband married a younger wife, my grandmother diplomatically accepted the younger wife, even welcomed her into the family. This earned her more affection from my grandfather and more respect from the community. After my grandfather passed away from sudden illness, she chose to start her own business, and without reading or writing, and speaking only Somali, she travelled frequently to Yemen to import goods to Somalia. Later, she enrolled in religious school and learned the Quran with women friends. Together they created a group called Sisters of Sheikha Faduma, after their Quran teacher who was a woman.

In these gatherings with my grandmother and her friends, I learned that women are not only strong but are resourceful and can survive many challenges. When I looked at my grandmother I saw intelligence, strength, and leadership, and I wanted to be just like her. She always found a solution to problems and always showed confidence and a strong sense of self. When I left my grandmother to be reunited with my mother, father, and siblings, I possessed knowledge about the Somali language that none of my siblings had. I knew many Somali proverbs and my genealogy from my paternal grandfather to thirty male ancestors (Somali culture is patrilineal and genealogy goes through the male line). I knew some of the Somali classical poetry and some of the modern additions. I preferred being in the company of people over fifty rather than with young kids. In this way, those early years with my grandmother greatly influenced the woman I grew up to be.

Even though my generation had many opportunities that women in previous generations did not have, I understood, at a young age, that as a woman I would have to fight for certain things. That was all around me growing up – one of my aunts who married three times always reminded me and my sister when we were little of a Somali proverb: "It is better for a woman to marry thirty times than live in a bad marriage." The story of my father's uncle was told in our yard many times – how his wife, after a bitter disagreement and while he was taking a nap, bought a very strong lock from the market, locked him in the house, and travelled from the village to the city without telling anyone. He was found hungry and exhausted a few days later. I was taught to love and respect my culture, but the women in my life also taught me that our culture had elements that disadvantaged women, and that these must be resisted. When I came to Canada in 1989 as a young refugee woman, exploring feminism and its role in women's equality was a natural step for me. However, my excitement was short-lived once I encountered descriptions of my grandmother that I did not recognize.

In university, I learned about Western women's journey to personhood and their fight for equality. The experiences and struggles of Western feminists were presented as complex and courageous. But the category of women I belonged to were presented in the same literature as victims of polygamy, female circumcision, and underdevelopment. My first reaction was confusion because I did not know about whom they were talking. Then, I became angry and decided to seek literature that affirmed what I knew. So I started reading people such as Nawal El-Saadawi, bell hooks, and many others to balance the one-sided accounts I was getting. At the same time, the stories of female circumcision and Somali culture started coming out in the mainstream media in Canada. It was a very sensational subject that became a marker for the strangeness and barbarism of African cultures, particularly Somali culture. At one point, in places like Ottawa and Toronto, you could not talk about Somali culture without female circumcision coming up. My grandmother, the fearless woman, was depicted as a victim of patriarchy, or an aggressor who mutilates her grandchildren. A strong need to change this perception replaced the anger. This is how my journey to community engagement and activism began in Canada.

At first I participated in activities organized by Somali students at Carleton and Ottawa Universities. I joined the Somali University Student's Association (SUSA). We organized conferences and workshops that focused on Somali people's history, culture, and resettlement in Canada. We came together to answer back, to provide education to Canadians about our culture, and to engage in dialogue. We understood that public education and conversations were very necessary. Even though they did not get rid of ignorance and racism, getting active made it possible for us to connect with each other as Somalis. Our efforts helped build relationships with Canadians and connect with our allies. I also joined non-Somali associations on campus to reach out to other student groups – for instance, the African Student Association. I later became a board member of the Somali Canadian Youth Society (SCYS), an organization that created leadership and mentoring opportunities for Somali-Canadian youth who were facing social and economic challenges as young refugees.

After I completed my undergraduate degree in sociology, I trained as a cultural interpreter, volunteered for different organizations, and joined other young Somali university graduates to create the Somali Centre for Youth, Women, and Community Development. In partnership with other established community organizations, we built an organization with the mandate to support Somali families in Ottawa. The centre provided settlement services, homework clubs for young students, support groups for women, and life skills development programs for youth.

I also engaged in advocacy by supporting and participating in efforts to lobby the federal government to revoke a law that required some Convention refugees (Somalis and Afghans) to have a valid identity document in order to get permanent residency status. I got involved in educating the public about female circumcision, and co-wrote an educational pamphlet for teachers and other service providers. I decided to focus my graduate research on Somali women and their formal political participation, and travelled back to what is now Somaliland (in northern Somalia) to do research on women activists and their role in rebuilding the country after the war. Since graduate school, I have been working in the not-for-profit sector. I am committed to creating more inclusive and equitable communities.

During this journey, I drew strength from my grandmother and the women I knew growing up; it was their feminism that gave me voice and the courage to believe in change. I strongly rejected the notion that my culture was something to discard, to simplify, or to be explained by those who never lived it. Instead, I completely accept and celebrate it as a complex system that presents me with comfort and strength as well as challenges. And while I support the eradication of practices such as female circumcision, I embrace my culture with the wisdom and grace of my grandmother as I continue to fight for change for the women in my community and around the world. Becoming a feminist, then, has been a journey that first started as a five-year-old in my grandmother's courtyard. It has continued and matured over the years, informed by my experiences in Canada as well as reflections on my Somali culture and lessons learned in my grandmother's courtyard.

Ikram Ahmed Jama is an educator, an activist, a storyteller, and a mother. Ikram has been an active member of the Ottawa community since 1992, working in various capacities. She is committed to creating a more accepting, inclusive community where social inequities are addressed effectively so that all can have the opportunity to share their gifts and achieve their potential. Ikram has a masters of political science from Carleton University.

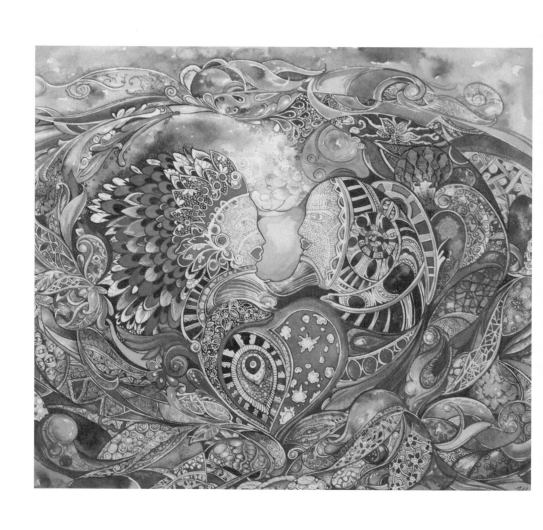

Section V
ACTIVISM: SHAPING OUR WORLD

INTRODUCTION
Vanaja Dhruvarajan

Reading the women's submissions in this section, one cannot help being impressed by their determination to work against the odds and make a difference. All of them are either first- or second-generation immigrants. Almost all of them experienced prejudicial and discriminatory treatment on the basis of culture, race, gender, and/or religion. The response more often than not was one of careful analysis and considered course of action with a firm conviction that things can be set right. The sites of struggles portrayed in the articles include the community, the academy, and the polity. The struggles are often national but can encompass the international arena in this globalized world of ours. The authors' dedicated efforts are exemplary.

Several themes emerge prominently in these submissions. One is the impact of prejudicial and discriminatory immigration policies and practices. Those who immigrated for economic betterment on the basis of Canada's immigration point system are taken aback by the devaluation, and sometimes dismissal, of educational qualifications earned in their country of origin. In spite of multiple efforts to integrate, some are left unable to use the expertise they have accumulated. Under these circumstances, the intense feeling of being treated as an outsider, one who does not belong, is exacerbated. Then there is the cultural devaluation of people as persons. Many of those who immigrated to escape from racism found more of the same. Poverty and deprivation, in addition to homophobia, are further blows to energy and spirit.

The specific responses to these challenges are varied. Some of the women are engaged in community activism to influence the politics of race and gender relations. Some have exerted

< Yulia Lisitsyna
Hearts & Souls
2014

influence within their workplace to change policies and practices. Others have struggled to change prejudicial attitudes and discriminatory behaviour. These struggles have been particularly difficult for those whose legal status is vulnerable. Structural adjustment policies often force vulnerable women from developing countries into exploitative conditions such as domestic work.

The exclusionary practices of knowledge production in the academy are another theme. With the firm conviction that inclusive knowledge is crucial to bringing about a just and caring society, the authors document the struggles to influence the process and content of knowledge production in the academy. Developing research tools to produce inclusive knowledge is one strategy. Questioning knowledge monopolies of hegemonic Western culture and organizing associations of academics to bring about inclusive knowledge production is another. Actively challenging the culture of the academy, including processes of decision-making, especially in determining curriculum content, is yet another approach.

Featured prominently in these contributions are the exclusionary practices prevalent in Canada on the basis of religion. The negative impact of these practices is elaborated in submissions by the followers of Islam who critique mainstream feminism and feminists for their narrow outlook. The authors show how being a feminist is not inconsistent with being a Muslim woman. They have chosen to educate the mainstream regarding Islam by participating in multiple activities on multiple fronts: working to improve communication between Muslims and the mainstream population; informing and educating everyone regarding the eating habits of Muslims; encouraging Muslim women to speak for themselves rather than be represented either by men in their communities or women from the mainstream; and finding ways and means to help Muslim women gain self-confidence.

The articles in this section enrich our understanding of the struggles of marginalized people against tremendous odds. The authors write with passion and commitment for the cause of justice and care in human relationships.

JOURNEY TO
CONSCIOUSNESS
Tania Das Gupta

July 13, 2012

You ask me what was the defining moment in my life? How was I transformed by my life experience? How did my life experiences shape my commitment to women's issues?

Life has always been full of contradictions from birth – being privileged and yet not privileged enough to be blind to the injustices of society.

As the eldest child in a middle-class Bengali family, I was the centre of the universe, attending an elite school in Kolkata and studying with the children of very rich and privileged families in the city. I was sheltered and protected, but "sensitized" to issues of fairness and social justice.

At the impressionable age of fourteen, I was aware of the injustice of poverty and colonial subjugation. My father and mother filled our ears with stories of the anti-colonial movement, about such great martyrs as Bhagat Singh, Sukhdev and Rajguru and Master Da, Tagra and Khudi Ram, about Sarojini Naidu, Udham Singh, of Jalianwala Bagh, and even Gandhi and Nehru. My brother and I heard stories about how the British colonialists would look down on Indians and treat them as inferior beings.

We heard the revolutionary poetry of Kazi Nazrul Islam and Dr. Harin Chatterji, which talked to me about never bowing down to oppression. We also heard songs on the radio filled with national fervour and patriotism, sat through all-night *jatras* (a form of Bengali folk theatre) that retold these same stories. We were inspired by the defiant and empowering poems of Rabindranath Tagore, who urged us to "walk alone if nobody joined us in the journey against oppression." We heard about the violence and irrationality of partition between West and East Bengal. We were taught that we are one people and that the division was artificially made. We saw with our eyes the abject poverty just outside our house in the *gali* where half-clad children played in the dust, and poor men and women eked out a living by working in people's homes as servants, or in precarious odd jobs.

Members of my mother's family had already immigrated abroad – to the UK, to the Caribbean, and to Canada. My parents had great hopes for us intellectually and, I suppose, professionally, although the latter was never explicitly mentioned. It was an aspiration to have scholarly children rather than successful professional ones. We were told stories of great scholars in our family – the famous historian of ancient Indian history and the renowned physicist who caused his professor to recommend dividing the Physics and Chemistry award into two separate prizes when he had tied with another great scholar. Immigrating abroad seemed to be a pathway to a world of opportunity for us.

Canada was, at the time, opening its doors to "other" immigrants, and many people were seizing the opportunity to migrate. "Why not us! It's worth an exploration," they thought. My mother was sponsored as a visitor by her sister and then applied for landed status. We followed a few months later. I distinctly remember my father saying that we would return in three years' time. He had never stayed in any city or town for more than three years at a stretch. Well, it's been exactly forty years, and we have lived in the same city – Toronto – for that entire time.

Immigrating to Canada proved to be a politicizing experience. Even though I was only fourteen years old, it was the first time that I became aware of what it is like to become the "Other" in the midst of white faces and bodies. I was struck by the fact that those people who had colonized India seemed to be around us in Canada now.

It was 1972 – the racism on the streets was palpable! Not a day went by when we were not called Paki – dirty Paki! Paki, go home! – on the streets, on public transit, in the schoolyard, in the public swimming pool, and outside our apartment building. I recognized it as the same "looking down" feeling that my father had talked about under British colonial rule in India. In one dramatic incident, I remember being harassed on the subway, along with my younger brother, by a group of white teenagers, all the way from Islington to downtown – nearly thirty minutes. When we retaliated verbally in our own way, using jokes and retorts, we were spat upon. I remember tears in my eyes after the group of white youth got off. I felt the anger in my bones and in my head. I felt what one feels when one is "put down." The scars don't heal.

While wandering around in a west-end mall with my mother, I saw a man wearing a T-shirt that said "kick a Paki." I felt a combination of shock and excitement in that here was a chance to do something about an overt example of racism. I discovered that there was a T-shirt place in the mall, where you could get whatever message you wanted put on the shirt. They had obviously produced the one that I had seen. I went there and asked them to make a similar shirt for me. I paid for it and they did it without any questions. Money was money! I folded it, put it in a yellow envelope, and mailed it to the Ontario Human Rights Commission with a note attached.

A few months later, I went to the same mall and noticed that the T-shirt stall had been closed up. I found out later that the chief commissioner was (black Jamaican Canadian civil rights activist) Bromley Armstrong. Could the demise of the store have been a result of my action and Bromley's?

There were other indignities. My parents who were educated, articulate, and fluent in English, with BAs from a large university in India, were assessed as having grade 13 educations and, as such, limited in their professional lives. In addition, they were blocked from pursuing higher education in Toronto by major universities because of administrative requirements they could not fulfill. I was enraged! They ended up working in precarious jobs and spending a decade or so recuperating somewhat their "lost" education and careers. That is another story.

I became an activist, first and foremost an anti-racism activist. My aunt was a big influence on me in this regard. She introduced me to the South Asian Working Group, of which she was a member, and which produced one of the first reports on racism faced by South Asian Canadians. It may have been one of the earliest articulations of a "South Asian" identity in Canada.

· · · · · · · · ·

Feminism was an academic endeavour for me. In my own life, I was not concerned by sexism. The women around me were strong people, even though most of them were in traditional roles as mothers, aunts, and grandmothers. As a girl child, I was made to feel that the world was at my feet and I could be whatever I wanted. As a young adult, I was never pressured to marry. In fact, to the contrary, my father and uncle impressed upon me that I must develop a career. My father would recall stories about all the brilliant women in his family being "destroyed" after marriage. He was anti-marriage even though he and my mother were given in an arranged marriage when she was sixteen and he was in his twenties. I knew that she had been admitted into medical school but could not follow through once married life and motherhood took over. She remains a dynamo! I was aware that my grandmother was so unhappy with my grandfather that her children sponsored her to Canada, and my grandfather never joined her. She lived and died here.

When I started graduate school, I was fortunate to attend a department renowned for its feminist scholarship. Strangely, I was never a part of the feminist culture in the department – I did not feel accepted or mentored by the feminist scholars, neither was I drawn to them, even though at the time I was researching women's issues in India. I was pursuing anti-racist, anti-colonial, anti-imperialist studies. I was part of the generation that pointed out that feminism as it prevailed in the early 1980s was a "white" feminism, which we did not identify with and which amounted to being racist and exclusionary in its formulation. The women's caucus in my department, which was an influential organization in terms of departmental affairs, needed a coordinator. It was suggested that I should take the position along with another graduate student. I accepted the offer and proceeded to expand the caucus to include other departments. I remember organizing a teach-in, along with other women graduate students, on the experiences and concerns of women of colour and "Third World" women and how these were different from those of white, European women. I began writing on the intersections of race, gender, and class for my dissertation. This politics made sense to me. In my activist life, I was in the thick of immigrant women's groups and anti-racist movements, which were at a high point in Toronto in the 1980s. I was involved in establishing a community organization named South Asian Women's Group (SAWG), later to be named South Asian Women's Centre, as well as the Coalition of Visible Minority Women in Ontario, all based in Toronto.

It was by focusing on the issues of women of colour, in the communities in which I was embedded, that I became more acutely aware of women's oppression. I heard about a number of violent deaths suffered by South Asian women in Toronto. That was a catalyst for the initiation of the SAWG. I looked around and found that although there were numerous community organizations dealing with immigrant settlement and racism, none focused on women's isolation and related oppressions, particularly for working-class women. Even the progressive organizations I had been active in were male-dominant. Often, I found myself to be the only woman involved, unless I brought my mother or friends along. My mother became a founder and solid member-volunteer of SAWG, without whose work the organization would have folded. There were many times when I would give up, and she would pick up the pieces and keep going.

It was also at this time that the International Women's Day Committee (IWDC) in Toronto issued a slogan in 1986: "Women Say No To Racism From Toronto To South Africa." That was the first time that the larger women's movement took racism up as its issue, but not without fierce contestation and decades of women of colour agitating for it. It was the first time that I felt compelled to participate in a "mainstream" feminist public action. This recognition of racism as a feminist issue galvanized many women of colour of my generation to join the movement, later to be known as the third wave of feminism.

Tania Das Gupta is a professor in the Department of Equity Studies, York University. Her publications, teaching, and research interests are in the following areas: South Asian diasporas, race and racism, anti-racism, immigration and refugee issues, state policies, and women, work, and families, as well as community activism. She has published widely in these areas, including Real Nurses and Others: Racism in Nursing *(2009) and* Racism and Paid Work *(1995). She has consulted with human rights lawyers and nurses' groups on numerous cases of racial harassment. Prior to entering academia, her many years of community work with immigrant women and anti-racism resulted in the 1986 publication* Learning from Our History: Community Development by Immigrant Women in Ontario, 1958–86.

A JOURNEY TO DISMANTLE
THE MASTER'S HOUSE

Jiyoung Lee-An

Scene #1

In an upper-level sociology class, a teaching assistant (TA) was han-
ding out graded assignments to students. A female student who seemed
unhappy with her grade asked the TA to increase it. The TA reviewed
her paper and refused to change the grade, explaining the marking
rubric she had used for grading. However, the student continued to
demand that her paper be re-graded despite the TA's clear refusal.
Finally the student stepped back and, turning to her friend, said, "My
TA is from Asia. She does not understand my English. That's why she
gave me a D." It was obvious that the student knew that her voice was
loud enough to reach the TA's ears.

I must confess, I was that TA. This incident took place within three
months of my arrival in Canada to study for my PhD in sociology.
It was my first direct experience with discrimination, where my
physical identity was used to blame me for the poor academic performance of the student. The student had no clue where I was from.
She simply assumed I was from Asia based on my appearance and
probably by my accent.

   I still remember that moment vividly. At first, I was just stunned.
My instinct was to tell her that her remark was problematic and discriminatory, but something inside me blocked me from responding
promptly. Only after my emotional turmoil faded away was I able
to think through what had happened, and, in particular, about why
I was hesitant to react.

   This incident hurt my self-esteem, dignity, and pride. However,
the issue was deeper than that. Why wasn't I able to talk back to the
student right away? Why couldn't I say to her, "Excuse me, what did
you say just now?" As time went by, my anger at myself deepened
and intensified.

   I have long defined myself as someone who is outspoken, opin-
ionated, and straightforward. I thought that I had at least a capacity

to resist injustice in any form. It was a surprising moment to observe how vulnerable, weak, and fearful I could be. Before coming to Canada, I had worked with different feminist and migrant groups in South Korea. It would be a lie if I said that I was not afraid to fight against injustice on the front line. However, I was less hesitant, less fearful, and less vulnerable there than I felt as an international student in Canada. Regardless of whether I recognized it or not, my stable legal status and taken-for-granted belonging to Korean society had provided a safer and more comfortable space and position to talk about the rights of immigrants and migrants in Korea. In Canada, where my legal status is not stable and my comfort zone, in terms of social and cultural belonging, is absent, my thoughts and actions seem constrained.

Then what does my journey to Canada mean for me? What has changed? Living in Canada does not simply mean a change of geographical location. It changed my status from citizen to foreigner holding a temporary visa. In fact, my everyday life is not that different from other Canadians. I live, study, and work here like other Canadians. I pay income tax, and my living costs always include paying 13 percent of indirect consumption taxes. However, my unstable status as a migrant exists as a potential or lurking threat. Thus, for me, the Canadian government shows its existence in its power to expel me rather than provide protection. Of course, I am still in a privileged position as an international student. People like me are more welcomed because we are expected to bring Canadian society financial resources. We are treated as "valuable" consumers in the Canadian education system and "potential human capital" in the future. Still, this rosy rhetoric toward international students does not protect us from our temporary status and vulnerable position.

Going back to my story, the worst part of the experience was how it continuously created and internalized inferior feeling inside me. My damaged dignity and pride made me doubt myself. Instead of treating that student's comment as problematic, I questioned my ability in English – that I might have a problem with English (which I now know is not the case). This tiny incident took away my confidence. This self-blame game is like a mobius strip that continuously circulates without an end. Once you fall into a trap of blaming, it is difficult to come out. I finally cut through that vicious and endless cycle, and the experience, in the end, helped me to start organizing international TAs who faced similar problems. I am not sure whether I will always be able to come out of this kind of situation easily, but I know that I have at least a capacity to face such discrimination in a straightforward manner and do something about it, not only for myself, but also for others.

Scene # 2

Four Korean men were standing at a bus stop in Ottawa one weekday evening. All of a sudden, three white girls and one white boy confronted them and started to beat them with their umbrellas saying, "You look like fish." This came out of nowhere, and the men did not know what to do. They were beaten until other people came and intervened. Only one of the four men started to fight back. First, they were worried about the impact of fighting back against girls. Second, they did not want to get involved in any trouble that might affect their status in Canada. Three of the Korean men were international students; the fourth had permanent residency – the one who fought back. The men did not talk to each other about what to do, but the three internatio-nal students behaved in the same way and the one who had permanent residence status fought back.

When I heard this story the first time, I was upset by the fact that these men faced an arbitrary racial attack in a public space – a bus stop. However, this case made me think not only about the attack itself but also about the vulnerable position that international students face as temporary residents in Canada. Nobody could argue that this was not a racial assault. This behaviour is punishable under the relevant Canadian anti-racism laws if the case is reported "properly."

Here I would like to emphasize the vulnerable legal status of international students as temporary residents and their immediate fear of being in trouble. In this case, they were "lucky" because the attack happened in a public space. Several people were around and a bus driver witnessed the event. It was clear that these four Koreans were victims. But what would have happened had there been no witnesses? What would have happened had these Korean guys started to fight back and, in the end, each side was injured seriously? Could the Koreans be recognized as victims? Whose voice would be accepted as legitimate had there been no "objective" witnesses? I see the unspoken and subconscious fear of those Koreans who hold temporary visas and live as racialized men in Canada.

This incident also made me think about the way East Asian men are racialized; it resonates with stereotyping of East Asian men as weaker and less masculine. Can you imagine different pictures of racial attacks, such as black men attacked by white girls in the dark streets, or white men attacked by Asian women in the middle of a public road? Visualizing different images makes it clear how Asian men – in particular East Asian men – are portrayed in Canada as more feminine and weak. A racial system is not a single hierarchical system stratifying people based on a single racial line. It combines with different intersections of social relations such as gender, class, ethnicity, sexuality, etc.

These are two cases of very direct and explicit racism I experienced or heard about in the last two and half years. Along with them, I've faced many more subtle forms of racism in my everyday life. Some are so subtle that they are very difficult to enunciate. In many cases, these subtle forms of racism are conducted in the name of "care" or in a "benevolent" manner. For the sake of this writing, I asked some of my friends from different parts of Asia about their experiences. Most of them started their stories by saying, "I am not sure whether this is racial discrimination or not. I may be too sensitive when I think in this way, but I have had to face many uncomfortable feelings." Many were hesitant to label their experiences as racial discrimination and emphasized that they might be too sensitive so that they interpret somebody's good intention in a negative way. Good intentions are decorated with language like "care." One of my friends told me she was treated like a "child" by her white, middle-class landlady. Although she is more than thirty, and the mother of a child in her country of origin, to her landlord her "younger" face, lack of cultural common grounds, and English-language skills are the basis for treating her like a child who needs care. I am also surrounded by "nice" people who want to give me advice about everything. I am not saying that all kindness and caring are bad. Sometimes I appreciate them. However, this type of paternal care consolidates unspoken structures of inferiority and superiority assumed between us and them.

If this "excessive" care is one axis of discrimination, exclusion stands at the other end of the spectrum. Even though direct and explicit racism may have been reduced numerically, social exclusion is still prevalent here. A 2013 Canadian Bureau for International Education survey on international students shows that about 58 percent of international students in Canada have very few or no Canadian friends. Isn't that surprising? This fact stands in stark contrast to the Harper government's recent announcement of planning a huge increase in international students to 400,000. Yes, no more official policies for segregation, but international students are still ghettoized within the "dominant" society.

When I was first asked to write my story for this book, I thought it would be easy. However, the writing process was much tougher than I expected. It required of me a great deal of courage to face what I have experienced. It was an onerous process because some parts of me want to adapt, accept, and conform to these discriminatory situations. If I have to resist all forms of discrimination every time they occur, I will be burned out. But it does not mean that I am avoiding facing the reality of discrimination nor the need for moving forward. Rather, I am choosing and experiencing my own journey to dismantle the master's house with my own tools and at my own speed. In that sense, Audre Lorde was absolutely right: "The master's tools will never dismantle the master's house." Our own resistance can dismantle the master's house.

Jiyoung Lee-An worked as a researcher-activist in the Network for Global Activism/School of Feminism (NGA/SF) and as a program officer for the Asian Regional Exchange for New Alternatives (ARENA) in South Korea. Currently, she is a PhD candidate at the Department of Sociology and Anthropology, Carleton University. She has also served as a chair of the International TA Caucus, CUPE 4600, and participated in organizing No One Is Illegal–Ottawa.

LOOKING BACK WHILE MOVING FORWARD
Rashmi Luther

Writing my contribution for this book has been difficult. I don't find it easy to talk about myself. Although as hard as it's been, it has also enabled me to pause and reflect, to think more deeply about my life, including how and why my values and beliefs were shaped, particularly around gender and race equity. These are not just areas of professional interest but are reflective of me as a person. Working in these areas has not been easy. It has taken an enormous personal toll over the years. I have found that gender and race equity are not topics most people want to talk about, or do more than pay lip service to. They involve introspection and a willingness to see that we are imperfect, that there is not always a convergence between what we say and what we do, that our taken-for-granted assumptions can be harmful to others. However, I also know that I would be untrue to myself, and my beliefs and principles, if I didn't continue to challenge and question social inequities shaped by race and gender privileges and exclusions.

At this juncture of my life, as I enter my sixties, I find myself doing what many others my age tend to do – journey into memories of the past. Maybe this is because I am acutely aware that the road I have travelled is longer than the one that lies ahead. Looking back, I am enormously grateful for the love, friendships, and opportunities that have filled my life. They have contributed to a very rich life, albeit at times a difficult one, filled with lessons learned and insights gained, especially from the challenges and roadblocks I encountered along the way.

My journey began in India, and then as a young girl I moved with my family to the United States for four years, and subsequently to Canada, which has been my home for the last fifty years. Home has become an interesting concept for me. In my mind, home is not just a physical place. It also has emotional attachments, involving significant relationships and experiences that have grounded me and given me a sense of identity and belonging. For me, despite having lived in multiple places, and calling each of them home, my strongest association with home has always been my mother. Home was not just where I lived, but where my mother lived. She was the beacon. She was home. She passed away a few years ago and I am still trying to recover from this loss, of her no longer being there to go home to.

At various points in my life, I have also found home, and a sense of belonging, among people with whom I have shared common political interests, beliefs, and struggles. Over the years, "home" has been with those advancing human rights and social justice, particularly for immigrant women and racialized communities. As I reflect, I have been trying to understand how these two areas became the dominant focus and driving passions in my life, in both my paid and unpaid work.

One major source of influence was my parents, who lived under and struggled against the last vestiges of colonial rule in India. Having been active participants in the independence movement, they witnessed and survived the bloody aftermath of Partition. These historic markers deeply imprinted their lives, reflecting and shaping their passions and beliefs in the importance of challenging domination in order to create a more just and egalitarian world, informed by Marxist philosophy. Another major influence has been the times in which I lived, informing the development of my critical consciousness. From the 1960s and beyond, they have been times of struggle and activism – for rights, justice, and equity.

In 1961, we arrived in Minneapolis, Minnesota, at the height of the civil rights movement, second-wave feminism, and activism around poverty, labour rights, Native rights, and opposition to the Vietnam War. In later decades, as greater numbers of immigrants and refugees from countries of the global South were permitted to enter Canada, struggles broadened to encompass immigrant, refugee, and migrant rights; anti-racism; gay, lesbian, and transgender rights; and rights for the differently abled, among others. As a child raised in a politically engaged family during the sixties and seventies, I seem to have absorbed a strong abhorrence for injustice, believing that it must be resisted.

While I didn't realize it at the time, my first eight years of life in India were where I was first introduced to the power of women. I remember being surrounded by an extended family in which women were strong, not the passive/subservient stereotype that is projected in the Western world. They were educated and had professional lives outside the home. They were my early role models – women who were politically engaged, astute, strong, bright, artistic, musically gifted, happy, and beautiful. Looking back, I think they were important guides in my life, showing me that women could be and do anything.

When we left India in 1961 this connection to the extended family and India as home was disrupted. Travel was expensive and telephones in India were unreliable at best. So my mother became the centre of my world. She somehow managed to juggle life in a new culture while being a graduate student, teaching assistant, mother, host of numerous dinner parties for friends and colleagues, and managing the household. I didn't appreciate then how difficult this must have been for her with no extended family for support. I remember her as strongly independent, talented, and resourceful. In many respects, she encouraged creativity, self-reliance, and independence in me. When I was in my late teens, I vividly remember her telling me, "Never depend on a man to look after you," and, "A woman is never independent unless she is financially independent." These beliefs are indicative of her fierce and feisty spirit that has somehow found its way into my core as well.

In her earlier life, my mother was also a rebel, rejecting the religious and cultural "traditions" such as the caste system, arranged marriages, and the dowry system for perpetuating inequities, especially for women. My father also rejected these types of restrictions and limits. His political beliefs were influenced by Marxist philosophy, especially its hope of achieving a more just, united, and egalitarian society in India. Sadly, the independence struggle ended up producing the opposite – the division of India and Pakistan. The Partition was violent and deadly, with mass displacement of people from one territory to the other, taking with them only what they could carry in suitcases or on their backs. As a consequence, many became refugees, including my father's family. They were forced to start anew, rebuilding their lives and dignities with limited means. The psychological scars were harder to heal, especially for my grandparents.

It is curious that, with this family history, my own critical consciousness about race/culture and gender did not really begin to form until I was in my late twenties. I can trace this back to several pivotal moments. With respect to race/culture, the first was in 1979 when my mother, father, younger sister and I visited India. This was my first trip back since we emigrated. On arrival at the Delhi airport, I vividly remember looking out at the sea of brown faces and realizing that everyone looked just like me. This was an "aha!" moment. It signified a sense of finding home while also realizing that it was not my home. Returning to Ottawa, I felt a strange disorientation because the contrast was so apparent. I couldn't blend in like I had in India, at least in terms of appearance. I wondered why the streets seemed so quiet and empty, and why there was so much space between people as they walked and talked, even in crowded situations. I longed for the colour and chaos of life on the street.

I consider this consciousness to be both a blessing and a curse. While it has shown me my roots, making me more aware of my origins, it has also made me feel more unsettled – a part of, yet apart from, both India and Canada. Over time, I have learned to value and navigate these in-between spaces of contradiction, tension, and ambiguity. These liminal spaces have given me a unique vantage point from which to straddle the two worlds as I look back while moving forward. Additionally, these spaces have made me more aware of how difference is constituted in Canada, and how this affects people's lives, positively or negatively. This awareness, in turn, has inspired me to spend most of my working life addressing the inequities produced by racial/cultural difference.

The next pivotal moment(s) concerning race also involved some travel. They are based on questions that directly or indirectly ask, "Where are you from?" On the surface these questions appear quite innocent and benign. However, they often irritate me, especially when they are posed in Canada, by mainstream Canadians. I wonder why they are asking these questions, especially as I have lived in Canada for almost fifty years and don't speak with a discernable accent. Is it because my skin is brown that I am deemed not to be a Canadian? When I respond that I am Canadian or from Ottawa, their usual follow-up is "But where are you really from?" I also get asked this question when I travel outside of Canada. For instance, I was asked this question by several Cubans when I was there with my partner and son on a family holiday. (I should explain that my partner is white, which makes our son biracial.) I responded as I usually do and said, "I am from Canada." However, this was not accepted as the right answer, so the questioning persisted. To my surprise, because I was brown, they thought I was Spanish or Mexican, not Canadian. On another occasion, while travelling through India with my family, taxi drivers, hotel staff, and others again asked me this same question. When I replied that I was Canadian, they too did not accept this response. They claimed that because I looked Indian, I was Indian, not Canadian.

There are probably many different explanations for this identity confusion, both positive and negative. It could be that despite Canada being known as a multicultural nation, it is still primarily believed to be a land of white people (with no acknowledgement of Indigenous peoples). Unfortunately, this belief seems to persist among mainstream Canadians and others around the world. It could also be that the questions posed, especially during my travels, were not meant to exclude but to make me feel included, as one of them, not an outsider. So who is asking the question, and of whom, does seem to matter, at least in terms of my reaction to it.

My critical consciousness about gender also dates back to the 1970s and 1980s, as I became more attuned to the women's movement in Canada. Women's groups and activities were also where I sought a community of belonging. This began as I was doing my undergraduate degree in English literature. At this time, I actively sought out women authors and enrolled in courses that were generally more women-centred or taught by professors who were women. While I loved the courses and soaked up stories about the lives, experiences, hopes, dreams, and concerns of North American and European women, I became increasingly uncomfortable with the absence of women's stories from other places like India, China, the Caribbean, and Africa. When I first went to local bookstores in search of these missing voices, there were very few on offer. This is when I first began to connect issues of race and gender and to raise questions about the Eurocentric nature of the education system and the mainstream women's movement. This realization firmly planted me in a tension-filled journey with feminism itself. And while I did not have a name for it at that time, my awareness about systemic aspects of race and gender exclusion was beginning to form.

Some of these tensions I felt with the mainstream women's movement were evident in 1981 when I attended the women's constitutional conference, organized by the Ad Hoc Committee of Canadian Women on the Constitution. I was excited by the opportunity to attend and learn from discussions where so many legends of the Canadian women's movement were present. It was a wonderful experience, and my commitment to gender equity was certainly strengthened because of it. However, I was also conscious that among the more than one thousand women present, there were not many who looked like me. I remember being unsettled by this and feeling quite self-conscious at being so "visible." These feelings not only made me question the evident "whiteness" of the mainstream women's movement at that time, they also led me to join with others to form groups reflecting the voices, issues, concerns, and aspirations of immigrant and racialized women in Ottawa. Through these different community-based involvements, we tried to challenge and inform mainstream feminism about these issues and concerns. We wanted the broader scope and understanding of the women's movement to be relevant to those whose lived experiences of exclusion were based on intersections of gender with race, class, culture, language, religion, and immigrant or refugee status. In this way, it is clear that my gender consciousness, including the activism it has inspired, has largely been formed through the lens of race.

It is through the convergence of different personal and professional experiences, as well as my involvement in issues of gender and race, that my understanding about power, privilege, and structural exclusion or discrimination has been shaped and enhanced. I must point out that this understanding has also evolved within a particular historical context – one where the presence of visible minorities or people of colour like me was increasing. As this happened, racist incidents also increased. Some were overt. They were in comments such as "Go back to where you came from" or the refusal to provide services, employment, or housing. Some were more deadly and involved pushing South Asians onto subway tracks, or innocent black men being shot by police officers based on racist stereotypes. Other incidents were more covert in nature, shielded by beliefs that existing systems are neutral and benign. Examples of these, then and now, are: the lack of recognition of foreign credentials;

requirements for fluency in both official languages; unstated preferences for Canadian experience; and culturally biased assessment procedures. As these incidents continued to escalate, all levels of government were increasingly pressured by community groups to intervene. The most common response became public education, policy and program development, and cultural sensitivity training. The focus of this training later shifted to anti-racism, and more recently still to anti-oppression.

In connecting this past with my present, for more than twenty-three years (until my recent retirement), I was located in the academy, in the field of social work. And after more than thirty years of active engagement in issues of race and racialization, I was still doing some of the same work I did when I started – making presentations and doing awareness raising in classrooms, among academic bodies, local agencies and institutions, and community groups. In doing this work, I was continuing to encounter defensiveness and a reluctance to move beyond tokenistic responses. When I was hired, it was into a faculty position that also carried the designation of race equity coordinator. I thought this was in recognition of the considerable knowledge and experience I had gained from doing race equity work at local, provincial, and national levels, and because I was already known to them, as a student and later as a sessional, having helped develop and teach their elective course on immigrants and race/culture. In thinking that my department's commitment to address race issues in all components of its work was sincere, and knowing that we were the only social work program to have such a designated faculty position, I was excited to take up the opportunity and challenge, excited also that I would not be the only "VM." However, I quickly discovered that what was said and what was expected were poles apart. In fact, I was not really expected to do much that would significantly change the culture of the program. In the first month I was reminded that as a faculty member, my loyalty was to faculty. The meaning of this was clear: I should back off and not rock the boat, I should be grateful for being allowed into the hallowed halls, and I should respectfully defer to others, but should not expect the same for myself. In sum, I was to be seen not heard.

I remember feeling utterly miserable and demoralized, spending the first few years in tears. Wanting desperately to flee, I chose instead to stay and fight. Supported by my family, friends outside the university, a small group of students, and an even smaller group of faculty, I would not cower. I could have chosen the easy path of being content to be a token, a showpiece to demonstrate how progressive we were for having created this position. But I didn't. Instead, I chose to give my loyalty to the racialized community and issues I was hired to address. I did this so that I could live with integrity and maintain my self-respect. I decided that if I were to be fired, it would be for upholding the principles of justice and equity. In the end, this was the best decision I could have made. It was liberating and empowering, then and now.

I wish I could say that it got easier over time, that after years of discussions at faculty meetings and retreats, different training and educationals about diversifying our courses and curriculum, the student body, and faculty composition, we had finally incorporated lasting changes in how we recognize and address questions of race. While there have been some positive changes with respect to student placement opportunities in more diverse agencies, in other respects I believe we have lost ground. We no longer have some of the institutional structures that were present in the early years. For instance, the position of race equity coordinator was eliminated a number of years ago. The explanation given was budgetary constraints. This exemplifies how vulnerable these positions are in institutional structures and how they continue to be viewed as marginal to the real work of departments and organizations.

The Anti-Racism Committee is also gone. It was originally made up of committed students (racialized and others), faculty, and community members. It was productive and had a large and active student presence. For the members, it was a community of belonging. It was where issues and experiences of race and racialization could be openly discussed and appropriate strategies and recommendations developed. It is gone because concerns were raised that a similar committee structure did not exist for other equity issues. Proposals were made that it be reconstituted under the umbrella of social justice to highlight the interconnections between the different issues. In theory this sounds great. In practice it meant that the commitment to race was weakened. As a result, race-related advocacy, monitoring, and review functions, particularly with respect to courses and their content, are no longer embedded into the department's formal organizational structure. These changes mean that the inclusion of race-related course content remains uneven across different courses. As well, the number of racially diverse students continues to be small, especially in the graduate program.

The course on race/culture, among the first to be introduced to social work programs in Canada, is in jeopardy. As an elective course, it is vulnerable if enrolment is deemed too low. This is what almost happened recently, in my final year as a faculty member. During a faculty retreat, I noticed that courses on race/culture and globalization were absent from the list of electives to be offered in the following year. After a series of heated discussions, a begrudging decision was made to offer the course on race but not the one on globalization. I remain astounded that, at a time of increased racial tensions, global crises, and movement of people around the world, these two courses were placed in jeopardy.

Lastly, with respect to our faculty complement, there also has been significant erosion. For instance, twenty-three years ago when I joined the department, there were four visible minorities – two Aboriginal people, one other woman of colour, and me – among the permanent faculty. In my final year there were two – one other woman of colour and me. With my recent retirement, the number dropped to one. I find this an appalling and regressive development, but it does fit the pattern of erasure and disrespect that has been unfolding for some time now. We continue to talk the talk but don't walk the walk.

Needless to say, my life as a faculty member, with additional responsibilities for bringing about "race equity," was quite a roller-coaster. The optimism and excitement with which I began quickly dissipated with each reminder that I was not really one of them. Unwilling to conform to expectations, I felt ostracized when I began, and that was how I still felt when I retired in 2014. The price I have paid for loyalty to my principles, beliefs, and values, for not relinquishing my dignity and self-respect, has been great. The discomfort was palpable when I was present in meetings and even more so when I spoke. Often I would sit alone with no one occupying the spaces on either side of me. I was not invited to contribute to different research or writing projects. I wonder if this is how my father experienced his life in the academy. He never spoke of it but when I first told him that I had been offered the position, he was both excited and apprehensive. He did say at the time that he hoped I would have a good experience because the academy could be a nasty place. Maybe this is why I chose to leave and retire early rather than stay. While all these experiences have made me stronger and given me valuable insights into the complexity of "doing" equity work, I was tired of being beaten up.

I will continue to stay active and involved in my life passions because they are an integral part of who I am. However, it will be in milieus that are supportive, creative, energizing, and joyful, ones that are reflective of home – a community of belonging.

Rashmi has been actively involved in social justice issues, especially those pertaining to immigrant women, broader immigrant and refugee groups, and racialized communities, for the last thirty years. Much of her work has focused on encouraging and assisting local agencies, institutions, organizations, and community boards to promote and support policy and program development, curriculum development, and changes to organizational cultures and practices that will further meaningful equity and inclusion for racialized communities in Ottawa. Now happily retired, she remains active and committed to advancing these important issues through her ongoing involvement in community-based projects and activities.

STRUGGLES OF RESEARCHERS AND ACADEMICS OF COLOUR IN CANADA

Vanaja Dhruvarajan

Over the years we, the women of colour faculty in the Canadian academy, have struggled to resist marginalization. These struggles have taken many forms. We asked ourselves how to articulate our concerns so that we would be heard and taken seriously. The answer eventually was to form an association to give strength to our voices and delineate strategies to realize our visions for a better future. Thus, the Association of Researchers and Academics of Colour for Equality (RACE) was formed.

Experiences of marginalization are not new to people of colour in Canadian society. Historical legacies of colonialism and imperialism have devalued our cultures. In this era of corporate globalization, issues pertaining to social justice are taking a back-seat. The few gains made to bring about gender and race equality, after decades of struggles, are gradually being eroded. In this "new world order," racism and gender discrimination are taking new forms of articulation. In this context, the establishment of RACE is a significant event. The association aspires to create conditions conducive to developing critical race scholarship, thus questioning the knowledge monopolies prevalent in the academy. It also aspires to support researchers and academics of colour as they endeavour to bring about changes at institutional, structural, and systemic levels in the academy. The hope is that such efforts will effectively confront the "new world order" and pave the way for a world that is inclusive, just, and caring.

Canadian academia has been, and to a large extent still is, Eurocentric and androcentric – it privileges men of European origins as producers and disseminators of knowledge. This same group has also controlled university administrations, thereby playing a significant role in curriculum decisions, as well as choice of university personnel and procedures. Feminists, particularly since the 1970s, have made some impact in addressing androcentric knowledge production and dissemination. The establishment of Women's Studies departments and programs has been one of the outcomes. The beneficiaries, to a large extent, have been white middle-class women who are represented in greater numbers (compared with the past) as teachers and administrators in the academy. In addition, knowledge production from white middle-class women's perspectives has also gained significance. But Eurocentric knowledge monopolies have been more difficult to address.

The struggles of non-European faculty to bring their perspectives into the classroom, and include their history and culture in the university curriculum, have been formidable. In my own teaching career (spanning more than thirty years at the University of Winnipeg), I can recount many instances when I was patronized, belittled, and my abilities and expertise questioned by administrators, colleagues, and students, as I attempted to question this Eurocentric monopoly. In my experience, even when there is clear evidence of our contributions to the academy it is difficult to get recognition.

I was actively involved in the struggles, along with a number of mostly white faculty members, to establish a graduate program and federally funded chair in women's studies at the University of Winnipeg. We were successful in both of these efforts. But when the time came to celebrate the success of these events, I was not included in the celebrations. My contributions were recognized by the community at large and I was awarded one of the "Woman of the Year" awards by the YMCA-YWCA in 1996. It was not until the end of my tenure that the university recognized my contributions by awarding me the Fellowship of United College, the highest honour it could bestow, in 2003.

In spite of such formidable environments, many academics of colour are making a difference in many fields through our research, writing, and teaching. Most of my research and publications are on women of colour in general and Hindu women in particular. In addition, I have published papers on the impact of corporate globalization on marginalized people. I developed and taught courses on these topics, and on knowledge monopolies in the academy, at graduate and undergraduate levels, at the University of Toronto, Carleton University, and the University of Ottawa.

As an executive member in professional associations, and a

board member of professional and community organizations, I have constantly endeavoured to bring forward perspectives of women of colour, and to highlight our concerns. This was particularly true during 1994–95 when I was in the federally funded women's studies endowed chair at Simon Fraser University. During that year, my main focus was on bringing to the fore critical concerns and perspectives of women of colour in the academy and the community. Because of such efforts by many women of colour scholars in women's studies, for example, issues of concern for people of colour are now included in some courses and textbooks. But these issues are not always integrated into the courses and are often added on at the very end. This "add-and-stir" approach to knowledge and professional development does not go far enough to establish the validity of different ways of knowing in the academy. Sometimes there are courses dealing with these issues listed in the academic calendar but they are rarely offered. This state of affairs persists because faculty of colour are not included in curriculum decisions, nor are there enough faculty of colour to teach these courses using perspectives that are appropriate to their content.

The chilly climate that exists for people of colour makes it very difficult to function normally in the academy. In spite of the fact that academic freedom is one of the cherished rights in the academy, it is not easy for this faculty group to exercise that right due to lack of support. As a result, many of these academics tend to practice self-censorship, even when they disapprove of policies and practices that negatively impact marginalized people, for fear of drawing attention to themselves and becoming targets for reprisals.

Under these circumstances the need for establishing an association that provides support to these scholars cannot be over-emphasized. In May 2001, the Race and Gender Teaching Advocacy Group in British Columbia (RAGTAG) invited researchers and academics of colour in Canada to a consultation meeting. I attended the two-day conference. It drew more than a hundred scholars, activists, and academics of colour who shared their experiences with the group and explored various strategies to address our collective concerns. The discussions were engaged and passionate. There was a convergence of ideas and opinions about the goals of the assembly, but there was considerable disagreement about the strategies to be adopted and the methods of implementing those strategies. The meeting ended with the establishment of a Planning Committee to look into these details, assess the wishes of the assembly, and come up with concrete suggestions for the next meeting, held in Toronto in May 2002. The committee had representation from each region of Canada and included an Aboriginal scholar and activist. I represented the province of Manitoba.

The Critical Race Conference 2002 in Toronto drew more than two hundred scholars and academics of colour. It was a roaring success judging by the enthusiasm and the scholarly merit of the papers and discussions. A proposal was made by the Planning Committee to establish a national association titled Researchers and Academics of Colour for Equality (RACE).

In brief, the goals of the association were to foster and promote critical anti-racist feminist thought by providing support to academics and activists of colour; providing conditions conducive to forming networks among activists and academics of colour to disseminate knowledge; pursuing institutional support to encourage and sustain efforts by academics and activists of colour; including academics and activists of First Peoples in all of these initiatives. To achieve these goals, a number of initiatives were suggested, including mentoring new entrants, acting as a clearinghouse for employment and research opportunities, promoting publications and activism, and facilitating collaborative activities in research and activism.

The association was formally established, but many outstanding issues still had to be dealt with. There were extensive discussions on determining the criteria for membership. The two major issues of contention at that time were whether to include male critical race scholars and academics, and whether to include female critical race scholars and academics of European origin. Regarding men, concerns were expressed that feminist orientations might be compromised since, more often than not, men involved in this area do not meaningfully include gender in their research and writing. Regarding women of European origin, the concern was that the rigour of dealing with issues pertaining to race and racism may be diluted for fear of offending them. Lacking consensus, these issues remain unresolved.

At the following conference – Canadian Critical Race

Conference: Pedagogy and Practice 2003, held in Vancouver – there was an even more active level of participation. Issues affecting the First Peoples were aired and discussed with considerable support. But there was also concern that we were not dealing adequately with issues facing people of colour in the aftermath of 9/11, the intensification of Arab-Israeli conflict, and invasions of Afghanistan and Iraq. There was considerable disagreement as to how these issues should be dealt with. The conference organizers did not want to make waves and draw attention to the association. Through their choice of speakers, and by limiting the discussion time, they tried to soft-pedal these issues and remain noncontroversial.

But there were many who made presentations on these controversial topics with the conviction that the Association must take a firm stand against racial profiling and against the imperial pursuits of Western countries, particularly the US. Concerns were also expressed about the negative consequences of corporate globalization now underway, and the underlying agenda to establish Western political, economic, and cultural hegemony around the globe. Calls were made to critically examine the routine practice of imposing Western models of development on different countries, without paying attention to their culture and history. Others challenged the growing environmental damage and threats to the safety and security of people around the globe, because of the aggressive imposition of the corporate globalization model.

Over time, the corporatization of universities has led to further marginalization of people of colour, as issues of inclusiveness, diversity, accessibility, justice, and equity were pushed to the bottom of university agendas. Under these circumstances, many participants felt that the association needed to take positions to serve the interests of people of colour and other marginalized people. The conference ended with many who were ambivalent about the actual achievements but resolved to work more diligently to address these outstanding issues at the next meeting, held at York University in Toronto in May 2004. By this time, my tenure on the Planning Committee was over. Because of personal reasons I had to withdraw from active involvement in the association at the end of 2003. However, RACE has continued to flourish.

Vanaja Dhruvarajan is an adjunct professor at Carleton University. She completed her BA *in India, and her Master's and* PhD *at the University of Chicago. Her teaching and research interests include globalization, family and socialization, gender, anti-racism, and knowledge monopolies. She has done research in India and Canada and has published several articles and books, including* Hindu Women and the Power of Ideology *and* GENDER RACE AND NATION: A Global Perspective, *co-authored with Jill Vickers. She has served as president of the Canadian Sociology and Anthropology Association, president of the Canadian Women's Studies Association, and Ruth Wynn Woodward endowed Chair in Women's Studies at Simon Fraser University. She has also served on the boards of several professional, university, government and community organizations.*

FROM ADVERSITY TO ADVANTAGE
Isobel Granger

"I can be changed by what happens to me but I refuse to be reduced by it" —MAYA ANGELOU

My primary passion in life has always been to help others reach their full potential. When I initially sought my purpose for being here on Earth, I realized my very existence must have been by divine design. It had to be because I was born in Zimbabwe, into a world of segregation – a system created by people who had lost sight of the reason mankind was placed here on Earth in the first place, people who had turned on each other in a desperate attempt to secure their own survival and maintain a way of life that excluded people different from themselves.

My earliest memories include a very stark awareness that I had a role to play in creating a better world.

In that oppressive environment, the community I was raised in had its own brand of segregation. The people were of mixed race and ranged in complexion from those much darker than I to those so fair-skinned, they could pass for white. The system killed the spirit of many people, particularly those with darker skins, who were constantly told, *"You are not good enough and you will never amount to anything."*

I was one of those people.

I have often said, my achievements result from the milestones throughout my life – disguised as adversity – which I had to overcome. In retrospect, I see that in times of adversity, someone would always appear at just the right time, or I would immediately see the lesson in the experience and resolve to learn from it. Sometimes someone would show up to help me through a challenge or learn a lesson I needed to learn, or they would say something that would catapult me out of my pity party, reminding me that giving up for someone like me is never an option.

Recently I was driving home after a difficult day, having commiserated with a close friend about some recent challenges I had experienced. Adversity has been a common thread throughout my life. That day I didn't feel like forgiving anyone or turning the other cheek or being positive. For once I wanted to just give up! And then I heard on the radio that Nelson Mandela had just died at the age of ninety-five. I stopped there and then to think about my own struggles and how minor they were compared to what he went through for most of his life.

The realization then was that we often forget that we all have a part to play, a calling in the quest to create harmony and a better life for all. Sadly, we often get caught up in ourselves, either accumulating "stuff" or trying to make sure that we "get the edge" on everyone around us so that we excel, sometimes at the expense of others.

The lessons I learned have stayed with me. I have used the experiences, negative and positive, as opportunities to turn adversity into advantage.

Any hardship or suffering I endured has built my character. I have strived, and continue to strive, to use the lessons from the challenges I faced to help others work through their own hardships. I try to be present, because being present keeps me aware, it helps me stay in touch with what is important, to me and to others around me. I would like to think that if what I share can help even one person, it will have been worthwhile and rewarding to have endured, persevered, and overcome.

One of my first defining moments happened when I was only eight years old.

From the time I learned to talk, I was known as a very talented singer. I sang in the church choir and at community events, sometimes for very large crowds. I was comfortable on stage, because I loved to sing. It did not matter what was happening around me, as long as I was singing. When I sang, it did not seem to matter that I had a dark complexion or that I was "not good enough." Very few children could sing like me. Even those who did not like me, teachers included, had to concede that they would have to travel far and wide to hear a voice like mine.

I also loved to read. I sometimes joke that I love reading so much that I would read a telephone directory if nothing else were available. When I read, I could travel anywhere and no one could tell me I was not allowed to enter because of the colour of my skin. Those days, even though most restaurants and other public establishments did not have signs like the ones in South Africa, which said, "No Blacks or Non-whites allowed," they did have signage that might as well have said the same thing. The restaurant signs in my city read, "Right of admission reserved." To us who lived there, those particular signs meant No Blacks or Non-whites allowed.

At the end of every year, my elementary school would put on a play. Rehearsals began in early September and, as the big day drew closer, those chosen to participate would attend daily rehearsals. The mayor and other important guests, mainly white, came to our segregated neighbourhood once a year to attend this big event. Members of my community considered the visits from the elite community an honour, so they would make sure to deliver a "top notch" production. Translated, "top notch" meant the lightest in complexion were given priority over the darker skinned, like me.

I was always chosen to participate, mainly to sing, and because I sang so well, I was one of the children who never had to audition. One year, the director of the play went away at the beginning of the summer season, which is when we usually began auditions for the end-of-the-year play. To my surprise, I was chosen to be a princess, with a very important solo part. Up until then, I hadn't noticed that my assigned roles had always been ones that required me to "cover up" so that I would only be heard. As an inanimate object on stage, or a farm animal, or shrubbery, I could sing and support whatever was going on, without diminishing the quality of the show.

Being chosen to play a princess was exciting and new, but it did not matter much to me. What mattered was that I was singing. The director returned a few short weeks before the night of the play. When she realized I had been given a leading role, she immediately replaced me with a long-haired girl with a lighter complexion. She told me I would sing the song from behind the curtain while the light-skinned girl mimed on stage. The teacher who had chosen me for the part was enraged. I remember her grabbing me by the shoulders and shaking me. Although her anger scared me, I realized she was fighting for me. To this day, I have never forgotten her words to me: "Isobel, never let anyone put you behind the curtain again."

I did not realize that up until the final show, she had continued to express dissatisfaction that the director had humiliated me by placing me behind the curtain.

I did not get to play the part and I did sing behind the curtain, but the important lesson I learned stayed with me. Although the circumstances may be different, there are so many people today who have had similar experiences that have changed the course of their lives. They find themselves behind curtains of doubt, insecurity, rejection, and other forms of oppressive conditioning. Some of them are hearing their own voices or those of others, which have reinforced the oppression by bombarding them with the message: "You're not good enough."

I share the lesson I learned from Phyllis Agnew, the woman who told me, "Never let anyone put you behind the curtain again."

I learned I am valuable, and it does not matter if, from time to time, people try to diminish me or to convince me that "I am not good enough." It is important to never let anyone set a ceiling for me or determine my worth. It is my God-given privilege to realize my full potential and live a rich and prosperous life.

Eleanor Roosevelt once said: "You gain strength, courage, and confidence by every experience in which you really stop to look fear in the face. You must do the thing which you think you cannot do."

In 1978, at age nineteen, I decided to challenge the status quo in my country.

Up until 1978, the British South Africa Police did not hire people of mixed race. Rhodesia had two rank structures for officers. White applicants were hired at the rank of patrol officer and any of them could advance through the ranks to the position of police commissioner. Black applicants were hired as constables and the highest rank they could attain was sergeant major. A white patrol officer on his or her first day of work was deemed to be higher in rank than the highest ranking black officer who held the rank of sergeant major and had many years of service.

I knew when they received my application at police headquarters they would assume I was white because of my surname. Shortly after I submitted it, I received a letter inviting me to meet with the recruiting officer. In those days, applicants from the black community had their own recruitment office in the west end of the city. There was no recruitment office open to people of mixed race. When I arrived at police headquarters to see the recruitment officer, my entrance caused quite a stir. The officers realized they had made a mistake, that I should never have been invited for an interview.

The recruitment officer's first question to me was, "Why would you apply? We do not hire coloureds." I took this as an invitation to discuss what I thought was a ridiculous rule. I pointed out that there was nothing that a white female could do that I couldn't. I also pointed out that it was not fair that white female police officers did nothing more than write parking tickets when, in my view, they had the potential to be fully operational, just as the men were.

At the end of my interview, I was satisfied and quite prepared that this was the end of my dealings with the British South Africa Police, since I had gotten what I came for – shock value. I had succeeded and, boy, did I have a story to tell my friends.

I did not anticipate that I would be called back. My assumption was that they were drawing a line in the sand. I was sure they would disqualify me before I disqualified myself. You can imagine my shock when, after my final board interview, my interviewers welcomed me as "the first non-white to join the white ranks of the BSAP."

This was by no means the beginning of an easy career.

On my first day at the training depot, I was surrounded by a group of white women who told me they thought it was wrong that they should be subjected to living with me, in addition to working with me. Some of the reasons they gave were cruel and demeaning, but by the end of our six months of training, some of them became the best friends I have ever had. For the first time in my life, and probably theirs, I was invited by some of them to sit at the dining room table in their homes, where someone of colour normally would have been in the dining room as a servant, definitely not as the guest being served.

I learned from this experience that my role is not to judge but to educate. People can change. One of my parents' favourite sayings was "Don't hate, educate." They taught us that it doesn't matter what people do to you. What matters are your actions. You can either take an adversarial stance or you can role model the behaviour you would like to see.

I believe it was Mahatma Gandhi who said, "Be the change you wish to see in the world."

This does not mean you allow people to walk all over you. I, for one, could not have survived a career in law enforcement if I had allowed people to bully me.

I left Zimbabwe in 1989 with a husband and three young children. We came to Canada because we did not want our children growing up in an oppressive environment. We wanted to give them the opportunity to be who they wanted to be, as long as they made an honest effort.

In 1994, I became one of the first five black women to join the ranks of the Ottawa Police Service. To my surprise, I experienced considerable challenges in Canada, some similar to those I had experienced in my first policing career. I drew on these earlier lessons. Whenever I was asked an ignorant or rude question, such as how long had it taken me to learn English or why I spoke with such a thick accent, I took the time to educate people on where I was from. I found that I had to work harder than some of my peers to gain the same respect.

In October 1997, while I was arresting an armed robbery suspect, I sustained a needle-stick injury from a needle inside the suspect's pocket. I soon discovered that even though he was considered high risk for infectious diseases, he could not be compelled to give blood for testing so that I could make an informed decision about the course of treatment I might follow to eliminate or reduce the risk of contracting a potentially life-threatening disease. It was then I realized that this was quite a common occurrence among officers, and many had endured the emotional trauma of not knowing whether or not they had contracted a potentially life-threatening disease.

I refused to accept the status quo. At the end of 1997, I embarked on a national campaign for a private member's bill to introduce a law to compel a person to submit to a blood test in the event that he or she exposed a frontline worker to bodily fluids during the course of duty, or in instances where good Samaritans, while performing acts of kindness, were exposed to bodily fluids with the potential of contracting life-threatening diseases. Many doubted that such a law could be passed, as it had been attempted before and failed, due to the impact on individual privacy.

The lesson I learned was, if a human issue is being addressed, it has to be supported by a human story. My story formed the nucleus for a national campaign that resulted in a law being passed in Ontario in 2002 that compels a person to submit to a blood test if he or she exposes someone to his or her bodily fluids, intentionally or unintentionally.

I worked within the Ottawa Police Service and assisted other police organizations across the country to establish best practices in the prevention of exposure to infectious diseases through bodily fluids during the course of duty. As well, I worked with other police organizations and emergency service organizations in other provinces to introduce similar laws.

The lesson I learned through these and other experiences is that greatness is often fuelled by suffering and adversity, and perseverance can be beneficial in overcoming obstacles and achieving goals. Even though the door seems closed, it's worth the try.

I would like to say that life improved after that, but I have continued to face challenges, as I am sure many do. In looking back at my life, it is evident that I have not walked alone. Through the difficult times, people have shown up to stand by me or walk with me. In times of joy and celebration, people have shown up to celebrate with me and propel me forward. It is no wonder that I call myself extremely blessed.

When you help others in their time of need, it not only momentarily takes your mind off what you are going through, it helps you grow, learn, and widen your support system. The person you help today may save your life tomorrow.

I am who I am because of what I have been through. I have faced several challenges on my way here but each one has only strengthened me. I continue to strive to be a professional who knows exactly what she wants – someone who sets her eyes on a goal and does not take them off it until it is achieved.

I could not have survived alone, and definitely not without the inspiration I have received from my mentors, friends, and family, for whom I have the deepest respect, and from whom I derived the strength to challenge myself and perform better at each stage.

The encouragement I now pass on to young Others is this: Say yes to your calling; your yes could be the catalyst to your greatness or the greatness of someone else, which could change our world.

S/Sergeant Isobel Granger of the Ottawa Police Service (OPS) is an international Gender-Based Violence (GBV) expert who is an advocate for women. She is a recipient of multiple awards who has made a profound difference in the lives of women in Canada and abroad. The first black officer to join the ranks of the British South Africa Police in Zimbabwe, and one of the first five black women hired by the OPS, Isobel is a veteran officer with a strong investigative background. She is certified to investigate GBV as a war crime by the International Criminal Court, delivers pre-deployment gender training for Canadian police officers, and has delivered GBV prevention training in many countries. Isobel has a BA in policing studies and an MA in leadership.

MIGRANT FEMINISM –
FOUR DECADES OF ACTIVISM

Dolores Chew

I arrived in Montreal, Quebec, close to four decades ago as a curious young woman, eager for whatever adventures life threw at me. Reflecting back, I can draw lessons that may be of use. One of the most inspiring things for me today is how youth, especially young women, are confronting current challenges. However, the wealth of knowledge and experience that people of my generation have gained is relatively unknown. Because of the pressures and immediacy of activism, not enough gets documented. As a result, at times it seems that the wheel is being reinvented. Collections such as this provide unique opportunities for documenting lessons, which may be helpful for future generations, and allow my generation to reassess and reposition ourselves as realities on the ground continue to change.

When I'm asked about my experiences with racism, I find that I haven't had much personal experience with it. Reflecting on why this might be leads me to recognize that growing up in postcolonial India as a mixed race person, and being educated in English, with the many "Westernisms" that were part of that package, I fitted in relatively easily with many aspects of Canadian society. In fact, an official from the Canadian High Commission who interviewed me in India for my immigration application assured me that settling into Canada would not be a problem. Later, in Canada, if my accent was commented upon, it was always in a positive vein as "a cute British accent" (though it's distinctly Indian, of a time and place). And even living in Quebec, where French should be important, my choices with education and work allowed me to live an enclaved life, like others from former British colonies who are fluent in English. Consequently, despite my many attempts to learn French, including taking courses over the years but with insufficient immersion to become bilingual, to my regret and embarrassment, I am unable to speak French. This also limits my ability to participate more actively in the vibrant political life of the province.

On the issue of racism, my pursuit of higher education, enabling my work as an educator, brought its own status and privilege. Though not initially explicit, it's now very evident to me how class privilege often trumps inequality based on race or language, even in a province where this is a very fraught issue. In other parts of Canada as well, I have heard how migrant women going to employment centres have automatically been sent to factories for packing jobs, or how the lack of facility in either "official" language resulted in migrant men and women suffering a loss of dignity. A friend from India narrated how, as a young doctor in British Columbia, a taxi driver, assuming she was part of the cleaning staff, drove her to the service entrance at the back. These comments are in no way indicative of any sense of superiority of mine with regard to the kind of work one does to earn a living. I am presenting them to demonstrate how, in my experience, language and occupation can confer privilege in racialized situations.

However, it's important to say that as a migrant from the Indian subcontinent, I am aware that in both the subcontinent and in the diaspora, we can be racist too. As a mixed-race person, I have experienced queries ranging from ordinary curiosity to patronizing judgment about my not being quite "Indian." I have responded in a variety of ways, depending on my mood at that time, but all essentially reminding the speaker, who might think that because Canada is "multicultural" he cannot be racially marginalized, that India is a very multicultural country as well. The reality is that as a mixed-race woman, I experienced more racializing in India than I have done in Canada, though as a community organizer and activist, I engage in and identify with struggles of the communities I am a part of, against racialism in Quebec and Canada.

Facility with English got me my first job as a secretary in the law faculty at a university, as well as a taste of how status and gender hierarchies operate in the everyday world. At that time, the secretaries, all women, were expected to prepare coffee on a rotational basis for the professors, who would come into the lounge mid-morning for a break. What irked me was that we could not have the coffee. A colleague and I got really exercised over this. We felt that if we were required to prepare the coffee, at least we should be able to drink it. Our coworkers, however, didn't see any inequity and regarded our outrage with a certain curiosity. We approached the professors with whom we worked, including two who are known as defenders of human rights. They were not interested. Therein was a gender and class lesson, as well as the lesson that the little things can provide a litmus test.

Implicit in the outrage I felt was an unconscious feminism. Today, in the courses I teach on gender, where I frustratingly encounter young women who see feminism as something antiquated and "uncool," I find the need to reaffirm its basic definition – equality for women with men. Feminism is at risk. Feminist rhetoric has been mainstreamed, but its essence has been forgotten. It's seen as something passé. My reading of history has led me to conclude that gender inequality ushered into place the first hierarchies and power imbalances, and until real gender equality is reached, other inequalities – class, race, economics, politics – will not be erased. The power imbalance that generated and maintained male power and privilege generated other powers that perpetuate their privilege through war, conquest, colonialism, imperialism, and neoliberalism.

My early experiences with feminism were atypical. I was raised in a family of strong women, and though to some extent there was a gender division of labour at home, my mother did not know how to cook and never entered the kitchen. Like many middle-class families in India, we had domestic help. The aunts I grew up with did not lead traditional lives. They were business and career women, independent and autonomous, and I assumed this was the norm. Though I found it bewildering on train journeys in India, where fellow passengers quickly elicit all the details of your life, that there would be a "tsk, tsk" on hearing that I had no brothers. "So sad." My father and mother, however, never conveyed to us three daughters any disappointment at not having a son.

Coming of age politically in the mid-seventies meant living with the reality of a dictatorship in India, which galvanized political opposition in the service of democratization. Around the world it was also the time of re-awakening, including a new wave of feminism, informed by the experience that winning the vote or independence from colonialism did not necessarily eliminate gender and other inequalities. Much more needed to be done. There was a surge of feminist engagement – organizing, re-framing issues, publishing magazines and newsletters. For me in Montreal, involved in expatriate politics for democracy in India, and informed by this new feminist awareness, I got to know like-minded women and we eventually founded the South Asian Women's Community Centre (SAWCC) in Montreal. The first organization of its kind in North America, it has withstood the test of time and is now more than three decades old. At the time SAWCC began, there was little in the city by way of political or feminist organizing for minority women. We felt a pressing need for a support and advocacy organization for South Asian women and their families.

From the start, we did not see ourselves engaged in a philanthropic endeavour. Implicit in our activism and organizing was the realization that we were also benefitting. To a large extent, our efforts were inspired by feminist organizing that was taking place in our countries of origin – in Pakistan, against the military dictatorship, where women were the only consistent and persistent political force, in part because Islamization directly affected the lives of women, and in India where there was a growing number of small, autonomous women's organizations across the country. Women organized as women, but were committed to making change that would positively impact their families and communities. For me, working on women's issues was about making connections with all aspects of women's lives. Working in solidarity and sisterhood with other women was very powerful, exciting, and sustaining. In the process, we forged our own understanding of feminism, which at times was challenged. For example, "Why are men also at the centre?"

By this time I was in graduate school and torn between organizing and academia. Eventually I realized both were possible, and it made sense to complete my master's degree in history. Unsurprisingly, my thesis was on an aspect of women's history in colonial India. This was a time when the discipline of women's history was still developing, and there was little available, theoretically or empirically. It was at times very disorienting to arrive at conclusions that seemed logical, but were such a radical departure from what had been written till then. There was a dearth of feminist work that might have reaffirmed or corroborated what I was discovering. At times I felt I was going over the edge. Today so much has been published. Young women have so much feminist and gender-based analyses to draw on. Thankfully, feminist research and feminist history are no longer as lonely and isolating as they once were.

My experiences in organizing and academia have taught me that one must have friends and allies who are a source of sustenance, solidarity, and strength. Living a life of resistance can be exhausting, lonely, and demoralizing. It's so difficult to go against the grain. And it's not that one chooses to be oppositional. It happens when you stay true to your understanding of reality, and when the conclusions you reach are informed by lived experiences and factors, such as in my case, a critical reading of history. The contradictions become apparent and then you have to choose to live with them or to challenge and change the imbalance of power and the hegemonic control of dominant ideologies – class, race, gender, economics, politics – wherever you find them.

For example, with the SAWCC, it would have been easier to stay with the mainstream and evolve into a service-providing organization. However, that would have meant abandoning our foundational objectives of service, support, and advocacy, which we saw as intertwined. And this meant at times taking on government policies and practices, questioning governments that might be our grant providers. We felt there was no option; we needed to bring attention to things that would not otherwise be aired. This also meant we had some rocky times, when some in the organization wanted it to become a service provider only. We struggled and survived and today are unique in comparison to many women's centres, in that we straddle different arenas.

A decade after 9/11, our communities are still under threat. Our work and track record had gained us respect and legitimacy. It was important that we used this to defend our communities against security certificates, increased racism, and other forms of oppression. This coincided in Quebec, as in other places, with the emergence of what I call "secular fundamentalism." In response to such attacks, when we applied the "choice" principle with respect to a woman wearing the hijab, it meant that we might have been accused of siding with the "oppression" of women. However, in tricky situations with respect to women's rights, the "choice" principle brings balance to debates and discussions. Of course choice itself is problematic, because it is impossible to determine how "free" one's choice is. Overt, covert, and emotional pressures can be brought to bear. When we spoke out in support of women's right to choose, without coercion, to be veiled, we could draw a parallel to marching with many Québecers, in 1989, in support of Chantal Daigle's right to terminate her pregnancy, a struggle that resulted in the Supreme Court striking down Canada's abortion law. "Choice without coercion" is also useful in determining where one stands on other issues that divide feminists, such as sex work and prostitution. Definitely, as with all debates and discussions, contextualization is most important. The privilege to "choose" is not afforded to all.

In these neoliberal times of globalization, flexibility and choice have come to mean different things to different people. In the pursuit of maximizing profit, businesses and corporations promote a race to the bottom as something advantageous and desirable. Flexible and contract work have become the norm. As women, we always pick up the slack. Cutbacks in spending and services mean that women are expected to do more with less. Whether we are living in a Canada reshaped by Harper or some other country, we find ourselves embattled on many fronts – economics, migration, the environment, racism. At times it's overwhelming. But as women organizers, we are committed and we are very effective. As we move in more visible ways out of the household, we are the victims of our own success, carrying multiple burdens and multitasking as never before, because there is still so much basic and essential change needed to smash ideologies and systems that are implicitly patriarchal – even as they don the rhetoric of feminism. We need to remember that what has sustained us, throughout decades, will sustain us in the future – working together in solidarity, finding kindred spirits, and laughing in struggle, together.

Dolores Chew was born and raised in Kolkata, India. She combines academic expertise with grassroots activism and finds "migrant feminism" the most apt description for what grounds her positions. She is a founding member of the South Asian Women's Community Centre in Montreal and the 8th March Committee of Women of Diverse Origins. In addition, she is an historian at Marianopolis College, a research associate at the Simone de Beauvoir Institute of Concordia University, and is on the editorial committee of the journal LABOUR, Capital and Society/TRAVAIL capital et société. *She is also a member of South Asia Research Centre, Montreal.*

MY CONTINUING STRUGGLE FOR PERSONAL
AND SOCIAL TRANSFORMATION

Cecilia Diocson

I take the view that my continuing political activism and community organizing are generally a product of my long years of social practice and study of the history of human society. They are an important part of my everyday life, and I try to practice them wherever I go. The past helps me understand and appreciate the present, even as the present allows me to glimpse the future. There is continuity and discontinuity in human history, including my own experience. There are significant events and certain junctures in my own personal history that push me to continue with my activism and organizing. The key is to be able to identify these events and conjunctures, and see the links between the past, the present, and future in the context of their particular place and time.

My political activism started prior to my coming to Canada. I had just graduated as a registered nurse in the Philippines when martial law was declared in September 1972. The military regime suspended civil liberties and committed massive human rights violations. Like many young Filipinos, I was immediately drawn into the struggle for human rights, social justice, and the restoration of civil liberties in the Philippines.

I was twenty-four years old when I immigrated to Canada in 1975 and worked as a registered nurse at one of the hospitals in Montreal. At that time, Quebec nurses, through our union, were engaged in an intense struggle with the provincial government for higher wages and better working conditions. We held rallies, demonstrations, and even strikes. We eventually succeeded in our efforts – a major victory that saw big improvements in our lives and working conditions. For me, this demonstrated the importance of collective struggle and organizing for working people. This was my first foray into political activism in Canada, and a reconnection with my political activism in the Philippines.

In the 1970s, especially the early period, social movements and radical protests were reaching their peak in North America, including Canada. While the Vietnam War was winding down, a newly arising neoliberal globalization, in the form of Structural Adjustment Programmes, was beginning to wreak havoc among the countries of the South. Second-wave feminism, the civil rights movement in the US, a global student movement, and support for national liberation movements were raging all over the world. All these helped sustain my involvement in political and social activism. In Montreal, I got involved with my partner in supporting the struggle for national freedom and democracy in the Philippines, and in international solidarity work against US imperialism. With other like-minded Filipino Canadians, we formed the Association of Progressive Filipinos. We subsequently transformed it into the Centre for Philippine Concerns, to include broader issues such as support for the struggle of Filipino women against class exploitation and gender oppression.

The economic crisis in the Philippines was brought about by Structural Adjustments Programmes imposed by the World Bank and the International Monetary Fund. These programs pushed Filipinos to find employment abroad. Many of the migrant workers created by these programs were women who left the country to work as domestic workers in various parts of the world including Canada. When I began working with these women, we shared our stories as migrants and immigrants. They expressed their difficulties in working in a foreign land, silently enduring gender oppression and racism. Feelings of loneliness, insecurity, isolation, and longing for family reunification were constant reminders of their emotional and mental states. Despite being a nurse and an independent immigrant, I began to realize that my experience as a working woman of colour in a predominantly racialized society was not much different from these women's. Eventually, I found myself confronting the issues of class, gender, and race. The intersection of these areas of concerns led to my further studies and understanding of women's issues, and my practical work of organizing Filipino women in Canada.

My husband, two young kids, and I moved from Montreal to Vancouver in July 1986. Immediately, we searched for a progressive organization where we could integrate and find people who were supportive of the kind of work we had been doing in Montreal. We found the BC Committee for Human Rights in the Philippines

(BCCHRP), a church and labour-related human rights organization. It was the appropriate place for us. Soon, the women members of BCCHRP saw a great need to form our own women's caucus to address women's issues in the Philippines.

Together with another member who was a domestic worker, we decided to organize the Philippine Women Centre of BC (PWC) to look at the concerns of Filipino women in Canada, particularly those who came as domestic workers. We showed the precarious situation of these women under Canada's Foreign Domestic Movement Program to the BCCHRP women's caucus and encouraged them to be critical of this program. As a result, the caucus was drawn more into the struggle and organizing of domestic workers.

The groundwork for the PWC began in 1987. Its main objectives were to support the struggle of Filipino women for national and social liberation and specifically to look at the conditions of Filipino women in Canada, especially those who have come under Canada's Foreign Domestic Movement Program, which was subsequently changed to the Live-in Caregiver Program (LCP). The three main pillars of its activities were education, mobilization, and organizing. We emphasized the concepts of class, gender, and race in our education program with the knowledge that we are part of the working class that happen to be women of colour, employed to work in the private homes of Canadian families.

Combining studies and social practice, PWC went on to mobilize Filipino women and their allies around particular issues of the day, including two key issues: Canada's LCP and our struggle for settlement and integration into Canadian society.

Filipino women who enter under the LCP constitute around 20 percent of all Filipinos in this country. Coming in under temporary status, without landed papers, women are vulnerable to various forms of exploitation and oppression. With hardly any support from the Filipino community or the Philippine government, women are left to fend for themselves. As women workers of colour doing low-wage work that most Canadians are reluctant to do, these women and their issues are concrete expressions of how class, gender, and race are intertwined and produced under the current neoliberal agenda of globalization. Under these circumstances, the process of educating and mobilizing can only be implemented successfully if there is an organized structure that systematizes and gives direction to this process. Hence, the need for organizing work that educates women about their issues and helps them take actions through political mobilization. This is the dialectics of education, mobilization, and organizing that sustains my commitment to political activism and community organizing. And our members are proud to say that we are the first Filipino women's centre formed in Canada specifically to address women's concerns through their empowerment.

Using the PWC as the base in our organizing and political work, we expanded nationally. The PWC became the reference point in our alliance work with other communities and women's groups. Contacts with progressive academics attracted to our comprehensive community program, including our community-based research and study using the Participatory Action Research (PAR) methodology, were established. Eventually I would lead our research team in collaborating with these academic allies, resulting in scholarly publications that would help further the work and issues of Filipino women in Canada.

In 1999, together with the other officers of PWC, I initiated the first national consultation of Filipino women in Canada. More than one hundred women from across Canada attended this affair, which had guest speakers from the Philippines and the United States. During this historic consultation, we reflected and learned about the experiences and struggles of Filipino women outside the Philippines. We identified the need for a national women's organization of Philippine women in Canada to coordinate and help advance our struggle for women's equality and intensify the campaign for the scrapping of the Live-in Caregiver Program – a policy and program which we defined as anti-worker, anti-woman, and racist. This was a major step in our national activities.

In 2002, we finally realized the formation of the National Alliance of Philippine Women in Canada as the umbrella of different Filipino women's organizations that members of PWC helped organize in several cities. Our issues and concerns had finally attained national focus and attention. Soon, I was invited to speak at various international conferences on women and the feminization of global migration. In 2010, together with some community leaders, we launched the formation of the Congress of Progressive Filipinos in Canada, with a mandate to help build or strengthen a socialist movement in Canada, mainly within the Filipino-Canadian community, particularly among youth, women, and workers.

My political and community activism took a major turn in 2008. Until that time, a big part of my work was supporting the struggle of the Filipino people for their national and social liberation. In many ways, this support work was the foundation of my activism in Canada, including participation in the struggle of Filipino live-in caregivers,

Over time, however, my years of work in women and community empowerment made me realize that these issues are mainly Canadian issues. For instance, our fight to scrap the LCP and the struggle for settlement and integration are Canadian issues that directly impact Filipinos in Canada and Canadian society. Both issues must be addressed and responded to by Canadians and the Canadian state. Thus, we refocused our work in the Philippines and put front and centre the struggle of Filipinos in Canada to stay, settle, and integrate into Canadian society.

I believe that Canadian feminism, or the women's movement in Canada, which, at this stage, seems to have distanced itself from progressive working-class politics, can make itself more relevant by seriously addressing the issues and struggles of working-class women of colour in Canada. Otherwise, the women's movement will remain in the halls of academia, among middle-class women, and almost irrelevant to the day-to-day politics of working-class women. There must be a real appreciation of the distinction between a women's movement that addresses general women's issues without class distinction, and a revolutionary women's movement that privileges working-class issues, first and foremost. Only the latter can lead to genuine social transformation in the struggle against neoliberal globalization.

The formation of the National Alliance of Philippine Women in Canada – whose role is coordinating and empowering women through the various women's groups under its umbrella – is another major highlight in my life and political activism. I hope to continue with this project, especially in encouraging and helping to develop a new generation of young people to become progressive leaders in the community. Guided by socialist and other progressive agendas, it offers a viable alternative to the present neoliberal agenda of globalization that continues to devastate the lives of the majority of the world's peoples.

I hope to continue doing the work of empowering women. I am fully convinced that, short of socialism, the condition of women in society will always be subordinated to patriarchy and the dominant classes in society. I am also fully aware that this struggle is a protracted process that helps set the foundation for future struggles. I have faith that the future generation will be able to improve or go further in what we have achieved thus far in the struggle for human liberation and an ecologically sustainable society.

Cecilia Diocson is a community researcher, organizer, and speaker. She currently heads the National Alliance of Philippine Women in Canada and Philippine Women Centre of BC. She researches with several academics on various community issues; organized the first National Consultation of Filipino Women in Canada and the first North American Conference of Women of Philippine Ancestry; and headed the Canadian PURPLE ROSE CAMPAIGN, an international campaign to end sex trafficking of Filipino women and children. She was a steering committee member (2002) with the International League of People's Struggles. She co-authored the following research papers: Workplace Rights for Immigrants in BC: The Case of Filipino Workers; Filipino Community and Beyond: Toward Settlement and Integration in a Multicultural Society; *and* Canada: The New Frontier for Filipino Mail-Order Brides.

ROOTS AND WINGS

Khadija Haffajee

The roots of my risk-taking and adventurous ways go back more than a century to my paternal grandparents, newlyweds who left a village in India for the shores of a new land thousands of miles away in South Africa. I am recalling my history in part for my nieces, nephews, and their children because it is important for them to know their roots. Most of them were born after I left South Africa so they only see me for short periods of time when I visit. I am now the elder in the family.

I am number nine of thirteen children, born to a child bride married at the age of thirteen. My mother must have had a difficult life, married so young and literally shipped across an ocean to a new land. A child bride who outlived her husband by some twenty-five years, she was widowed at age thirty-nine and was left no choice but to listen to and follow instructions of the male relatives in the extended family. I learned early on that one had to be confident and speak up for oneself.

She raised her children with strong values of loyalty, honour, and integrity. Education was of paramount importance although she herself was illiterate. Yet she instilled in us the importance of education and acquiring knowledge, together with the value of being financially prudent. These were valuable lessons. My father must have been a feminist, because in his last will and testament he said he wanted his daughters to be educated, to be specialized in their particular field of study. This was at a time when Muslim women did not even complete elementary school!

I was the maverick child who pushed my mother to the limits. She once told me, "The biggest mistake I made was to give you an education!" Why? Because it enabled me to leave home and country nearly fifty years ago.

I quit my teaching position and left South Africa in 1964, travelling to England by boat. Within two days of my arrival, I reported to my new position at a grammar school in Bristol. A day earlier I had been interviewed by the superintendent – a formality to check my proficiency in spoken English.

This period in my life was a time of adjustment as I tried to let go of the indignities of my apartheid upbringing. Apartheid had also taught me the values of self-confidence and the importance of the equality of humanity. I soon started to feel more comfortable in my interactions with my colleagues, having overcome skin-colour politics such as being told to leave restaurants because I had the wrong colour skin.

Two years later, I was ready for another drastic change. The English weather got the better of me. The cold and damp was too much. I decided to leave for Canada – a land of immigrants. In April 1966 I left on another voyage, a weeklong sojourn at sea across the Atlantic. There were incentives for immigrants to come to Canada. My passage was paid by the government, with the agreement that I would repay within a year. This was all explained to me at my initial interview with the Canadian authorities.

On April 18, 1966, the ship docked at Quebec City in the midst of a longshoremen's strike. There was the problem of offloading the luggage from the ship. The one bright light was a letter delivered to my cabin on arrival. What a godsend. It was a letter of welcome to this new land from Peggy and Bill Tyson in Toronto, a Canadian couple I had met the previous summer at the Edinburgh Music Festival. I sent them a telegram explaining what had happened and asked if I could stay with them for a night as I did not want to arrive in Hamilton, my destination, late in the evening.

So it was that I made my way to the train station and boarded the train to Toronto from Quebec City. Peggy and Bill were there to receive me. What a relief to see faces I knew when the train got into Toronto. The next morning I was back on a train to Hamilton. I had booked into the YWCA in downtown Hamilton. I was all alone; I did not know a soul in the city. I made an appointment with the superintendent at the Burlington School Board and managed to find my way there. I was hired on the spot and offered a full-time position for September and as an occasional teacher until then. I could not accept the occasional teaching offer as it meant commuting from Toronto and I did not know how to drive!

My next step was to find some other means of earning a living until September when school started. The first priority of immigrants is to ensure financial security. I checked the classified ads and found a position as a housekeeper with a family in Burlington until the fall, when I would assume my teaching job. This was my introduction to family life in Canada, albeit very upper class. We dressed for dinner. The oldest daughter was sent to finishing school in Switzerland and, of course, we all went off in the summer to the cottage in the Lake of Bays area – sailing, canoeing, etc. All the people I met were very friendly.

My three years at the school in Burlington were spent adjusting to the school system and settling into my new home. I had an apartment on Lakeshore Drive, with Lake Ontario as my backyard. How fortunate can one be? In 1969 there were significant changes to the education system in Ontario. Small municipal school boards were amalgamating into larger county boards, and so it was that I found myself looking at possible moves. I chose Ottawa as the newly formed Carleton School Board was hiring many teachers.

I came to Ottawa in April for the interview. What was I thinking? In Burlington the grass was green. Here in Ottawa, the snow banks were taller than me! I was offered a position, but it was not what I wanted so I negotiated another. Such was the climate in 1969.

My move to Ottawa in July 1969 was the most significant one I had made to date. Many new opportunities presented themselves. Once settled, I explored various avenues. I was elected to the executive of the local teachers' federation.

The seventies were my time for change. I was an unmarried, professional, Muslim female living on her own, which at that time was almost unheard of. It was also a period in my life when my faith became my modus operandi. I decided to wear the hijab. I think I was the first teacher in the public school system in Ontario to do so. There was no public outcry, a contrast from today's constant negativity surrounding the issue of Muslim women and their dress.

I had skills that would benefit my faith community. I was elected president of the local Ottawa Muslim Women's Auxiliary. This was a stepping stone as the board introduced new ideas and moved the organization ahead, and it drew the attention of a national organization, the Council of Muslim Communities in Canada (CMCC), which asked me to head its Women's Committee. This led to travels across the country, to Edmonton, Winnipeg, Montreal, and within Ontario to address Muslim women. I actually sent out a questionnaire to survey how Muslim women were participating at local mosques. I knew that there were challenges as, in Canada, a new role was emerging for these women and I wanted to help them any way we could. Ottawa was used as a model. During this time, women were encouraged to participate as speakers at monthly meetings, to empower them to learn and to present their ideas.

At the same time, I also saw the need for our involvement in mainstream society, so I tried as much as possible to be a part of organizations that promoted women's issues. To this end, I became a member of a minority women's organization and eventually its treasurer. It was an uphill struggle to get other Muslim women to attend these gatherings. Most were expending energy settling into a new environment and had challenges with family and children, as do women of today. In the seventies we were a small community, and access to services was limited and difficult to come by.

Faith played a significant role in my decisions. I joined the World Conference on Religions for Peace (WCRP) in the late seventies. (For a time, I let my membership lapse due to other commitments and rejoined in the nineties. In fact, I represented Canadian Muslim women at the conference held in Amman, Jordan, in 1999.)

In 1986, an opportunity arose that enabled me to travel to Malawi and Zimbabwe to offer leadership training for young Muslim women. At this time I was active in national Muslim organizations, working with women. I had always been committed to empowering my fellow sisters of all ages and had done many youth camps during my summer vacations in Canada and the US.

As a teacher, I had portable skills. What was lacking was solid Islamic education, so I closed this gap by attending seminars and lectures and doing personal study on topics pertaining to women's issues. During the 1980s and 1990s, I was on the lecture circuit at Muslim conferences, addressing women's issues to male and female audiences. I had taken a stand in 1972 that when asked to speak at a conference, I would agree only if I addressed a mixed group. On that occasion, when I was introduced and arrived at the podium, a group of men protested in a loud voice and walked out. I just continued. Today I feel a sense of pride when I see women of all ages up on stage, speaking on issues that affect us as citizens living in this beautiful country.

At a 1995 Beijing conference, we Muslim women were not really accepted by the other groups. My sense was that the others wanted to speak on our behalf, stereotyping us as submissive, veiled women who had to be saved from our oppressors. However, we were present and could speak for ourselves. There was much tension, which was most unfortunate. On my return to Ottawa, the tension was still present when I attended the follow-up meetings. In fact, I was ignored when I tried to speak at the local meetings.

September 1997 was a momentous occasion for Muslim women in general and for me in particular. I was the first woman elected to the decision-making body of the Islamic Society of North America (ISNA), the oldest and largest Muslim organization in North America. A press release was sent out to newspapers. I had entered a bastion of men – twenty-three in all. I served for a decade as I was re-elected twice. In fact, I decided not to run again as I felt very strongly that younger women should step forward.

There is a dearth in the encouragement of creativity in our community. It was an obvious hole waiting to be filled. So in 2008, I invited a group of younger Muslim women to an open brainstorming discussion on meeting this challenge. Out of this initial gathering, we formed Expressions of Muslim Women (EMW). To date we have held four very successful sold-out events celebrating the creativity of Muslim women. We are expanding our efforts by organizing a display and sale of creative arts by Muslim women.

Some positive inroads have been made, but not enough. There are visible signs of inclusion. I sincerely hope they are not just cosmetic changes. What is needed is a system of mentoring young Muslim women so they may have opportunities to learn from more experienced women who take a personal interest in them and help them gain self-confidence – the wings to fly on their own.

Canada is not the welcoming country it was when I landed at Quebec City in 1966. Compared to more recent immigrant stories, mine is more positive. Today, immigrants, especially Muslims, are under the microscope. Over forty years, I have seen the efforts made by my co-religionists to contribute to society; however, the public is deprived of this information. Acceptance of the Other can only come from knowledge, understanding, and most importantly, interaction with dignity and integrity – all, unfortunately, lacking.

Originally from South Africa, Khadija Haffajee has resided in Ottawa for more than four decades. As a retired educator, she uses her skills to promote an accurate understanding of Islam and build interfaith dialogue. In 1997 she was the first female elected to the decision-making body of the Islamic Society of North America. Khadija has long been active in the local community, working with the Children's Hospital of Eastern Ontario, Ottawa Police Services, Children's Aid Society and the Council of Aging, among others. In recognition of her contributions she has received numerous awards for her community leadership and for promoting interfaith dialogue. In 2009 Khadija received the City of Ottawa's Distinguished Civic Award for Humanitarianism.

I'M WITH THE BAD GIRLS:
A FEMINIST LIFE IN FRAGMENTS
Chelby Marie Daigle

GENDER: My hair wouldn't grow long so people thought I was a boy. Strangers would come up to my mother and say, "What a cute little boy." She decided to get my ears pierced and have me wear dresses. I hated dresses and I hated earrings. I also didn't like having to play with girls. At eight, I decided to be a loner. My teachers freaked out and tried to get me to make friends. They were not concerned with all the boys my age who were loners, but there was something that deeply disturbed them about a girl with no friends. I was just so bad at being a girl, from my short hair, to my desire to be alone, to my hatred of boy bands. When I discovered punk and grunge and the character Darlene from the TV show *Roseanne*, I was able to re-imagine a way that I could be a girl on my own terms. I didn't have to have long hair, wear pink, be pretty, date boys, or have friends if I didn't want to. So I spent my teens stomping around in used Doc Marten boots, baggy jeans, plaid shirts, a Korean Army jacket, with short puffy hair, reading Virginia Woolf, and listening to

Hole. My mother wasn't happy, but by that time my D-cup breasts had come in so she didn't have to worry about anyone thinking I was a boy anymore.

CLASS: I grew up on welfare in a social housing community full of single mothers. I wanted to be a single mother when I grew up. When I had to clean my room, I would play the game "The Children's Aid Worker is Coming to Visit" because I grew up with Children's Aid workers coming to visit, and when they came over, you really needed to clean up your house because you never knew where they were going to look. Sometimes the children in the neighbourhood across from ours, where people owned their houses, called us "White Trash." My friend and her mother got cut off of welfare when her mother's boyfriend moved in because of the "Spouse in the House" rule – which meant, if the government thought you were living with a man you should be completely financially dependent on him. In my early twenties, when I decided to move back in with my mother after a period of being homeless, she begged me to apply for social assistance so that I would get drug benefits. At the Ontario Works office, they asked if I had been living with a boyfriend for more than three months. I left without answering. I would find another way to cover my medication.

RACE: In 2002, at the second Colour of Violence Conference organized by INCITE Women of Colour Against Violence in Chicago, I attended the Black Women's Caucus. I was the only Canadian in a group of about twenty black American women. We went around in a circle introducing ourselves and I said I was half-white. Immediately, a woman in the circle shouted at me that I was trying to claim white privilege by saying I was half-white. I shouted back that I was just being honest about my experience. My mother was white; I was raised in a white family in a predominantly white neighbourhood. I also explained that even my black identity was different from theirs because I knew my father's last name and where my ethnic group came from in Nigeria; my ancestors weren't stolen from Western and Central Africa and given the last names of their white slave masters. I wasn't trying to claim privilege; I was refusing to appropriate other black peoples' experiences.

This stirred up a lot of debate within the circle. Eventually, the woman who shouted at me admitted that she had grown up saying she was Puerto Rican because her parents told her it was better to be Puerto Rican than black. After the arguing and debating, we all started crying about different things. One woman cried about not being able to tell her grandmother, who had raised her, that she was a lesbian for fear that she would disown her. One woman cried about how her mother never believed her when she told her she was being sexually abused. One woman cried about all the young men who had died in the gang wars in her neighbourhood. I cried about growing up not knowing what to do with my hair and not knowing any black women who could teach me what it meant to be a black woman. I cried about having never known my father along with all the other women in the circle who were also crying because they had never known their fathers. After we cried a lot, we started clapping and singing and decided that the next day we would do a traditional West African libation (a ritual pouring of liquid, usually palm wine or water, as an offering to the ancestors) at the opening plenary, which I volunteered to participate in even though I had no idea what a libation was.

VIOLENCE: Growing up knowing that my grandfather was able to sexually abuse his children, grandchildren, and foster children with impunity because he was the "Head of Our Household" made me want to live in a world where women and children were NOT dependent on men. I gravitated toward spaces that supported survivors of sexual violence. I volunteered on crisis lines at Carleton University's Women's Centre and the Sexual Assault Support Centre, counselling women who had been recently sexually assaulted or were coping with past experiences of abuse. At the time I was involved with these organizations, I had not received any counselling for my own trauma. I think this is often true for young feminists; we want to help others facing the problems we ourselves are grappling with, or avoiding grappling with. Sometimes I think taking on the roles of "crisis counsellors" or even "social workers" is a comforting distraction from dealing with our own trauma. I have always found it easier to help others than to help myself.

"Coming out" as a survivor of incest has been pretty liberating. I refuse to feel ashamed about something that isn't my fault, but I know that sometimes people see this as a piece of information that is too personal to be shared, particularly within professional feminist circles. I agree that you shouldn't tell clients about your personal trauma because that will just focus attention on you when it should be focused on them. But I do think speaking publicly as a survivor is important, particularly as a way of supporting other survivors. Because I have spoken publicly about my experience at conferences or even in casual social circles, other women have felt safe to come out to me about their own experiences – not for support, but just because it is nice to know you are not alone, that you are not a freak, that this "dirty secret" doesn't have to separate you from others, it can actually connect you to them.

BEAUTY: I am fat and ugly. Women always get so upset and try to shower me with compliments and advice when I say this. "No, Chelby, you are so cute." "No, Chelby, I think you are actually losing weight!" "No, Chelby, a lot of black men think fat women are sexy, so go marry a black man!" When I try to explain that I'm okay with being fat and ugly, everyone just gets confused. We still live in societies that equate a woman's worth with her physical beauty and her ability to attract a man. I have even found many "feminist" spaces to be quite "lookist," where it's seen as fine to insult a woman by calling her fat or ugly: "She's such a second-wave feminist...and she's so ugly!"

CITIZENSHIP: Through my work with First Nations, Métis, and Inuit communities, I have been trying to learn how I can work in solidarity with their struggles, unlearn my prejudices, and unpack my settler privilege. It's hard to look at our prejudices and privileges, the ways in which we are complicit in other people's marginalization. It is always easier to point the finger at others – White People, Capitalists, the One Percent. I am no longer interested in delineating all the ways in which someone else is a horrible oppressor. All I have control over is myself and what I do, so I need to take a good hard look at myself and change.

SOLIDARITY: Since my late teens, I have always had queer friends of colour. Many of my friends have had to struggle with both the homophobia of their ethno-cultural and religious communities and the racism and anti-immigrant sentiment within queer communities. Needless to say this totally sucks. I feel that the homophobia within communities of colour goes beyond religious arguments and actually questions the cultural authenticity of queer members of our communities, as if the Somali woman who is queer doesn't care about the famine, or the Tamil woman who is queer doesn't care about Tamil Eelam (Sri Lanka), or the Palestinian woman who is queer doesn't care about Self-Determination, or the Jamaican woman who is queer doesn't care that it's the 50th anniversary of Jamaican Independence! But they do, and why wouldn't they? I really hope to see more feminist of colour spaces in Ottawa and Canada actively work at becoming safer and more inclusive of queer women of colour, otherwise I don't see how they can think that they at all reflect the true diversity of women of colour's lives in this country.

FEMINISM: When I hear that a woman has become the president of a country or a corporation, I'm, like, "meh." I do want to see women become leaders in politics, business, religion, sports, etc. but this doesn't inspire me. Besides, these women are often just as likely to be complicit in the oppression of marginalized women as men are. I get excited when I hear that Nigerian sex workers organized a march in Lagos in honour of International Sex Workers' Rights Day. I am inspired more by the achievements of women who are often shamed in our societies by both men and women, and even some feminists – the Bad Girls. I'm more inspired by their activism, their resistance, their resilience – because it's harder.

Chelby Marie Daigle has been working and volunteering to support survivors of sexual violence for more than a decade. She worked as a facilitator for the Ottawa Rape Crisis Centre's Girls' Chat program in local high schools for more than five years, and chaired their advisory committee to support youth, service providers, concerned family, and community members on issues related to violence framed as honour and forced marriage. As a feminist, she is inspired primarily by black feminist thinkers (Audre Lorde, bell hooks, and Angela Davis), and the activities of Sub-Saharan African feminist organizations (Baobab for Women's Rights) that address intersection and divisions of race, class, gender, sexuality, religion, and ethnicity. She also works as an anti-oppression educator for local non-profit organizations.

BUILDING THE IMMIGRANT WOMEN'S MOVEMENT: REMINISCENCES OF AN ACTIVIST AND ACADEMIC

Roxana Ng

In the early 1970s, the early years of the second-wave women's movement in Canada, I was a new immigrant, having arrived in Vancouver from the British Colony of Hong Kong in the late summer of 1970 with my family (my parents and two younger brothers). I was in my late teens. Almost overnight, I changed from being a confident, middle-class young woman who knew her place in the world, to being an immigrant "child" who was patronized at every turn, treated as if my English wasn't good enough; ironically, I spoke with a British accent at the time, having spent two years of boarding school education in England. In college, especially during the first year, I was seen as the shy, reactionary, conservative, slightly backward young person who had to be civilized. This was a blow to my sense of self. I did, over the next few years, become reticent and silent. I was isolated and silenced.

Meanwhile, family dynamics also changed. Patriarchy in the Chinese family, previously hidden, reared its ugly head. My father, who I considered extremely liberal and who had always encouraged his children to be social, educated, and out in the world, became controlling and fearful. No doubt this was due to his own sense of insecurity and experiences of discrimination and racism, although he never mentioned them. He was a social worker by training and by profession, having obtained his BSW and MSW at the University of

Toronto in the 1960s. He had achieved the highest attainable administrative position as a Chinese in colonial Hong Kong. However, like many professional immigrants, then and now, his extensive work experience was not recognized; it took him more than six months to obtain an entry position as a social worker in the BC government. Starting all over again in his midforties, he never regained his former status, and was forced into early retirement due to restructuring just before he turned sixty. He became bitter and angry. We were the recipients of his frustration, which still flares up.

My mother didn't want to immigrate, because for her it would mean isolation and loss of status. She came from a large, well-to-do business family. Growing up, we were surrounded by uncles, aunts, and cousins. We had domestic help. Not only did my mother enjoy and receive support from her extended family, she had a responsible position in a government-run home for juvenile delinquents prior to immigration. In Canada, she became a housewife in the truest sense of the word. When she attempted to find paid employment, the only work she could get was temporary menial jobs in restaurants, factories, and occasionally clerical positions in Chinese-run agencies, due to her lack of proficiency in English. She, too, became bitter and angry, and blamed my father for her unhappiness.

In many ways, my family story is a typical one for immigrants. But I was not to know this until much later, when I began to do research on immigrant women – a silent group whose experiences I was determined to expose. I graduated with a master's degree in anthropology in 1975. I have always loved school and enjoyed learning. Unfortunately, my post-secondary education was a lesson in sexism and racism. Here are two unforgettable incidents: First, although I was an A student, the message I received was that I wasn't good enough academically. My memory of receiving my first and only C, in a third-year undergraduate anthropology course, is etched vividly in my mind. Upon getting the poor grade, I met with the teacher to see how I could improve my work. The instructor, a prominent anthropologist, told me that I had a very analytical mind, but no intellect. Since the latter was something one was born with, there was nothing I could do about it. The fact that I couldn't tell the difference between intellectual and analytical abilities was proof that I couldn't cut it as a scholar.

The second incident occurred during my master's study. A history professor gave me a B for a course where my average was an A throughout. When I spoke with him, he told me in all seriousness that he couldn't give everyone (five in the class; I was the only female) an A, so he gave me a B because, as a woman who would soon be married, I didn't need the grade to go on with my education. These were my early, blatant, encounters of racialized sexism. I say "racialized" because I now have no doubt that the instructors' perception of me as a lesser student was not only rooted in sexism, which of course it was. It was furthermore influenced by my status as an ethnic minority in a white-dominated society. Had I remained in Hong Kong, my educational outcome would have been very different.

I left the University of British Columbia (UBC) in 1975 with two degrees, vowing never to enter the academy again. I got a job in Strathcona – Chinatown – at first as a researcher. I then became a counsellor cum community worker in a demonstration project funded by the federal government. The idea underlying the project was to prove that indeed Chinese immigrants had special needs not addressed by the mainstream service delivery network. The project was spearheaded by community leaders and supervised by a social work professor from UBC. The staff consisted mainly of young professional Chinese immigrants who, in spite of their training and education, could not find paid work in the mainstream system – indicating another way in which racialized minorities were marginalized and relegated to ethnic enclaves.

My university education was not entirely negative. The highlight of my time at UBC was the introductory course on anthropology and sociology, which exposed students to current issues in Canadian society. The course was co-ordinated that year by eminent feminist sociologist Dorothy Smith. In addition to weekly lectures in a huge auditorium, we also had weekly tutorials to discuss the issues covered in the lectures. The hand of fate put me in a tutorial led by Dorothy Smith. Through her, I was exposed to feminist ideas. I listened with interest to the many issues covered in the course: women and sex roles (yes, it was called that at the time), Aboriginal people (we were told the term "Indian" was derogatory), the FLQ crisis (which erupted right after we arrived in Canada, shattering the myth that Canada was a peaceful country), and the US domination of Canada. I don't believe racism was part of the discussion then. But in this course I began to question the role of women in Chinese and Canadian societies and my upbringing – how did I come to be the person I was? Was it nature or nurture? What were the options open to women? Recall that the male professors, whom I met later on, suggested that biology was immutable, but this course had sowed the seeds of doubt in my naive mind.

Working as a researcher/counsellor/community worker, I quickly realized that women's experience of immigration was different from that of men's. While my main role was to compile statistics on the clients the program served, the receptionist began to send me women who came in for service. She sensed that they needed to talk to a woman and I would be empathetic. I discovered that women all over the world share many similar problems. Non-English-speaking Chinese immigrant women encountered isolation, had problems with in-laws, faced abuse by their husbands, and were neglected by the mainstream service delivery system. Some of these issues, especially those pertaining to negative family dynamics, were brushed aside by my male and some female colleagues as cultural and hence "normal," although there was a recognition that immigration might have exacerbated these problems. I was stymied by simple cultural explanations, but didn't have alternative theories to make sense of what I was witnessing.

In search of answers and explanations, I went to see Dorothy Smith, who, surprisingly, remembered me. Dorothy was in the process of setting up the Vancouver Women's Research Centre (WRC), a feminist research collective outside of the academy, which would work with women to do research on their communities, using an approach that would eventually be coined "institutional ethnography" (IE). She recruited me to be part of the collective, and we established a committee on immigrant women, looking into the conditions I found in my work. Through the WRC, we organized a series of four workshops in the summer of 1977, which brought together immigrant women working in the service delivery system to share experiences as immigrants and as women working with immigrant women to identify commonalities and gaps in our understanding of, and work with, immigrant women. Although we did not arrive at definitive conclusions, our meeting opened up spaces for questions, dialogues, and further investigation. The series was compiled in a report published by the WRC. The following summer, with a small grant from Health and Welfare Canada, the Immigrant Women's Committee of the WRC conducted a study, informed by IE and feminist theory, on the experience of family violence among immigrant women in Vancouver. Another report was produced that was circulated informally among immigrant women's groups beyond BC.

By the time I began my doctoral study in Toronto in the fall of 1978, immigrant women in many Canadian cities were voicing their concerns and demanding the establishment of appropriate services to address their needs. My intent in returning to the academy was to make "immigrant women" a legitimate field of study and to participate in the emerging movement that would put us on the social and political map of Canada. With Judith Ramirez of the Immigrant Women's Centre, I conducted a study that began in 1979 that would become one of the first published books on immigrant women. I was learning and honing my skills as an IE researcher, and this method would become a leading approach to most of my research in the years to come.

The decade from the late 1970s to the late 1980s was a heady one as we analyzed and contextualized the conditions of our lives. Riding on the momentum created by the second-wave feminist movement, we organized and built communities in cities large and small. We demanded that the state respond to our needs in education and in society. Although we participated in the feminist movement, we also challenged its racism and class bias. I completed my doctorate in 1984 and became a migrant academic; that is, I was going across the country in search of employment. But unlike my isolation when I first immigrated, this time, I met other immigrant women who took me into their fold wherever I went: in the Prairies, in Central Canada, and in the Atlantic region.

When I returned to Toronto to take up my current position at the University of Toronto in 1988, the social landscape was much different from the one I found when I had arrived ten years previously. Not only were there immigrant women's groups in different parts of the city; many were for specific communities and addressed specific issues (e.g., domestic violence or employment). Some specialized in advocacy while others were resource centres. Immigrant and racialized women had also made inroads into mainstream women's organizations such as NAC (the National Action Committee on the Status of Women) and CRIAW (the Canadian Research Institute for the Advancement of Women). But there were also more divisions among us: we had to confront the differences within, be it religious, social, political, or economic.

As neoliberalism gained momentum as an economic and ideological force, state funding began to dry up. Since the late 1990s, we have witnessed the demise of many women's groups in general, and immigrant women's groups in particular. Many of us have been absorbed into the mainstream, myself included. The condition of our lives, albeit much improved in some ways, is putting new limits on our participation in civil society. Speaking personally, as I become more entrenched in the university system, the demands of my job and the high cost of living in a metropolis (with longer and longer commuting time) mean that I can no longer participate as readily in what I have come to identify as my community. As I get older, my energy is more limited. However, I am comforted by the fact that we have changed the social landscape of Canada irrevocably, and that I do have a network of women with whom I am connected, if only in spirit. This collection is an indication of the achievement and enduring strength of our movement. I am also optimistic that the movement is being carried forward by younger women who are continuing the work begun in the heyday of the immigrant women's movement and who are finding new ways of building alliances and communities ahead.

At age 19, Roxana emigrated from Hong Kong to Canada with her parents and two brothers. She passed away in Toronto in January 2013 after a short and courageous battle with cancer. As a professor of adult education and community development at OISE and the director of the Centre for Women's Studies in Education, her work shaped the field of immigration studies, especially by drawing links between race, gender, class, and the experiences of immigrant women. Roxana's passion for human rights and social justice encompassed her professional life as well as her community-based activism. Even as her body weakened from cancer, she shared her research findings about foreign-trained professionals with her caregivers (many of whom were immigrant nurses) – encouraging them to study for their certifications while she napped.

(Adapted from "In Memoriam: Roxana Ng," *U of T Magazine*, Autumn, 2013) downloaded from: magazine.utoronto.ca/ life-on-campus/in-memoriam-roxana-ng/

ACKNOWLEDGEMENTS

For all of us, working on this collection has truly been a labour of love. We have worked as a collective for almost four years to guide, shape, coax, and nurture this book to life. The journey has been long but it has also brought us much pleasure, forging new friendships, strengthening old ones, and opening new networks and resources. From the outset, we were blessed with a shared sense of purpose and excitement, as well as deep commitment to the project directed at giving voice to racialized women's life stories in Canada. This solidarity with the project's vision, and the strength of our personal friendships, is what kept us meeting month after month to discuss, plan, and problem solve around the book, and to share recent ups and downs in our own lives. Even when circumstances made it difficult to meet in person, we maintained regular contact through emails, contributing our perspectives on issues being discussed.

In that we are all women from diverse cultural backgrounds who hold a strong sense of "community," our meetings and social interactions inevitably involved food and brewing some tea. This social component enabled us to share laughter and get caught up on each other's lives. Although a pre-developed agenda was always in hand to guide our discussions, outside observers might have wondered how we managed to cover all the agenda items when we all wanted to speak at the same time and discuss issues in a non-linear fashion. Being strong women, at times we were passionate and firm in expressing and defending our ideas and disagreeing with others. At other times, we were equally passionate in supporting and defending each other's positions.

In many respects, we became a family. We worked hard together and we had fun together. In hindsight, this is likely what kept us going for the almost four years it has taken to give wings to this collection. With our shared sense of purpose and friendship, meeting and working together was fun, not onerous. Our gatherings nourished us socially, psychologically, and spiritually.

Our greatest reward and inspiration was receiving these life stories from racialized women across Canada. What is truly remarkable about this collection is its inclusion of experiences and voices of everyday women, from all facets of life, who are too often overlooked or marginalized in Canadian women's history. Therefore, we are first and foremost indebted to all the women who took on the challenge of writing their personal narratives so that they could be shared with the broader public. We appreciate that for many, this was the first time they had taken time to reflect and write about personal aspects of their lives and that this likely evoked varying degrees of anxiety and trepidation. For some, this might have been reluctance in exposing aspects of their lives that could be judged or misunderstood by others. Several may also have experienced uncertainties about expressing ideas and emotions in a language that was not their mother tongue. Being aware of these tensions, we are grateful to all the women who contributed to this rich collection.

We are equally indebted to the Feminist History Society, particularly Diana Majury and Constance Backhouse for encouraging us to pursue this project and for hanging in there with us for the long haul. In the project's final few years, Diana Majury became our primary link with the Feminist History Society and its publisher, Second Story Press. In this capacity, she became a friend and mentor, providing support, advice, encouragement, and constructive criticism along the way. She also became a regular member of our collective, joining in our meetings and discussions and sharing of food and laughter. As we entered into the editing phase, she and Rashmi Luther also collaborated closely in fine-tuning the manuscript, getting it ready for publication.

We are also grateful to two Ottawa-based organizations: Immigrant Women Services Ottawa (IWSO) and Ottawa Community Immigrant Services Organization (OCISO) for generously offering us meeting space, not to mention food and countless cups of tea over the years.

A special thank you is also extended to Benilda Formoso Ladouceur and Caroline Lavoie. Benilda took on the challenge of tracking down and organizing photos and artwork, some of it from IWSO. Caroline supported the project by generously translating all our "call out" materials into French.

Finally, we are indebted to our publisher Margie Wolfe of Second Story Press. She received a very preliminary and unedited draft of the manuscript and immediately recognized the project's value, including its potential to share experiential insights and knowledge with a broad and varied readership.

—Rashmi Luther, Vanaja Dhruvarajan, Ikram Ahmed Jama, Yumi Kotani, Monia Mazigh, Peruvemba S. Jaya, and Lucya Spencer

SPECIAL ACKNOWLEDGEMENT

We would like to thank Rashmi Luther for her wonderful energy, enthusiasm and drive in spearheading this project and inviting us all to be a part of it. Her leadership, friendship, warmth, and team spirit inspired us all. Thank you, Rashmi.

—Book Project Collective: Vanaja Dhruvarajan, Ikram Ahmed Jama, Yumi Kotani, Monia Mazigh, Lucya Spencer, Peruvemba S. Jaya

APPENDIX A

Racialized Immigrant and Refugee Women's Stories about
Significant Life Experiences in Canada (1960s to the Present)

We are writing to you as members of a diverse working group of
women who are developing a collection of stories about women who
have been racialized in Canada as "visible minorities" or "women of
colour." We encourage stories about your personal, professional or
activist life experiences, as well as involvement with women's issues,
movements and organizations in Canada since the 1960s. This collection will be a part of a series of books being published by the
Feminist History Society in Ottawa. It will contribute to broadening
our understanding about the lives of racialized women in Canada,
including their challenges and contributions.

We see this as an exciting opportunity to celebrate the voices
and lives of many diverse women who have experienced differen-
tiation based on our "colour" and/or "dress." This includes women
who may be earlier or more recent immigrants or refugees and their
daughters, as well as second or third generation "Canadians." We are
also interested in contributions that reflect on your struggles with
feminism and feminist terminologies with respect to culture, race,
language and religion. As well, stories that capture your involvement in feminist/women's movements, organizations and issues are
also encouraged.

One hope is that the collected stories will enable us to more fully appreciate and theorize about the richness of women's experiences, the creative ways we have tapped opportunities and overcome challenges, as well as the insights we have gained as women. Another is that we will be able to share, with each other and the broader Canadian public, some of the lessons we have learned about ourselves and women's lives based on our individual and collective experiences. We also hope that this collection will help us further value and celebrate our many strengths, talents, creativity and contributions to enriching lives, our own as well as our families, communities, other women in Canada, and those in our respective "homelands."

To contribute to this important collection, please send us your written submissions, up to 2,000 words in length, by July 15, 2012. The stories can take the form of essays, letters, poetry, drama or drawings. These will be collected and edited, as autobiographical texts, in a book we hope to publish by the end of 2012. Some questions that might help you to identify what aspect to write about include:

- How did you address the struggles/challenges you encounter in Canada? What suggestions would you have for others facing similar experiences? What skills did you use or develop in the process?

- What was a defining moment in your life? What was its significance? How did this shape you?

- How were you transformed by your life experiences? How did this affect others around you? How did your life experiences shape your commitment to women's issues? What insights did you gain?

- In reflecting on your life to date, what stories would you like to tell your grandchildren or future generations? What legacy would you like to leave behind?

- What people or events inspired or influenced you and your life's direction? How would you like to inspire or influence others in your life?

- What significant insights have you gained? How might these help other women?

- What do you hope for in your life? What is your hope for future generations?

- In recognizing that there are many "feminisms" due to the plurality and diversity present among women, what does the term feminism mean to you? What is your relationship with it (positive or negative)? How has it influenced you and your life either personally or professionally?

- From the 1960s onward in Canada, women were asserting their rights and society was changing rapidly. How did you relate to the women's movement in Canada in those years? Did it make a difference to how you led your life or your own choices?

- What women's organizations or community-based organizations that worked with women have you been active with? What were your experiences and how did this influence you as a woman?

We hope that you are as excited about this project as we are and that you will consider sending us your story. We also ask that you tell your friends and colleagues about this project and send us their names and contact information so that we can encourage them to write as well.

Thank you,

RASHMI LUTHER Community Activist and Faculty Member, School of Social Work, Carleton University, Ottawa

VANAJA DHRUVARAJAN Adjunct Professor, Pauline Jewett Institute of Women's Studies, Carleton University, Ottawa

LUCYA SPENCER Executive Director, Immigrant Women Services Ottawa

PERUVEMBA S. JAYA Associate Professor, Department of Communication, University of Ottawa

MONIA MAZIGH Human Rights Activist and Author, Ottawa

YUMI KOTANI Community Activist and Graduate Student, Carleton University, Ottawa

IKRAM AHMED JAMA Community Activist and a Program Manager at Ottawa Community Immigrant Services Organization (OCISO)

BIBLIOGRAPHY

Angelou, Maya. *Letter to My Daughter*. New York: Random House, 2009.

Bannerji, Himani. *Thinking Through: Essays on Feminism, Marxism, and Anti-Racism*. Toronto: Women's Press, 1995.

Berry, J. Phinney, J. Sam, D., & Vedder, P. *Immigrant Youth in Cultural Transition: Acculturation, Identity and Adaptation Across National Contexts*. NJ: Mahwah, Lawrence Erlbaum Ass., 2006.

Birman, D. "Biculturalism and Perceived Competence of Latino Immigrant Adolescents." *American Journal of Community Psychology*, 2008, 26(3), 335–354.

Da, W.W. "Development of Social-Support Networks by Recent Chinese Immigrant Women with Young Children Living in London, Ontario." *CERIS* Working Paper no. 66. Toronto: Centre of Excellence for Research on Immigration and Settlement, 2008.

Dirie, Waris. *Desert Flower*. London: Virago Press, 2001.

Dossa, Parin. *Politics and Poetics of Migration*, Toronto: Canadian Scholar's Press, 2004.

Esquivel, L. *Malinche: A Novel*. New York, Atria Books, 2006.

Essence Magazine. "Maya Angelou: Her Phenomenal Life and Poetic Journey." August 2014.

Lamba, N., and H. Krahn. "Social Capital and Refugee Resettlement: The Social Networks of Refugees in Canada." *Journal of International Migration and Integration*, 2003. 4(3), 335–360.

Miedema, B. and E. Tastsoglou. "'But where are you from, originally?' Immigrant Women and Integration in the Maritimes," *Atlantis*, Vol. 24.2 (82–91) Summer 2000.

Razack, Sherene. "'Simple Logic': Race, the Identity Document Rule and the Story of a Nation Besieged and Betrayed." *Journal of Law and Social Policy*, vol. 15, 2002. pp. 181–209.

Roosevelt, Eleanor. *You Learn by Living: Eleven Keys for a More Fulfilling Life*. New York: Harper-Collins Publishers, 1960.

Rushdie, Salman. *Step Across This Line: Collected Non-fiction 1992-2002*. Toronto: Alfred A. Knopf 2002.